PRINCIPLES
PROMISES
and
POWERS

STERLING W. SILL

PRINCIPLES
PROMISES
and
POWERS

STERLING W. SILL

Published by Deseret Book Company, Salt Lake City, Utah 1973

ISBN Number 0-87747-506-7
Library of Congress Catalog Card Number 73-877

Lithographed by

DESERET PRESS

in the United States of America

PRINCIPLES

To know the law

PROMISES

To expect the blessing

POWERS

To develop the abilities

PRINCIPLES

There is a divine principle governing every human activity.

PROMISES

Every principle has a divine promise inseparably attached.

POWERS

The Lord giveth no commandments unto the children of men save he makes available to them the power for their accomplishment.

PRINCIPLES

I teach them correct principles and they govern themselves. —*Joseph Smith*

Nothing puts so much order into human life as to live by a set of sound principles.
—*Dr. Henry C. Link*

PROMISES

Given for a principle with promise.—*D&C 89:3*

Whereby are given unto us exceeding great and precious promises: that by these ye might be partakers of the divine nature. —*2 Peter 1:4*

POWERS

But as many as received him, to them gave he power to become the sons of God. —*John 1:12*

For thine is the kingdom, and the power, and the glory, for ever. —*Matthew 6:13*

The powers of heaven cannot be controlled nor handled only upon the principles of righteousness. —*D&C 121:36*

Contents

Preface

Someone once wrote an interesting article entitled "How to Get More Out of a Book Than There Is in It." If one is a good reader, he may be able to get out of a book all there is in the book, but with a little imagination and some ability to analyze, he may get much more. The article pointed out that every good reader has the experience of having his mind strike some particular idea, causing it to ricochet out into space. Under some circumstances, one should not be too quick to draw his mind back into the book, because frequently if he gives his mind a little rope it will lead him to some related ideas that will be very helpful.

Most great men discover that their most important ideas are those that they themselves think. And as a mind follows its own chain of thoughts that are linked together, it will make some inspiring discoveries. Then when it has exhausted itself, it can be drawn back into the book to continue its reading. In that way, a person can get out of the book all that there is in the book; in addition, the book will cause him to make some decisions about a great many things that are not in the book. This business of managing one's thoughts is one of our most profitable enterprises.

Sir Isaac Newton once explained that he had discovered gravity by thinking about it all of the time. By this thinking process he discovered a great many things that had never been written in books. The point is that if Sir Isaac could discover gravity by thinking about it, we can also solve some of our problems that are just as important by that same procedure.

One of the first and most important steps leading to any success is to think about it. This process also leads to understanding it and believing in it and taking action about it. And when we have good ideas leading to good activities, then accomplishment is placed within our easy reach. When Lord Bacon said "Knowledge is power," he had in mind that kind of knowledge which is supported by some strong motivations.

Ralph Waldo Emerson has often been referred to as being one of the greatest thinkers that America has ever produced. And in one of his wisest statements, he said that his greatest personal need was for someone to get him to do those things that he already knew that he ought to do. This is one of the most urgent needs that most of us ever have, and we should learn to work at it a little more effectively.

Knowledge by itself is wonderful, and yet none of us ever come very close to living up to those truths that we are already completely familiar with.

As Moroni, the last of the prophets of pre-Columbus America, was finishing his great volume of scripture in preparation for its transmittal to us, he wrote a note through which he now speaks to us, in which he said: "Behold, I would exhort you that when ye shall receive these things, . . . that ye would . . . ponder it in your hearts." (Moroni 10:3.)

The dictionary says that to ponder is to appraise and to evaluate. It is to weigh an idea in our minds and then to analyze it in order to determine its most constructive use. To ponder is to examine carefully, to view with deliberation and careful consideration. The dictionary says that we may ponder *over,* or ponder *on,* or ponder *about.* By our pondering we may get answers on the most momentous issues so that we are prepared to take action right down the road toward the target.

The great apostle Paul was a ponderer, and he said, ". . . whatsoever things are true, whatsoever things are honest, whatsoever things are just, whatsoever things are pure, whatsoever things are lovely, whatsoever things are of good report . . . think on these things." (Philippians 4:8.) And with a good pondering program we are able to get more out of situations and things than there is in them, and this is the process by which we lift ourselves above the ordinary.

Many people have referred to Alexander Hamilton as a genius. And Alexander Hamilton tells us how he became a genius. He said: "Men give me some credit for genius, but all of the genius I have lies in this: When I have a subject in mind, I study it profoundly; day and night it is before me. I explore it in all its bearings. My mind becomes pervaded with it. The result is what some people call the fruits of genius, whereas it is in reality the fruits of study and labor." Study by itself may not be very important, but a good study *habit* can make us almost all-powerful. Then about the other part of Mr. Hamilton's formula, Leonardo da Vinci said, "Thou O God doth sell us all good things at the price of labor."

The great driving forces of the world are not only intellectual; they are primarily moral and emotional. When our minds are made up, our emotions aroused, and our souls set on fire, then every accomplishment is placed in our own hands. Mere ideas as such may not be worth a dime a dozen, as there are millions of really great ideas that are wasting away in our success books. There are dozens of great programs gathering dust in our libraries. There are hundreds of pages that contain the word of God himself that presently are unknown to and unused by us. However, even the greatest ideas don't do us very much good unless we digest them, get them circulating in our bloodstream, and make them a part of our bodily strength.

Victor Hugo has said that nothing is as powerful as an idea whose time has come. And an idea's time comes only when it has been harnessed and set to work. Therefore, we ought to get out the great success books and practice the art of pondering and accomplishing. This can give us a more productive appetite for study, investigation, thinking, learning, believing, motivating, and practicing.

The chapters of this book were written on a one-a-week basis. There are some who may want to read them on that same schedule. If what is found in this book does not satisfy you, so much the better. You may rewrite the chapters to your own specifications in such a way that they will leave nothing to be desired. By our effective pondering processes we are able to make some firm decisions and form some strong motives on the important issues. Then we may realize Mr. Emerson's ambition of getting ourselves to do the things that we ourselves know that we ought to do. This will put us well on our way toward becoming a genius in carrying forward our part of the work of the world and also in doing that part of the work of the Lord that he has given us to do.

Principles, Promises, and Powers

EVERYONE WHO dwells upon our great earth is involved from his first minute of life to his last in this all-important process of making the most of himself. He also inherits a full responsibility for that part of the work of the world that life has given him to do. This great gift of human life should not be taken lightly, as it is a very important one. Life was given for a purpose, and it entails many responsibilities that are wonderfully and terribly important.

President Joseph Fielding Smith once said that in one very important way this short period of mortality is the most important part of our total eternal lives. Our presence in this mortal probation indicates that we passed with flying colors the requirements of our long and important first estate. And if we make the most of these intermediate years of our second estate, then we can look forward to a brilliant, everlasting, successful, and happy third estate where we will have glory added upon our heads forever and ever. Therefore, the big question that will determine much of the value of not only what has gone before but also what will come after depends upon what we do now. It is thought that the three all-important key words that will represent the quality of our eternal success are *Principles, Promises,* and *Powers.* And to get the most good out of ideas, we need to learn as much as possible about each of them.

Just think what advantage it gives us when we understand the principle on which our desired success is based. And then we add another part of the success triumvirate when we develop the power to effectively carry out the principle. Both of these are focused in those great promises that God has made for our ultimate accomplishment and happiness.

God is all wise; he has all knowledge. He is the author and master of the fundamental principle on which every achievement is based. But no success is ever predicated on weakness, and one of the important characteristics that makes God God is that he has all power. And we close the Lord's prayer by saying to him,

"For thine is the kingdom, and the power, and the glory, for ever. Amen." (Matthew 6:13.)

God started us on our journey of learning correct principles when he permitted our first parents to eat from the tree of knowledge of good and evil that God himself had planted in the Garden of Eden. And after man had eaten, God said, "Behold, the man is become as one of us, to know good and evil. . . ." (Genesis 3:22.) And I would like to point out in passing that the right kind of knowledge still tends to have that effect upon people. To know good from evil still tends to make men and women become as God. But even though many of us know what is right, we may still miss the mark by shooting under it because we are too weak to carry out the divine program. And more than about anything else, most of us need that great power to do. The apostle Paul said to Timothy, ". . . be strong in the Lord, and in the power of his might." (Ephesians 6:10.) Whether we realize it or not, that is one of our greatest ideas.

Isaiah talked about an interesting combination of principles and powers when he said, "Wash you, make you clean; put away the evil of your doings from before mine eyes; cease to do evil; Learn to do well; seek judgment, relieve the oppressed, judge the fatherless, plead for the widow." (Isaiah 1:16-17.) This requires both of these great abilities for knowing and doing. We need to understand the great principles on which all success is based. And we need the powers necessary to bring them about. We have some great powers of the mind and spirit that need to be developed. Most of us also have some unused heart powers. We have been given some miraculous "will power."

Someone has said:

> The human will, that force unseen,
> The offspring of the human soul,
> Can hew away to any goal
> Though walls of granite intervene.
> Be not impatient in delay
> But wait as one who understands;
> When spirit rises and commands,
> The gods are ready to obey.

Surely no one who craves excitement or information or opportunities could help but feel grateful for the privilege of living now. Our great knowledge explosion gives us the ability to know almost everything we want to know about almost anything that we want to know about. Because of the restoration of the gospel, we have new and everlasting promises that make learning the principles and developing the powers extremely worthwhile. He has promised us the greatest blessings. We may know about God and the details of his program for our salvation, and the power is available for us to reach almost any objective, including those that reach beyond the boundaries of this life. What a day, what an opportunity, and what a challenge! His principles are wise, his promises are sure, his powers are great.

Objectives and Responsibilities

THERE IS one thing that I believe in more than about any other thing and that is the proposition that "the one business of life is to succeed." I am perfectly confident that God did not go to all of the trouble of creating this beautiful earth with all of its laws, resources, utilities, and opportunities without having in his mind some very important destiny for those whom he would permit to live upon it. I am equally certain that God did not create us in his own image, endow us with these potentially magnificent brains, these miraculous personalities, this astonishing power to grow, and this godly ability for procreation, and then expect us to waste our lives in failure.

God did not give us these godly ambitions to mock us. He did not build a stairway leading nowhere. However, the greatest waste there is in the world is not the devastation that goes with war; it isn't the cost of crime; it isn't the erosion of our soils or the depletion of our raw materials or the loss of our gold supply. The greatest waste there is in the world is that human beings, you and I, live so far below the level of our possibilities. Compared with what we might be, we are just partly alive. The most widespread disease in the world is the inferiority complex. We load ourselves up with guilt, lethargy, weakness, and sins by thinking little thoughts and living too much of our lives on that low level of fractional devotion, marginal morals, and misunderstandings that result in our turning in too many minimum performances in our lives.

There is a cure for our problems if we follow that great line in the scripture which says, "And this is life eternal, that they might know thee the only true God, and Jesus Christ, whom thou hast sent." (John 17:3.) We must not contaminate our success with the destructive belief that God is dead or that he has lost interest in us or that he has given up in his purpose. By indulging in any of these, we do ourselves a damaging injustice. It is important for us to remember that God is God and beside him there is no Savior. How important to have him as our guide when he has all knowledge, he has all power, he is all good, he has all wisdom. He is not only our Eternal Heavenly Father, but he also has an incomparable program for our eternal progression, our eternal glory, and our eternal happiness.

The great God who fashioned us in his own image and created this earth as a place for us to serve our mortal probation does not deal in trifles. He does not waste his time working on unimportant projects that are not worthwhile. We may desert him, but his purposes will not fail nor will any of his programs fizzle out and come to naught. And as the apostle Peter said, God has given to us "exceeding great and precious promises: that by these ye might be partakers of the divine nature. . . ." (2 Peter 1:4.) And the greatest of all human opportunities is that we shall put ourselves in harmony with his program and make the greatest capital out of his excellence and magnificence.

To reach our maximum destiny, we must believe in him who created us. And we must also believe in ourselves. God has said, ". . . this is my work and my glory—to bring to pass the immortality and eternal life of man." (Moses 1:39.) But to achieve the best results, he must have our complete cooperation based on an effective understanding of his program. We should know what his objectives are for our lives and what our responsibilities are in carrying them out. When we fill our lives with sins and weaknesses, we are bound to miss the mark by erring in our aim.

Jesus announced the purpose of his own mission by saying, "I am come that they might have life, and that they might have it more abundantly." (John 10:10.) And for us to get the most comprehensive and comprehending view of the magnificence and desirability of that intended abundance for both here and hereafter is one of the greatest of all possible objectives. It is interesting that it has always seemed very difficult for us to believe in our own importance or our destiny.

The Pharisees accused Jesus of blasphemy when he told them that he was the Son of God. Then in trying to get them to understand their real situation he quoted their own earlier scripture that projected one of those precious promises in which it was said, "Ye are gods; and all of you are children of the most High." (Psalm 82:6.) Then he said, "If he called them gods, unto whom the word of God came, and the scripture cannot be broken: Say ye of him, whom the Father hath sanctified, and sent into the world, Thou blasphemest; because I said, I am the Son of God?" (John 10:34-36.) He was saying to them, "Ye are the children of God, and according to the divine law of heredity the offspring of God may sometime hope to become like their eternal parents." He has outlined for us a great program of eternal progression. Even God does not stand still. The poet said:

> We serve no God whose work is done,
> Who rests within his firmament;
> Our God his work has just begun
> Toils evermore with powers unspent.

However, it has always been the besetting sin of the inhabitants of our world to belittle their own importance, to disbelieve in their own destiny, and to destroy their own chances for glorious eternal success. Throughout the holy scriptures and through the work of the Church and by the whisperings of the Holy Spirit, God is pleading with us to make the most of our own possibilities.

In that great Sermon on the Mount when Jesus said, "Be ye therefore perfect, even as your Father which is in heaven is perfect" (Matthew 5:48), he was saying to us, "Ye are the children of the Most High, so go out there and amount to something." It was for this purpose that he put in each one of us this magnificent upward reach, this great self-improvement instinct, this ambition to aspire heavenward. The primary thing that our parents, our teachers, and our employers are also saying to us is, "Go out there and amount to something." This is also the message that we get from our conscience, our ambition, and our faith. And it is thought that the most profitable of all success procedures would be for us to sit down and read his sacred promises and determine what God's real objectives for our lives are, what they ought to be in our own hearts and ambitions, and what responsibilities we bear in relationship to them.

James G. Harboard was a very successful general in World War I. Before going into the service, he had been the president of the Radio Corporation of America. After the termination of his military service, he went back to RCA as chairman of the board. And he once said that before anyone under his direction undertook any accomplishment, either in business or the military, he must do four things in writing:

1. He must make a written detailed statement of his objectives.

2. He must make up a complete inventory of his resources.

3. He must make a thorough calculation of the resources of the enemy.

4. He must prepare a written plan as to exactly how he intends to use his resources to overcome the resources of the enemy so that his objectives can be accomplished.

When we form the habit of writing our objectives down in detail, we usually do a much better job of thinking them through and making them definite and decisive in our own minds. Then we accept them as our own, we believe in them, and we prepare to do something about them. But, of course, we should also be fully aware of all of the possible resources that are available to us in bringing about the greatest possible accomplishment. We should also be conscious of those opposing forces that will tend to prevent us from achieving our goals. And finally we ought to formulate an effective permanent plan giving all of the details for the accomplishment.

Someone has said that planning is the place where man shows himself most like God. Nothing is more godlike than the planner, the thinker, the organizer. He is the one who draws the blueprint for success. He is the one who builds the roadway on which accomplishment will travel. It is likely that our greatest opportunity is to have a good set of definitely worked-out objectives that are fully believed in and about which firm determinations have been made. There is an old axiom that says, "All the world stands aside for the man who knows where he is going and how he is going to get there."

And when we come into this great world of benefits and opportunities we must also carry a share of the responsibilities for bringing them about. These two must always go together. No one gets very far who insists on having all of the benefits without carrying any of the responsibilities. And when we enthusiastically accept the responsibility, we get a much greater proportion of the benefits. Under the overruling program of our free agency, God has set up at least four great institutions to help bring about his objectives for us. These are all pointed toward the greatest of all objectives, which is, that if we are faithful, then the offspring of God have his promise that they may sometime hope to become like their own eternal parents.

These four primary inventions of God designed to help us accomplish our purposes are:

1. We know "that governments were instituted of God for the benefit of man, and that he holds men accountable for their acts in relation to them, both in making laws and administering them, for the good and safety of society." (D&C 134:1.) God is unalterably opposed to dictatorships. Great destruction always follows the rule of wicked men. God tried to help the ancient Israelites avoid the evils involved in having a king. However, they insisted on a king, and as a consequence their nation was finally destroyed. One of the greatest gifts of God to modern-day America is that he himself raised up wise men to establish its constitution and lay our national foundations on Christian principles.

2. He has organized his church upon our earth so that he could more effectively teach us those divine laws necessary for our group and individual success. He has prescribed the necessary offices and appointed the officers in the Church. He has given to them the necessary appropriate authority to administer in all of the ordinances of salvation. He has not only given us the holy scriptures to teach us righteous principles, but also to tell us of God's dealings with the inhabitants of the earth in every dispensation of our 6,000 years of world history. The Church and the scriptures make it possible for us to understand the purpose of God, to repent of our sins, to be baptized into the Church, to receive the gift of the Holy Ghost, and to live according to the prescribed principles of the gospel.

3. One of the greatest creations organized in our interest was when he established the family and ordained that each one of us should come into the world at the invitation of two parents and should enjoy the advantages of membership and the intimate relationships provided by this small but important group. In the very beginning God said, "It is not good that the man should be alone" (Genesis 2:18), and he might have said that it is not good that woman should be alone. Certainly it is not good that children should be alone. And so he established the family to be the source of most of our education, love, and eternal blessing. One of the greatest titles of God himself centers in his parenthood. And one of our most valuable blessings is that he has shared this privilege and ability with us. When the first marriage was performed, death had not yet entered the world and the family unit was designed to be eternal.

4. God himself established our occupations, and he instituted the great gospel of work as the source of most of our blessings and the ruling principle in our lives. When the Lord closed up the Garden of Eden so that the real work of the world could get underway, he gave to our first parents this fundamental law of accomplishment, saying, "In the sweat of thy face shalt thou eat thy bread. . . ." (Genesis 4:19.) However, that is not a command of punishment; that is a command of opportunity. That is not just the way we get our bread; that is also the way we build our characters, develop our personalities, build our temples, do our church work, provide for our families, build our faith, and motivate our ambitions.

The Lord has said that all things unto him are spiritual and that he has never given any command that was temporal. In this same spirit, Elbert Hubbard once said that "business is the process of ministering to human needs. Therefore," said he, "business is essentially a divine calling." The farmer who grows the food to maintain the lives and health of our families is ministering to a human need, and therefore he is entitled to say that he is engaged in a divine occupation. The doctor who provided me with nine blood transfusions was ministering to a human need, and therefore he is entitled to say that he is engaged in a divine calling. And as we take hold of our share of the work of the world, we ought to think about it in that way and do it in that spirit.

Principles

MANY YEARS ago while taking some college courses concerned with educational training, I was enrolled in a class where one of the prescribed textbooks was entitled *Principles of Education.* This book was written by a man who had had some very successful teaching experience. He had also done extensive research and spent a great deal of time trying to learn how to solve the problems involved in acquiring a successful education. A few years later in my life, I read another book that was entitled *The Principles of Successful Salesmanship.* And since that time, I have become aware of the importance of this great word *principle* in every one of our projected successes.

The dictionary says that a principle is some fundamental truth that never varies. It is a governing law that can be depended upon. It is a settled, proven rule for successful action. It also has reference to a divine doctrine. It is one of those attitudes or beliefs that exercises a directing influence in our lives and behavior. It is a fundamental proven assumption and a dependable maxim or axiom. Sometimes we hear people say, "It is the principle of the thing," and usually we ourselves are good or bad, successful or unsuccessful, according to those principles that we believe in. Our most important talents are our religious talents, and our most important principles are our religious principles. Thomas Carlyle once said that a man's religion is the most important thing about him. That is what he thinks about and believes in and works at and fights for and lives by.

Dr. Henry C. Link once made a helpful success statement when he said, "Nothing puts so much order into human life as to live by a set of sound principles." And certainly the most sound of all the great principles to be found in the world are the principles of the gospel of Jesus Christ. In any area of our projected accomplishment, the principles of the gospel furnish us with our most profitable human concepts and our finest success ideas. Dr. Link himself grew up in a religious household, but as he climbed the educational ladder, he decided that he might make a more intellectual approach to life through his education. And, therefore, he somewhat relaxed his hold on his religion. However, when he was thirty-two years of age, with his Phi Beta Kappa key on his chest and his name in *Who's Who in America,* he became the head of the Psychological Service Center of New York, where it was his job to advise thousands of troubled people as to how to solve their problems. Then he made one of the greatest of all discoveries, and that was to the effect that the difficulties of every person in the world can best be solved by following the principles enunciated in the religion of Christ. As a consequence of his discovery, he wrote his great book entitled *The Return to Religion.*

Just suppose that everyone in the world enthusiastically believed in and lived each one of the Ten Commandments, the Sermon on the Mount, the Word of Wisdom, and all of the other great laws of God. Then almost all of our problems would almost immediately disappear. If we followed the morality, the fairness, the honesty, the industry taught in the holy scriptures, the great divorce carnage that now desolates our land could be immediately wiped out. To follow the scriptures, obey the laws of the land, and utilize the other important principles of success would prosper us in our occupations, make us happy in our families, and give effectiveness to our social relationships. Following these great Christian principles would make us good citizens and pleasant neighbors, and would also lead us along that straight and narrow path to the celestial kingdom.

There is a life-saving Article of Faith in which we say, "We believe that the first principles and ordinances of the Gospel are: first, Faith in the Lord Jesus Christ; second, Repentance; third, Baptism by immersion for the remission of sins; fourth, Laying on of hands for the gift of the Holy Ghost." (Article of Faith 4.) In another one we say, "We believe in being honest, true, chaste, benevolent, virtuous, and in doing good to all men; indeed, we may say that we follow the admonition of Paul—We believe all things, we hope all things, we have endured many things, and hope to be able to endure all things. If there is anything virtuous, lovely or of good report or praiseworthy, we seek after these things." (Article of Faith 13.) In giving the Word of Wisdom, the Lord said that it was "given for a principle with promise" and that it was "adapted to the capacity of the weak and the weakest of all saints, who are or can be called saints." (D&C 89:3.) But every one of the principles of the gospel also has a promise attached, and all of them are "adapted to the capacity of the weak and the weakest of all saints, who are or can be called saints" if we have the spirit of the gospel.

In speaking about the principle of tithing, the Lord has said that if we obey it, he will open the windows of heaven and pour us out a blessing that there will not be room to receive it.

The people who keep the Sabbath day holy will be a different kind of people than those who do not. From the top of Mount Sinai God said, "Honour thy father and thy mother"; then he attached the promise when he said, "that thy days may be long upon the land which the Lord thy God giveth thee." (Exodus 20:12.) We have many other thrilling principles that can raise our life to any accomplishment. Ralph Waldo Emerson once said, "Nothing can bring us peace but a triumph of principles." As we hope for success, we must have a good understanding of those great principles of eternal marriage and of eternal progression and the other great laws and doctrines of Christ.

We hear till we are weary about the temptations of our day. Some say that it is too difficult for one to live his religion and that we cannot be expected to practice the principles of the gospel. However, no temptation is a temptation at all unless we are entertaining it. God never forces us to do right, and Satan has no power to force us to do wrong. Someone has said that God always votes for us, and Satan always votes against us, and then they ask us to vote to break the tie. It is how we vote that gives our lives their significance. And if we always vote according to the principles of the gospel, our lives will have great power behind them.

If one desires to be a great teacher, or a great doctor, or a great citizen, or a great child of God, he ought to get out the great success books. He ought to know the great scriptures and study the principles of power, the principles of righteousness that are the principles of success. The Prophet Joseph Smith was once asked how he so successfully governed the large group of Latter-day Saints who had come from so many widely different backgrounds and cultures. They had different temperaments, different loyalties, and spoke different languages. The Prophet said, "I teach them correct principles and they govern themselves." And he has been the instrument in reestablishing the Church upon this earth, and the Church is the proponent of the fullness of the gospel. It is the chief fosterer of those great principles of eternal marriage, the literal bodily resurrection, eternal progression, salvation for the dead, and the atonement of Christ.

There are some who claim that it is difficult to understand the principles of the gospel, but it is also difficult to understand how the grass grows, or what sunshine is. We do not understand all of the principles of science, but we can understand how to get their benefits. We can run electrical currents for thousands of miles along copper wires and transform the energy into light, heat, or power, and we can learn to push the switch and pull the lever to give ourselves the benefits. We can make ourselves successful and happy and qualify ourselves for eternal life by understanding and obeying these great principles of the gospel which are adapted to the understanding of the "weak and the weakest of all saints, who are or who can be called saints." But certainly its importance makes it worthy of our best thought and finest attention.

The gospel is the good news, it is God's story; it is the plan of life and salvation. It contains the greatest success principles, and it is founded on the wisdom and mercy of God. It is our only safe guide in the universe.

The Law and the Prophets

THE SCRIPTURES are frequently called by various names, some of which may make a stronger appeal to us than others. They are sometimes referred to as "the law and the prophets." Since time began, God has given us many fundamental laws on which our success depends for both here and hereafter. He has also made available the stimulating words of his prophets. Jesus judged the philosophy of people and the people themselves by how they harmonized with these principles of truth.

After giving the great laws of love, he said, "On these two commandments hang all the law and the prophets." (Matthew 22:40.) He admonished teachers to stay within the general limits by saying: "To the law and to the testimony: if they speak not according to this word, it is because there is no light in them." (Isaiah 8:20.)

The scriptures are called by such other names as the law and the testimony, or the God story, or the good news, or the commandments, or the principles of the gospel. Each of these has some peculiar significance to us. But whatever they may be called, each one of these commandments or truths represents a saving principle designed for our eternal benefit. None of these were intended to restrict our growth or happiness; in fact, the very opposite is true.

The Golden Rule is a basic fundamental principle of success. The Lord has given us the Word of Wisdom, the ordinance of baptism, and the principle of faith. He instituted the family relationship, the literal bodily resurrection, the immortality of the personality, the eternal glory of the human soul, and the principle of eternal progression. None of these, or any of the dozens of others, are superfluous or unnecessary, and we ought to be thoroughly familiar with them.

The Lord has said that in order to reach the perfection that he has projected, we should live by every word that proceedeth forth from the mouth of God. In every age the cry of the prophets has always been, "Keep the commandments," "Live by the law," "Be obedient to the great principles of truth."

Recently at a family home evening the father was discussing with his children the importance of keeping all of the commandments of the Lord, for even one exception might be disastrous. One of his young daughters held up her hand and asked her father a very comprehensive question when she said, "Daddy, how many commandments are there?"

The father was a little taken offguard, and he had to confess to his daughter that he did not know. And so, they took as the project for their next week's family home evening to count the commandments and to make up a list as large as they could think of. They reasoned that it might be a little bit difficult to keep a commandment that they had forgotten or didn't even know about or could not fully understand. And each one of us might also ask ourselves, How many principles of the gospel are there? We might find out that this question would prove to be somewhat comparable to asking how many laws we have on the statute books, or how many principles of success there are, or how many principles of truth, or how many principles of science, or how many laws of health, or how many good ideas there are, or how many promises of blessings God has made to us.

If we were going to be completely informed on the laws of successful farming or horticulture or animal husbandry, how many facts would we need to know and understand? Or how many laws of medicine are there and which one is so unimportant that we can afford to neglect it? If a good law firm is going to completely protect the best interests of all of its clients in court, it might be necessary for it to have a library of several thousand law books.

There are some people who may go through their entire lives without consulting a doctor or a lawyer more than a few times. But almost never does a day go by when we don't have some very important use for the constructive principles of truth and righteousness. We need to know all of the doctrines of salvation and all of the principles of righteousness. And we need to remember all of the commandments of God. If we forget any of his laws, we will be a different kind of people than if we remember them.

When I was ten years old, I had a brother who was nine years old. One afternoon while with a group of children his own age, something happened that involved a principle of morality. My brother came home and reported the occurrence to my mother, and my mother sat down with my brother and me and discussed this idea in its many ramifications and the great importance it had in our lives. I had a great love for my mother and a great confidence in her wisdom, ability, and righteousness. I made a firm determination that my mother's teaching on this subject would always be one of those fundamental principles that would guide me in my future life. Even when we are young, we can make some firm decisions that will hold us true against the ugly pressure of evil.

To help us to make good decisions is also the reason that our eternal Heavenly Father has given us the holy scriptures. Then, so that we would not get too many conflicts, he came down onto the top of Mount Sinai and said to us, "Thou shalt have no other gods before me." (Exodus 20:3.) That is, he was saying the same thing that my mother said, that there is no other acceptable conduct but righteousness. And if we disobey these principles, we can be certain that unpleasant and unprofitable consequences will follow.

There is a law of agriculture that says that if a farmer prepares a good seed bed with the proper fertility and if he follows all of the other laws of successful farming, he may have real hopes for an abundant harvest. But if he plants his corn in the chill of the December blizzard, he will surely find that the laws of successful farming have turned against him.

But more important than the laws of farming are the laws of life, and the Lord has indicated that we should study those important principles that determine our eternal salvation and happiness. He has had them written down for our benefit in the holy scriptures, and only when we understand and follow them are we on safe ground.

Abraham Lincoln was an unschooled, backwoods boy. He was isolated from most of the sources of culture and learning. His mother died when he was nine. Even books were very scarce and hard to get. But Abe said, "My best friend is the one who will get me a book I haven't read." In the evenings after the work of the day had been finished, he used to lie before the open fire and read the Bible and the one or two other good books that he had access to. He said, "I will prepare now and take my chances when the opportunity arrives." And when his chance came, Abe was ready.

There are many other great men who owe their success in life to the habit of regularly reading the scriptures and being familiar with other important ideas. It is also necessary that a good scientist study every day if he hopes to learn the secrets of science.

Jascha Heifetz, the great violinist, once said: "When I fail to practice for one day, I can tell the difference in my playing. When I fail to practice for two days, my family can tell the difference. When I fail to practice for three days, the whole world can tell the difference."

Practice is one of the fundamental principles of every other success. When even for an hour we forget God and these great laws that he has established for our benefit, we also immediately begin suffering some losses. The Lord has given us several other learning opportunities. One is that if we properly train our conscience, it will always prompt us as to what is right and what is wrong.

For another, we have the privilege of building great character power within ourselves so that we may always do what is right. We also have the prompting of the Spirit of the Lord speaking to us. On one occasion, Jesus said, "My sheep hear my voice. . . ." (John 10:27.) In our antemortal state, we were taught the principles of the gospel, and while the specific memory of the details has been temporarily taken from us, yet when we try to do right and listen to the Spirit's prompting, we receive directions from God and from our subconscious understanding. Good things have a familiar spirit in the ears of good people. And we bring with us from the past an important heritage that we may call instinct or character, natural intelligence, or inspiration. And all of these are for our individual protection and profit.

William Wordsworth put part of this idea into verse when he said:

> Our birth is but a sleep and a forgetting:
> The soul that rises with us, our life's star,
>   Hath had elsewhere its setting,
>   And cometh from afar:
>   Not in entire forgetfulness,
>   And not in utter nakedness,
> But trailing clouds of glory do we come
>   From God, who is our home.

If we listen to those echoes from the spirit and the past, we may know that immorality, dishonesty, unkindness, unfairness, and all other kinds of unrighteousness are wrong. And certainly the best way to be a good teacher or a good salesman or a good doctor or a good lawyer is to be a good man. Just think what our world would be like if every one of us knew and loved and obeyed every principle of the gospel. Then the prayer of the Master would soon be realized when he said, "Thy kingdom come. Thy will be done in earth, as it is in heaven." (Matthew 6:10.)

If we disobey God's laws half of the time and keep them the other half, we are doing just as much to tear down our eternal success as we are to build it up. We ought to have a great catalog of those important truths that we believe in so that we would not overlook any of them; then we ought to develop the skills, the attitudes, the aptitudes, and the courage involved in the power to follow through with them. Certainly we cannot hope for success while thinking negative thoughts or unrighteous thoughts or thoughts of failure. We can destroy our success by pouring fear into our bloodstream and filling our muscles with lethargy, disobedience, and sloth. But more than about anything else in our lives, we need to learn the principles of success and stamp into our brain cells those powers designed for greater accomplishments.

Religion is much more than theology. Religion is how to live successfully, not only for now but for eternity. There is nothing so profitable as to follow the principles of truth. There is nothing so Godly as righteousness. If the principles of the gospel of Jesus Christ are lived, we will become as God is.

Promise Books

RECENTLY A story appeared in the newspaper about a newly married young woman who gave an overworked mother next door a small notebook containing forty perforated slips of paper. On each slip this young woman had written: "I promise to give to Mrs. John Jones any time during the next year one evening of free baby sitting—date to be arranged." She then signed her name.

This interesting example of helpfulness inspired a Girl Scout to make up her own version of what she called her "Promise Book." It contained a great number of slips that she had made out to her mother and on which she had promised her mother to give certain services, such as washing the dishes, making the beds, and doing a lot of other helpful things. This would not only greatly please her mother but it would be of even greater benefit to the daughter herself. To this young Girl Scout these promise slips were all sacred pledges and they were backed up by the character and integrity of a very responsible maker. They were guaranteed by her firm determination that in no case would they ever fail to be honored in full. I do not know what anyone else may think about this situation, but if I know a great idea when I see it, this is it.

However, in the world around us, there are a great many promise books containing important promises to pay. For services received, the government has accumulated a vast debt of approximately five hundred billion dollars for which it has an obligation to pay. The government currency is made up of slips of green paper on which has been written a promise to pay the bearer a certain sum of money. On the bills themselves are shown the pictures of some great men, most of whom are American presidents. On the other sides of these slips of paper are emblems and significant insignia. A one-dollar bill has the picture of George Washington; two dollars—Thomas Jefferson; five dollars—Abraham Lincoln; ten dollars—Alexander Hamilton; twenty dollars—Andrew Jackson; fifty dollars—Ulysses S. Grant; one hundred dollars—Benjamin Franklin; five hundred dollars—

William McKinley; thousand dollars—Grover Cleveland; five thousand dollars—James Madison, ten thousand dollars—Salmon P. Chase; and one hundred thousand dollars—Woodrow Wilson. A great amount of our energy and a large portion of our time are spent in earning the right to possess these slips of green paper. And of all of those mentioned above, we seem to prefer the ones having the likeness of Woodrow Wilson.

The greatest promises that have ever been made are not on the faces of $100,000 government bills nor even the promise book of a wonderful Girl Scout, but the greatest promises have been made by the God of Creation himself. And our holy scriptures are the most magnificent of our great promise books. In fact, someone has compared the sacred scriptures to a great collection of promissory notes. God has never given a commandment to which he did not attach the promise of a blessing. The value of this blessing always far exceeds the amount of the service given. For example, through Malachi he said that we ought to pay our tithing. He said: "Bring ye all of the tithes into the storehouse." That is the command. Then the blessing was attached when he said, ". . . and prove me now herewith, saith the Lord of hosts, if I will not open you the windows of heaven, and pour you out a blessing, that there shall not be room enough to receive it." (Malachi 3:10.) That is, if we keep his commandments, the blessings will be so great that we will be unable to contain them.

From the top of Mount Sinai, God said, "Honour thy father and thy mother." That is the command. Then the blessing is attached which says, "that thy days may be long upon the land which the Lord thy God giveth thee." (Exodus 20:12.) He has said that if we obey the Word of Wisdom, we will receive the invaluable blessings of health. He referred to the Word of Wisdom as "a principle with promise," but all of his principles have promises attached. And if we live the celestial law, we will receive all of the blessings of the celestial kingdom, including the privilege of resurrecting celestial bodies and having celestial minds and celestial personalities.

Isn't it interesting that we can't even keep the Sabbath day holy without receiving a reward. We can't even think a good thought without being paid. And we can't think an evil thought without suffering a penalty. That just is not possible.

In one of his greatest promises, he has indicated that the success and welfare of our eternal lives are based on what we do in these few years of mortality. That is, the basic law of the universe is this immutable, inexorable, irrevocable, unchangeable law of the harvest that says, ". . . whatsoever a man soweth, that shall he also reap" (Galatians 6:7), multiplied. It is one of the fundamental laws of our existence that everyone will be judged according to his works.

It is very interesting to try to place a figure on the number of God's commandments. It is even more exciting to try to place a value or a number on his promised blessings. And so far as I know, these numbers will be about the same. What an inspiring thought to know that we can build up the most tremendous eternal estate and bind the great God of heaven, the Creator of the universe, to the most magnificent promises possible. He himself has said: "I, the Lord, am bound when ye do what I say; but when ye do not what I say, ye have no promise." (D&C 82:10.)

One of the great characteristics of God is his desire to be bound in our service. In every age and with every people he has desired to make contracts or covenants of behavior through which it is possible for us to bind him to the most fantastic agreements in our interests. As a natural corollary to this idea, just think how profitable it can be for us to make out some promise books to God.

Robert Frost once wrote a striking poem entitled "Stopping by Woods on a Snowy Evening." He described the life's promises of a man who lived in the days before the automobile. One winter evening very late at night he was traveling through the woods in his horse-drawn sleigh. He stopped for a few minutes on a lonely road to enjoy the beauty of the snow falling so softly among the silent trees. He said that he was watching the woods fill up with snow. However, he could not linger for very long, as he had some important duties to perform. Whether he was a doctor out making late calls or doing some other important human service, I do not know, but he might have been representing any one of us when in concluding his poem he said:

> The woods are lovely, dark and deep,
> But I have promises to keep,
> And miles to go before I sleep,
> And miles to go before I sleep.

Abraham Lincoln said: "I am not bound to win, but I am bound to be true. I am not bound to succeed, but I am bound to live by the best light that I have. I will stand with anyone who stands right, and I will part with anybody when he goes wrong." There are many wonderful promises that we may make and keep. We make some sacred promises to God at the waters of baptism. We make others when we are ordained to the priesthood or called in any important divine service. We go into the holy temples and make God a party to our sacred marriage promises. We promise God that we will be righteous. We give some promise books to our wives that we will make them happy. We give some promise books to our children that they will be loved and educated.

Governments were instituted by God for the benefit of man, and he holds each of us personally responsible for our acts in relation thereto. We reaffirm those promises when we sing our national anthem and take our pledge of allegiance to the flag. Each of us who lives under the stars and stripes has inherited a responsibility for our country's safety, and one of our greatest opportunities is to make our nation greater and better than it would have been. Nathan Hale gave a promise book to his country and just before he was hanged by his government's enemies, he made the last entry in which he said, "I only regret that I have but one life to lose for my country."

Martin Treptow was also a great soldier and was killed in the battle of Chateau Thierry in 1918 in World War I. In the diary found on his body were written these words, "I will work, I will save, I will sacrifice, I will endure, I will fight cheerfully and do my utmost as though the entire conflict depended upon me alone." Such patriotism should inspire us as the young wife did the Girl Scout.

In 1852, John Ruskin wrote in his diary, "Today I promise God that I will live as though every doctrine contained in the holy scriptures was true." And if each one of us were inspired to emulate his example and with great integrity and character back up our promise that we would live by his every word, this earth would soon be God's paradise, and we would be the greatest generation that has ever lived upon it. And why not?

To begin with, God created us. He has granted unto us our lives, for which we will be forever indebted to him. But when we do any righteous thing, he does immediately bless us with manifold blessings, and our debt is increased. He has told us the sure way to eternal exaltation and eternal happiness, and if we make our covenants and keep our promises, no blessing will be withheld from us. In one of the greatest of all his promises the Lord said, "For he that receiveth my servants receiveth me; And he that receiveth me receiveth my Father; And he that receiveth my Father receiveth my Father's kingdom; therefore all that my Father hath shall be given unto him. And this is according to the oath and covenant which belongeth to the priesthood. Therefore, all those who receive the priesthood, receive this oath and covenant of my Father, which he cannot break, neither can it be moved." (D&C 84:36-40.)

Try to think of something more exciting or worthwhile than to be a part of that great enterprise in which God himself spends his entire time. How much better it is for us to be great human beings, to obey the law, to keep the commandments, to build up our balance with God, and to qualify for his promises. Before we can keep his commandments, we need to know what they are and have strong convictions about them. The kind of promises we make to God will not only determine the kind of people we will become, but they will also determine his promises that will be fulfilled in our behalf. And so we say again with Robert Frost:

> The woods are lovely, dark and deep,
> But I have promises to keep,
> And miles to go before I sleep,
> And miles to go before I sleep.

The Age of Power

THE PARTICULAR period in which we live has been called by many names, both good and bad. Our day is noted for its delinquencies, its crimes, and its sins. Jesus looked down to our time and made some rather uncomplimentary comparisons for us when he said, "But as the days of Noe were, so shall also the coming of the Son of man be." (Matthew 24:37.)

He also pointed out that our age should be characterized by its destructive wars and the serious disturbances that would be taking place in nature. The apostle Paul also saw our day even better than some of us do and he said, ". . . in the last days perilous times shall come. For men shall be lovers of their own selves, covetous, boasters, proud, blasphemers, disobedient to parents, unthankful, unholy, Without natural affection, trucebreakers, false accusers, incontinent, fierce, despisers of those that are good, Traitors, heady, highminded, lovers of pleasures more than lovers of God; Having a form of godliness, but denying the power thereof: from such turn away." (2 Timothy 3:1-5.)

Other prophets have seen our day and have held up for view a great long list of our problems. It may be true that we constitute the most wicked age; if that is so, it may be that life is trying to keep the balance even because our age also has the longest list of positives.

The world's greatest knowledge explosion has taken place in our day. We are also the beneficiaries of the most fantastic inventions. We enjoy the greatest comforts, the finest luxuries, and the biggest food supply. It is also one of the most important religious ages. While looking forward to our day, the apostle Paul called it "the dispensation of the fulness of times," when God would "gather together in one all things in Christ, both which are in heaven, and which are on earth; even in him." (Ephesians 1:10.) It was in our day and for earth's present people that the gospel was restored in its greatest fullness. It is the people of our present age who have split the atom. And certainly one of the most apt descriptions of our day would be to call it the Age of Power.

It is interesting to remember that our forefathers lived on a flat, stationary earth and plowed their ground with a wooden stick, whereas we live on an earth of power steering and jet propulsion. It was not many years ago that most of the work of the world was done by the puny muscle power of men and animals, but now our giant power equipment can literally move mountains. Almost every inch of our earth is loaded with potential power both on its surface and in its depths. God buried in the ground for our benefit billions of tons of coal, oil, and uranium.

The earth itself is a giant magnet with its great lines of force producing tremendous power. Both the water and the air are filled with electrical power. There is power in the rays of the sun, and the sixteen miles of atmosphere over our heads are also loaded with power. The air furnishes us power for our lungs and our combustion engines, and it keeps our airplanes aloft. God also gave another great gift of power to our earth when he covered it with sixteen inches of topsoil. Our topsoil has enough production power that over a few years it can produce a pile of potatoes twenty feet high and still have its sixteen inches of topsoil left. Scientists have now discovered how to produce vast amounts of heat and power by burning water. The great powers of our earth have produced some fantastic miracles.

We fly through the stratosphere faster than sound. We can live in the depths of the sea or sail under the polar ice cap. With our tremendous farm machinery, our fertilizers, and our know-how, one man can produce more food than thousands of those men represented by the parable of the Sower. Jesus told of the man who went forth to sow and some of the few seeds thrown out by his hand fell among the rocks, some got mixed up with the thorns and the thistles, and some lay upon the hard ground until they were eaten up by the birds. Any good farmer can imagine the starvation return that would result from this back-breaking, lackluster toil.

However, God did not put his greatest power into machinery or even into the atoms. He put his greatest power into the man who makes the machinery and splits the atoms. But above all of these, by far the greatest power in the universe is the power of God. By his power he created and controls the universe. The night before his crucifixion Jesus said that he could command the services of twelve legions of angels to fight in his behalf. However, during his antemortal existence he did many unimaginable things. God said: "And worlds without number have I created; . . . and by the Son I created them, which is mine Only Begotten." (Moses 1:33.) John mentions this same idea when he said of the antemortal Christ, "All things were made by him; and without him was not anything made that was made." (John 1:3.)

Jesus himself said: "All power is given me in heaven and in earth." (Matthew 28:18.) And we might try to imagine the extent of his present power. Through his power worlds come into existence and others pass away. At his decree nations rise or fall. The time is very near when he will come to the earth again with great power and glory, accompanied by his mighty angels in flaming fire. Jesus has power over life and death and every detail of our existence. He is the light of the sun and the power by which it was made. One of the primary purposes of his life is to give us power. And more than almost any other thing, that is what we are in greatest need of both here and hereafter. We have the power of repentance, the power of excellence, the power to be like God. Emerson said, "Do the thing and you shall have the power." That is, we learn to do by doing. Certainly our age of power is no place for incompetents, cowards, and weaklings. But the apostle John gives us a profitable direction for attaining power when he says of us and of Christ: "But as many as received him, to them gave he power to become the sons of God. . . ." (John 1:12.) We need the power to build character, the power to overcome temptation, the power to destroy the weaknesses and sins in ourselves.

The two angels who were sent to destroy Sodom and Gomorrah had the power to call down fire and brimstone upon those two ancient, wicked cities, and God has given us the power to destroy every vestige of wickedness and trouble from our own lives. Paul said to Timothy, "For God hath not given us the spirit of fear; but of power and of love, and of a sound mind." (2 Timothy 1:7.) And with these three we can work almost any miracle.

The Lord gave the sealing power to Peter when he said, "And I will give unto thee the keys of the kingdom of heaven that whatsoever thou shalt bind on earth shall be bound in heaven: . . . and whatsoever thou shalt loose on earth shall be loosed in heaven." (Matthew 16:19.) And the dictionary says that power is the physical, mental, or moral ability to act. It is that capacity for extraordinary performance that we ourselves may develop. This great power has to do with such mental and bodily functions as thinking, believing, judging, willing, and progressing. Because of the increased evil of our day, we need a much greater power to overcome our more difficult problems. We need more thinking power and more character power, and more doing power.

We see some people who have political power, some who have financial power, and some who have physical power. There are many ways that we may develop greater personal power. Each of us has within himself fantastic abilities and potential powers that may presently be unknown to him. These may be aroused by a little study and exercise. We can wield a much greater power of example. There is a great power in love. There is a great power in godliness.

Tennyson's hero called Sir Galahad said, "My strength is as the strength of ten, Because my heart is pure." A roadside billboard for an oil company says, "A clean engine produces power." And so does a clean mind, a great ambition, and a righteous heart. We have a great power in our ability to plan. No one generates more power than the planner, the thinker, the organizer, the doer. He is the one who draws the blueprint for success. He is the one who builds the roadway on which every accomplishment will travel.

It takes power to overcome any evil and bring about every righteous accomplishment. Jesus said of his own mortal life, "I have power to lay it down, and I have power to take it again." (John 10:18.) And if we live by his principles, God will also give us the power over death. We may also have all of the power necessary to bring about God's promises of an eternal life, an eternal success, an eternal happiness, and our own eternal progression.

It should be of utmost interest to us that all powers are based on obedience to the laws of righteousness. It is the natural law of weakness that when one becomes drunken, disobedient, dishonest, he is enslaved by his evil habits and therefore loses his power. Satan is evil and the full consequences of his deeds will sometime catch up with him. Then he will lose his power and will be confined forever in hell, chained to the evil that he has developed. But in various degrees, this same situation will also prevail with those of us in this life who let weakness and sin rule our lives.

Then if we are to be saved, even in the lowest kingdom, it must be through the cleansing fires of hell. But those who follow God will develop the strength and power of righteousness with the natural consequences of those blessings of happiness, everlasting life, and eternal progression. And of us it may then be said, as it was of God himself, "For thine is the kingdom, and the power, and the glory, for ever." (Matthew 6:13.)

The Will to Do

IN PLANNING for any successful accomplishment, we should include in our research some studies having to do with those great potential powers that God has made available to us in our own minds and personalities. One of the most exciting of all of our human opportunities is our tremendous God-given gift of free agency. In one of his most significant declarations, God said to man: ". . . thou mayest choose for thyself." (Moses 3:17.) But in addition to giving us the right to choose, he has also given us the ability to bring any of our projected accomplishments about. We sometimes refer to this giant human power as "will power."

The dictionary says that will power is that energy or force of will that we express in our purpose, our resolution, our determination, and our strength of mind. Tennyson referred to someone with an "iron will." And we think of one who is strong-willed as one who has some definite goals that are supported by strong convictions and real enthusiasms. It is the will that moves the intellect to action. It is by our wills and our intelligence that we are able to overcome evil. It has been said that appetite is the will's solicitor and the will is appetite's controller.

Any worthwhile accomplishment involves a strong desire or a powerful intention or a resolute determination strong enough to control our activities. By the power of one's will he may also control his emotions, his thoughts, and the outcome of what he does. We sometimes speak of the will to win, the will to live, the will to endure, the will to grow, the will to excellence, and the will to make our lives successful.

Ernest Hendly was a helpless cripple when he wrote "Invictus." He said:

> Out of the night that covers me,
> Black as the Pit from pole to pole,
> I thank whatever gods may be
> For my unconquerable soul.

> In the fell clutch of circumstance,
> I have not winced nor cried aloud;
> Under the bludgeonings of chance
> My head is bloody, but unbowed,
>
> Beyond this veil of wrath and tears
> Looms but the horror of the shade
> And yet the menace of the years
> Finds and shall find me unafraid.
>
> It matters not how strait the gate,
> How charged with punishments the scroll,
> I am the master of my fate:
> I am the captain of my soul.

It is by this power of the will that we overcome all indecision and uncertainty. We settle all internal conflicts by the act or the experience of willing.

Great character values are always lost when our wills lose their tone or become flabby and weak. With a weak will we become like the weathercock that is blown about by every passing wind or the chameleon that changes its color in every environment, where it has no goal and no destiny.

The will becomes inoperative in the case of those who are feebleminded or intoxicated or who lack a sense of responsibility. Sometimes people can be hypnotized and placed under the control or the will of somebody else. It is easy to become enslaved by evil and weakness. On the other hand, a firm continuous exercise of a stable will builds up power that makes us stronger than anything that can happen to us. Will power eliminates danger.

Someone has expressed the philosophy of his will by saying:

> Night swoops on me with blackest wings,
> But I'll succeed.
> I see the stars that darkness brings
> And I'll succeed.
> No force on earth can make me cower
> Because each moment and each hour
> I still affirm with strength and power
> I shall succeed.

That is a marvelous philosophy of success. It is by the will that we establish goals and build habits around them. As it has been said, the strongest power in the world is the power of habit. It is stronger than education or discipline.

Someone has said that what the rails are to the streamliner, habit is to our success. As the rails support and guide the streamliner, so habit supports and guides our success. One of the chief exercises of the will is to bring about our own success by establishing in ourselves those habits of thinking, planning, working, and believing.

God is all-wise and all-powerful, and we can learn what his will is concerning us and then build strong habits around our obedience to it. What an exciting idea to try to understand the will power of God or how it would improve us and our world to join with Jesus, who is our example in following God's will concerning us. To do the will of his Father was probably the most important principle involved in the Master's success. On all occasions he said to his Father, ". . . not my will, but thine, be done." (Luke 22:42.) If we can develop great convictions and a great appetite to do the will of the Lord in every detail, then the greatest success is fully assured to us.

Sometimes we make this serious mistake of being spasmodic and uncertain in the control of our will. When we allow too many exceptions to success, we are doing as much toward tearing it down as we are toward building it up. One secret of the Master's excellence was that he allowed no deviations or exceptions to righteousness. There were no leaks in his enthusiasm and no chinks in his armor where weakness or evil could get a foothold.

Will power is made up of many things, such as appetite, ambition, desire, love, and industry, but it should not be confused with those elements of conflict and struggle. For many persons, will power has come to signify strain, tension, repression, misery, and compulsion. We sometimes think of will power as the unpleasant way to get ourselves to do something that we do not want to do. Jesus said. ". . . he that endureth to the end shall be saved." (Matthew 10:22.) And endurance has come to mean a time of suffering and unpleasant hanging on to our ideals by sheer force. There are some people who do not like to get up on time in the morning, and so when their conscience or necessity tells them to get up and their flesh and lethargy tells them to stay in bed, they lie there and carry on an unpleasant battle that almost always ends in failure and a kind of nervous instability. A much better way would be for one to point out to himself all of the advantages of wanting to get up on time and make it pleasant for himself to get up on time. If we were going to get a thousand dollars each time we got up on time, that would make us really *want* to get up, and our accomplishment would then be certain.

An effective assertion of the will makes all things not only easy but pleasant. Because we don't understand this principle of willing, we very frequently defeat ourselves by saying it is hard to live our religion, and to live a good life is so difficult and unpleasant that we cannot be expected to do it. This may be true if we have already given evil activities and unholy ambitions such a great power over our lives that we are enslaved, intoxicated, or hypnotized by them. But it is not true that evil is more pleasant than good or that the state of failure is happier than success.

It is just as easy for an honest man to be honest as it is for a dishonest man to be dishonest. It is much easier for a good man to do good than for a good man to do evil. However, it is much easier for an evil man to do evil than for an evil man to do good. A life of sin and unrighteousness would have been the most difficult path for Jesus to have followed. On the other hand, goodness and righteousness would be impossibly difficult for Satan. We are not paying ourselves compliments when we confess a greater desire to be traitors than patriots, or to be criminals than good citizens, or to be lazy than industrious. We are selling ourselves short when we make such false and evil generalities as to say, "Everybody's doing it" or "I suppose it would be more pleasant for me to go to hell because most of my friends will be there." The original meaning of will was desire, wish, to prefer; and to build up a great will power would mean that we cultivate a strong love of righteousness and success and a firm determination to avoid every evil and every failure.

If one allowed himself to get very sick with lung cancer by smoking cigarettes, then he might truthfully say it is very difficult to get well, but if he would prevent or dispose of the evil before it causes the disease, health would be the natural result even without effort. And so it is that by breaking the commandments of the Lord we produce stronger appetites for evil in ourselves. Then we might properly say that it is difficult to live our religion, or we cannot be expected to keep all of God's commandments. No success is easy if we first build up a lot of alibis, rationalizations, and antagonism to fight against it. If one wants to be successful, he must make success easy to attain. We always have great power to do those things that we love to do and that we do well, and the secret of will power is in building up a great love for accomplishment and righteousness.

There is also a great opportunity to strengthen the will by increasing our knowledge, our understanding, and our good judgment. Will power is that process by which the mind makes the right choices and is prepared for any effort to overcome the obstacles that would bar the way or the contrary desires that would neutralize effort. We ought to set the machinery of our life toward developing will power instead of won't power. We ought to love God instead of Satan. We should gear our life to success instead of failure, mediocrity, or neutrality.

A psychiatrist once asked a mental patient if he ever had any trouble in making up his mind. The mental patient said, "Well, yes and no." This is probably our own biggest problem. There are too many yes-and-no people who have not made up their minds between good and evil, right and wrong, failure and success.

Recently a man with a serious moral transgression was discussing his problem. It was said to him: "What do you think is going to happen when the next temptation presents itself?" He said, "How can I tell what I will do until I know what the temptation is?" It is easy to predict the future result of such irresolution. That is, because he hasn't made up his mind to begin with, if the temptation has a strong attraction to him, he will fall. If the temptation has only weak appeal, he will be able to resist.

We should thoroughly understand what is good and what is bad in life and then make some firm determination to accept the one and reject the other. The greatest example of success is God. He does not vacillate nor does he fall down before every temptation, because his mind is made up. He "cannot look upon sin with the least degree of allowance." (D&C 1:31.) God has will power. He loves righteousness, and by learning his will we can make its power our own. In yes-and-no people the will and the judgment are in continual conflict, and they are consigned thereby to the lower levels of success unnecessarily.

If we desire to develop this miraculous ability called will power, then we need to develop good judgment and fine convictions and the ability to eliminate conflicts. Then every success is placed within our easy reach.

Action and Reaction

ONE OF the greatest ideas in our world is represented by the little three letter word *act*. Nothing has very much significance until something has moved. The battle cry of success is action. The power to act is the power to accomplish. To act is to work, to function, to operate, and to become. An act is the mainspring of existence. It contains the seeds of motivation and the fruits of achievement. We generate fears and failures while we sit, whereas courage and success are born out of activity.

One of the greatest compliments that can be paid to anyone is to say that he is a man of action. Where there is no activity, there is nothing. The chief characteristic of life as well as the greatest of all of our possessions is the power to do things. A stone may lie unmoving and unthinking on the mountainside for a billion years, and it accomplishes nothing. But God created man in his own image and gave him these miraculous gifts of movement, thought, love, and joy, which altogether we call life.

Life is that mysterious primal element in which God himself has his being. It was said of God: "In him was life; and the life was the light of men." (John 1:4.) The Creator has also placed that godly intelligence and the ability to take limitless action in his greatest creation—man. Through our great gift of free agency we have an unlimited ability to make any desired movement in any direction at any speed. However, action has a kind of opposite motion that is called reaction. Instead of our responses coming from our minds and wills, they sometimes come from our prejudices or emotions. Our responses frequently come as rebounds from some other things. Then instead of acting, we are being acted upon.

The dictionary says that reaction is to exert a reciprocal or counteracting force or influence. In one of his excellent articles entitled "Do You Act or React?" Sydney J. Harris says:

The other night I walked with my Quaker friend to the newsstand. He bought a paper, and politely thanked the newsie. However, the newsie didn't even acknowledge it.

"A sullen fellow, isn't he?" I commented.

"Oh, he's that way every night," shrugged my friend.

"Then why do you continue to be so polite to him?" I asked.

"Why not?" inquired my friend. "Why should I let him decide how I am going to act?"

As I later thought about this incident, it occurred to me that the important word was act. My friend acts toward people whereas most of us react. My friend has a fine sense of inner balance which is lacking in so many of us. He knows who he himself is, what he stands for, and how he should behave, and he refuses to let anyone get him off the track. If he should return incivility for incivility he would lose command of his own conduct.

Nobody is more unhappy than the perpetual reactor, because he is always at the mercy of everyone else's whims. His center of emotional gravity is not rooted within himself where it belongs, but it is in the world outside him. His temperature is always being raised or lowered by every social climate in which he finds himself, and he becomes a mere creature at the mercy of these elements.

False praise gives a reactor a feeling of groundless elation. Criticism depresses him. Real or imaginary snubs hurt him, and the merest suspicion of unpopularity generates bitterness in him. Serenity cannot be achieved in us until we become the masters of our own actions and determine our own attitudes. To let another person decide for us whether we shall be rude or gracious, elated or depressed, successful or unsuccessful is to relinquish control over ourselves, and control is ultimately about all that any of us possess. The only true possession is self-possession. One of the profitable projects of our lives is to learn to conduct our activities according to that God-given intelligence within us instead of throwing away our self-control and allowing ourselves to react according to what goes on around us.

A few years ago I had an ordinary cold. Because it seemed to hang on a little longer than it should have done, I went to a doctor who gave me a shot of penicillin. Instead of the medicine taking the curative action of killing the disease, as the doctor had intended, my whole system set up a violent reaction to the penicillin itself and induced in me a far more serious sickness than the one brought on by the disease. The reaction caused a rash to break out that completely covered my body and put me out of commission for several days.

But our problems become even worse when we get into the habit of substituting reaction for intelligent action. We bring many of our most serious diseases upon ourselves when we spend our energy reacting to the faults and failings of others. About this subject in our own day the Lord has said:

My disciples, in days of old, sought occasion against one another and forgave not one another in their hearts; and for this evil they were afflicted and sorely chastened.

Wherefore, I say unto you, that ye ought to forgive one another; for he that forgiveth not his brother his trespasses standeth condemned before the Lord; for there remaineth in him the greater sin. (D&C 64: 8-9.)

Someone has posed this question: "Suppose that you were bitten by a rattlesnake and had your choice between the following two courses, which would you take? First, you could chase and kill the rattlesnake, or second, you could get the poison out of your own system." Suppose that there was plenty of time to do either one but not enough time to do both. You can sit down quickly, open the wound, suck out the poison, and save your life, in which case the rattlesnake would get away. However, if you chased and killed the rattlesnake, by that time the poison would have gone all through your system and you would swell up and die. The right solution to that question may not be as simple as it sounds. Many people have such a strong sense of reaction that they even lose their eternal lives while killing rattlesnakes.

Some people react to their problems by getting drunk or becoming bitter or cursing God. There are people so burdened down with inferiority complexes that instead of curing the disease, they chase the rattlesnakes. Those people who want to tear down the establishment, overthrow the government, turn to crime, and join the hippies are reactionaries.

Recently a young woman came to talk about her problems. She was nice-looking and seemed like a very intelligent young woman, but she was a reactor. She had been immoral with three men, and each of her evils was a reaction to a disagreement with her boyfriend with whom she had never been immoral. She had always thought of herself as one with high principles and a good church member. However, because she now finds her actions in conflict with her beliefs, she has decided to try to solve her problem by withdrawing from church activity. If she took proper action, she would relieve the conflict by repenting of her sins. She merely reacts against her sins by committing more sins. She seems to think that by striking at her boyfriend and the Church, she might solve her problem, but each time that she kills a few more rattlesnakes, she herself will bloat up a little more.

In early days some Indians and some white men used to react to the death of one of their number by killing the next one of the opposite group that came within range. This reaction or rebounding, or this attempt to get even or to punish someone, causes many of our most serious difficulties. A reactor lives by rumors, impulses, senseless marches, and name calling when even the source of his problem is often in doubt.

Shakespeare was speaking of a thoughtful, righteous man of action when he said: "This above all: to thine own self be true, and it must follow, as the night the day, Thou canst not then be false to any man." (*Hamlet,* Act I, scene iii.)

When a person intelligently decides what is right and what is wrong, he is then able to use his mind and his will to take effective action. When anyone does anything right, he always has a feeling of peace and that his life itself is worthwhile. However, when one abandons his principles and becomes a reactionary, he gets into all kinds of troubles. When one can't tell whether he is responding to something because it is right or because he is a reactionary, then he gets all mixed up and doesn't know how to handle his problems.

A man was recently killed in an automobile accident, which naturally was a terrible shock to his wife. But instead of trying to solve her problems in the best possible way, she began a chain reaction. She somehow seems to have felt that her husband's death was God's fault. Therefore, she quit going to church. She began spending her tithing money for liquor and tobacco. She didn't like liquor or tobacco, but this seemed to her to be the best way to get even with God for letting her husband die. We can never solve our problems by offending God and making sinners out of ourselves.

One of the most important services that we might perform for ourselves is to build up our ability to take appropriate action in all things instead of turning ourselves into reactionaries. Such great words as *ask, seek, knock, pray, love, work,* and *believe* are action words, whereas *hate, anger, revenge, lust, fear,* and *doubt* indicate reaction.

There is a story to the effect that the President of the United States once asked Robert E. Lee to give him his opinion about the capability of a certain man who was being considered for a public office. Robert E. Lee gave the man a good report. Someone said to General Lee, "I can't understand why you have said so many nice things about that man when you know that he is saying many uncomplimentary things about you." General Lee said, "I understood that the President wanted my opinion of him, not his opinion of me."

So many of our sins are not because we want to do wrong, but because we are not using our best judgment. We are merely reacting to someone or something. There is a very constructive philosophy that we should remember that says, "I will not let mine enemy make me sin." Rather, we should make good out of every situation. Edgar A. Guest identified both of these situations in his poem "The Trick." He said:

> I noticed as soon as I opened the door
> that the fellow was surly, and so
> with a frown just as black as the one that he wore
> I angrily told him to go.
> Now I hadn't the slightest intention to be
> as surly, uncivil and hateful as he,
> but that was the trick that he played upon me.
>
> Another chap came to my doorstep that day,
> and a twinkle he had in his eye.
> With a smile on his face he began in a way
> that prompted a gentle reply.
> Though a stranger he was, I was eager to be
> as gracious, good-natured, and kindly as he,
> and that was the trick that he played upon me.
>
> Since those visits I've thought in this life that we live
> and the lesson seems simple to learn:
> We get back a smile for the smile that we give
> and a frown brings a frown in return.
> If I chuckle, with chuckles I'll surely be met.
> Just as I set my lips, so all lips will be set.
> And that is a trick that I mustn't forget.

There is another wonderful action story told about a little slave girl on the auction block during the Civil War. A prospective buyer approached her and said, "If I buy you and give you a good home and feed you well and treat you kindly, will you promise me that you will be honest?" This wonderful little slave girl said: "I will promise to be honest whether you buy me and treat me kindly or not."

We have a great concern about protecting our material treasures and possessions, but our greatest treasures are the possessions of our own person. It is with our judgments and the kinds of decisions that we make that all good things are determined. All of us will be judged according to our works. This makes taking proper action the greatest of all of our opportunities. It is by our power to act that we may become even as God is.

The Agenda

O NE OF the most effective means by which any leadership accomplishment can be brought about is the habitual use of a good, well-planned agenda. An agenda is usually thought of as a list of items arranged in logical order with necessary information attached so that certain subjects may be taken up and discussed at a meeting called for that purpose.

The dictionary describes an agenda as a memorandum of responsibilities to be performed. It is a list of important duties that should be taken care of. Of course, before the agenda can be prepared, the matters to be decided have to be fully planned so that the agenda can be put down in writing. When the agenda has been thoughtfully prepared, the problems will have been partly solved. The dictionary points out an interesting relationship between the word *agenda* and the word *credenda*. An agenda is a list of duties that should be taken care of, and a credenda is a list of doctrines that should be believed in. In these two words we see something of the traditional conflict that has always been going on between our deeds and our creeds. Usually a good business practice dictates that when a meeting is called so that important matters may be discussed, a letter should be sent out with the call outlining the matters that are to be considered.

A written explanation of what will be on the agenda will encourage those planning the meeting to more carefully think through the matters that will be considered, and those involved may have all supplementary material available and on hand. It will also enable those attending to make all necessary preparations to protect their own interests and those of the company.

However, if those conducting an important meeting do not have a well worked-out agenda in writing, the meeting may not be nearly as productive. Those present may then have to guess at the pertinent facts and depend upon their memories, which may not be very dependable. A good agenda also has several other uses. I know a very successful salesman who makes up a written agenda for himself before he undertakes any important sale. He usually has a fact-finding interview with the prospect, and then in a kind of sales rehearsal he makes a written outline of the specific points that he feels should be made. Every good salesman needs an agenda of facts, thoughts, and reasons as to why and how the sale can best be made.

In addition to making an agenda for every sale, a good salesman may also make an agenda for each of those days, weeks, months, and years that are soon to become a part of his career. A good agenda, prepared and written down well in advance of its date of use, will help to mature his thinking and keep him on course so that his program will not be disrupted by unscheduled attractions.

I know a man who does a great deal of personal interviewing. He has an agenda of questions to use that have been well worked out in advance. This way he is certain that he will get all of the necessary information, and when he fills in the prospect's answers to these well-considered questions, he also gets written minutes of the interview. And in addition to the answers, he also gets the prospect's attitudes and ambitions.

However, there is at large a conflicting philosophy to the agenda that allows many people to hold their meetings, conduct their business, and make their sales on a kind of hit-and-miss basis. Because these people do things only as they occur to them, they never put very much planning or thought into their work. Rather, they just act on their impulses with whatever may come into their hands or minds. This lesser philosophy, featuring a lack of planning, is expressed in the recurring theme of the song which says, "Doing What Comes Naturally." Such people allow themselves to be governed largely by conditions or by whichever wind may be blowing at the moment.

Dr. Leon Tucker, a great teacher of the Bible, used to tell a story of a lady who had poor health. As her friends would ask her how she was, she would usually reply, "I am feeling as well as could be expected under the circumstances." Then in making a comparison to another kind of poor health, Dr. Tucker said that "far too many people, including a lot of Christians, allow themselves to live most of their lives 'under the circumstances.' " Everyone is far more successful when he lives above and ahead of and beyond the circumstances. Someone once said to Napoleon, "How are conditions?" The great emperor replied, "I make conditions." When we live at our best, so do we make our conditions.

As Julius Caesar was in the process of conquering the world, he was once crossing a rough sea during a severe storm. The captain of the boat was expressing his serious concern for the safety of those for whom he had responsibility. Then his famous guest said to him, "Fear not, thy boat carries Caesar." In the beginning God created man in his own image and gave him dominion over everything upon the earth, including himself. When we fail to control our conditions, our conditions will control us. When we succumb to our temptations or allow ourselves to be overpowered by our weaknesses, we are living under the circumstances.

In excusing his mediocrity, a salesman once said to his sales manager, "I think I did pretty well under the circumstances." His manager said, "What in the world were you doing way down there?"

That is a good question for many of us to ask ourselves. However, if we had a good agenda, planned well in advance, thoughtfully considered and completely followed, we would always be the master of our circumstances. But when we have no recognized official agenda, we then let all kinds of unauthorized activities get into our programs.

Frequently we wait to see what our circumstances are going to be before we make up our minds about what kind of people we are going to be. We wait on luck, chance, conditions, and the devil.

Often when one associates with those who drink or smoke or take dope or tell lies, he feels that under the circumstances it might be well for him to do these things also, no matter how unprofitable they may be. We excuse our lack of judgment by saying, "When in Rome, do as the Romans do." As a result, when someone breathes the air of dishonesty, atheism, or immorality, we frequently have a strong inclination to take up the habit. We reason that if others are doing it, it must be all right. However, the philosophy of "everybody's doing it" is a doctrine of weakness and evil.

Someone once said to his friend, "But for a jerk, don't you think that I have come quite a long way?" Jerks and sinners don't have a strong, well-planned agenda to which they have made a whole-hearted commitment. A good agenda greatly reduces the chances for errors and the necessity for making snap judgments. Our agenda tells us what should be on the program and what should be left off. It is sometimes illegal, unconstitutional, and unfair to take action on any matter that is not listed on the agenda in advance. It is also unprofitable and unwise.

Somebody has figured out that there are at least two ways to pack a trunk. One way is to have a place prepared for everything and then see that everything goes into its place. One compartment may be prepared for your shoes, one for your shirts, and all of the other items are exactly fitted in those places where they belong. Then all available space will be utilized to the best possible advantage. The other way to pack a trunk is to dump all of the contents into the trunk helter-skelter, with no order and no priorities. That is, the trunk has no agenda.

I know of a doctor who packs his office by loading it helter-skelter with patients who are required to wait for hours before their turn comes. I don't know how successful he may be in his efforts to save their health, but he is certainly very successful in wasting their time. This doctor would do well if he were to learn a little more about how to organize his day. A lot of us would do well if we were to learn how to better organize our lives.

Therefore, what are we going to do about organizing an agenda for ourselves? Certainly there isn't time for us to make all of the possible mistakes personally. This is also a luxury that we can't afford. And when we say "Everybody's doing it," we are just kidding ourselves. Some people are doing some wrong things and some are doing other wrong things, but no one ever does all of them. Because it is impossible to take advantage of all of the good experiences, we therefore need some kind of a system of priorities. We ought to sit down and work out what we want on our own life's agenda.

Somebody has said that the four most important dates in anyone's life are these: (1) the day he is born, when a new life comes into being; (2) the date that he is married—that is, when a new family is organized; (3) the day he selects his life's work, which will determine the amount and kind of his service and his own self-development, and (4) the date on which he dies—that is, the day he graduates from life with either honors or dishonors.

Henry Thoreau once said that we should thank God every day of our lives for the privilege of having been born. Then he went on to speculate on the rather unique supposition of what it might have been like if we had never been born, and he pointed out some of the excitement and accomplishments that we would have missed as a consequence. However, what Mr. Thoreau may not have known was that one-third of all of the children of God never were born and never can be born because they didn't comply with God's agenda prepared for their first estate. When Lucifer rebelled against God, someone in the propaganda field said, "Everybody's doing it," and as a consequence all of them failed to graduate into their second estate.

Every spirit child of God hungers for a body. Those unembodied spirits who appeared to Jesus in his day preferred the bodies of swine rather than to have no bodies at all. However, with our present battery of birth control pills and our high abortion rate, we are making it pretty tough even for those who passed the requirements of their first estate to be born.

Among many other success devices, we ought to have a good education placed high on our life's agenda. We should follow the instruction of Jesus and be born again so that we could become devoted members of his kingdom. We should put a godly character and a temple marriage on the agenda. We ought to make sure that the quality of our faith and our works will entitle us, upon graduation from this life, to enter into the celestial kingdom. It is important that we understand that every principle and every ordinance of the gospel has to do with the celestial kingdom. That is, if we are only interested in the lower kingdoms, it is not necessary to keep our minds healthy and our bodies clean. However, if we plan to qualify for the presence of God in celestial glory, we should put all of the Ten Commandments on the agenda to be lived under the strictest discipline, and we had better leave off the agenda all of those things about which God has given us those stern warnings, saying, "Thou shalt not."

If the enticement of liquor and atheism and immorality were forbidden by God when he stood on the top of Mount Sinai, then we had better not include them in any program for our lives. We should never make a decision in anger or fear or undue haste. A great businessman once said that one of the best aids to success was for everyone, before undertaking any accomplishment, to make up a list of those things which he just must not do under any circumstances. The Lord thundered one such list from the top of Mount Sinai some 3400 years ago. If we definitely make up our minds about those things that we must not do, then we will have all of our time free for those things that we should do.

Every one of God's great commands comes to us with a blessing of righteousness, prosperity, and happiness attached. The scriptures are just a great collection of promissory notes. We ought to make sure we have the ability to plan, organize, and follow the great agenda that God has prepared in the holy scriptures.

Alienation of Affections

I T IS likely that the most important influences in our lives are determined by what we like the most. Life's quality depends on what we are attracted to, and whom we fall in love with, and what we have an appetite for. When we have some definite desires propelled by strong motivations, we can reach almost any planned objective. An unwavering desire for good things produces a power that God himself recognizes. A great prophet once said: "God grants unto every man according to his desires."

The primary principle of any success is to believe in it effectively and to want it vigorously. On the other hand, the chances for any accomplishments being reached are seriously reduced when our attractions and loves and appetites and desires are reduced in size or when we are working with a confused focus.

Of course all contrary influences tend to destroy our interests and turn our ambitions in some other direction. There is an interesting phrase found in the dictionary called "the alienation of affections." This refers to a destructive estrangement that makes one indifferent, unfriendly, or hostile to that which he had previously loved. This phrase describes a condition in which some previously profitable attachment is broken.

Then an existing love may be withdrawn or a faith may be liquidated or one's affections are transferred to another by being diverted from their natural channels. Many years ago this phrase, "alienation of affections" used to be a common court pleading in divorce lawsuits. Some third party was named as having broken up the happy relationship between a man and his wife. It was often claimed that an accused person had caused a transfer of a spouse's affections to himself from the plaintiff, who had a better right to them. Many have claimed that their spouse's love for them has been destroyed because she was improperly or unfairly persuaded that she had married beneath her station, or that her husband was too stingy or too selfish. Some women have been accused of taking advantage of some other woman's husband by flattering him about virtues that he did not possess or offering him charms with which the wife was not able to compete. All kinds of insidious alienation of affection campaigns have been carried on to pervert the minds of people with lies and enticements and every other kind of consideration.

One of literature's classic examples of alienation of affection is found in Shakespeare's tragedy of *Othello*. Othello was very much in love with his beautiful and virtuous wife, Desdemona. Othello was a famous general in the wars conducted by the Venetians against the Turks. However, Othello had one serious weakness in that he had a very jealous nature.

Capitalizing on this fault, his crafty and traitorous friend, Iago, poisoned Othello's mind against his own wife. In philosophizing about jealousy, Shakespeare says, "Trifles light as air are to the jealous confirmations strong as proofs of holy writ. . . . Dangerous conceits are in their natures poisons, which act upon the blood and burn like mines of sulphur."

Finally, blind with rage and certain that his most virtuous wife had been untrue to him, Othello strangled her. His jealous, unreasonable mind told him that he must destroy her before she betrayed someone else. Almost immediately after her death, Othello learned the truth, and he stabbed himself and died by the side of his wife.

Othello's affections for his wife were alienated by jealousy incited by misinformation. But, alienation of affections, while not frequently mentioned in our own day of easy divorce, still leads the list as the reason for broken homes. The causes of divorce are not only jealousy; mental cruelty, immorality, dishonesty, nonsupport, boredom, and incompatability have all been added to the list.

Nowdays we don't need to wait for some third party to alienate our wife's affections, as there are so many interesting ways to make ourselves financially, religiously, and personally offensive to each other. Suppose that we had some way of registering what the affections of a wife may be on a thermometer ten feet high that we could read. We would find that everything that happened between the marriage partners would change the readings in proportion either up or down.

Suppose that when we had been at our best the reading was at its maximum of 100. But then suppose that we gave the wife a good punch on the nose. In all probability we would discover that the mercury would drop off a few points. All of our inconsiderations, unfairness, untruthfulness, temper, unkindness, scorn, unrighteousness, negative attitudes, personality faults, and irresponsibilities would cause the mercury to continue to retreat until it reached the bottom.

Alienation of affections takes many other forms. A great proportion of the success that the Communists have had in building up their power has come to them as they have alienated the affections of other people from their own government. Satan is the father of lies and misrepresentation, which are the chief tools of alienation, and in this field the Communists are probably his most capable students. They have been called masters of deceit. Over and over again they have proven their superiority in stirring up trouble for other governments and sowing discord among other peoples. They know how to cause divisions among those they are trying to dominate. They are masters in causing rebellions and strikes against constituted authority. As soon as their victim's strength has been exhausted by internal alienation, they walk in and take over because their prey is now too weak to resist.

The Communists may be far behind us in agricultural production, in manufacturing, in individual enterprise, in religion, in freedom, and in self-government, but they lead all peoples in their various programs of subversion and misrepresentation. They have made great progress in their announced goal to make slaves of as many people as they can, and they are able to collect enough vassal tribute to make their evil enterprises profitable. It seems incredible that many intelligent groups of people are not able to figure out that a free enterprise among a free people is much better than force, slavery, and oppression. The long suit of the Communists is alienation of affections, the inspiration for which comes from Satan, the father of all evil.

In the grand council of heaven before this earth was, Lucifer rebelled against God and led one-third of all of the hosts of heaven after him. Satan was the originator of this idea of ruling people by force and is still its chief exponent. In several ways, we who live in America are very vulnerable to having our affections alienated because of the great amount of freedom that has been granted to both friend and foe alike.

Everyone is permitted full liberty to promote his own doctrine, whether it is good or bad. But we should remember that it is by this process of alienating the affections of good people from good things that the Communists hope to destroy both our freedom and our country. Above most other things, Satan and the Communists want to alienate us from our ideals. They want to destroy our love of liberty. They want to kill our respect for law and order and our love of beauty and harmony. They would like to turn us so strongly against war that we would rather serve as slaves than protect our rights as free men.

The dictionary says that an alien is a person of another family or another race or another place. An alien is a stranger who pays his allegiance to some other country or some other ideology. And many of these aliens, who owe their allegiance to other countries and other ideologies, are now trying to pervert our minds with falsehoods and misinformation from within our own ranks. They would like nothing better than to make us dislike ourselves. By the things that we are doing in our crime waves and our sins, we are not only destroying our own self-respect, but we are also doing things that will estrange us from God.

With our help, the Communists have already gone a long way in this endeavor. The scriptures foretell the fact that the people of our present world will so seriously offend God that he will finally be impelled to personally come to cleanse the earth of its sin. The alienation causing all of these problems is actually our own fault because of our own gullibility. Anyone who deliberately permits himself to be led into a wrong must also bear the responsibility and suffer the evil consequences.

There is an interesting companion word for alien in the dictionary called *alienability*. It refers to those who are easily fooled. It doesn't take much to persuade some people to transfer their allegiance to the alien powers of Satan and the Communists, even though slavery and death are plainly marked as the final result. Shakespeare says of one person: "He would not serve God if the devil bid him." Cain was one of those who wanted to play on the devil's team. The alienability of Cain is indicated by the scripture that says: ". . . Cain loved Satan more than God." (Moses 5:18.) Many people in our day also want to get into the devil's act and serve as a sponsor for evil, ugliness, and crime. The increase in crime indicates the acceleration with which we are transferring our allegiance away from God.

There are many to whom it may seem a small thing to throw away their love of God and their prospects of eternal glory. The number one success law of the world says: "Thou shalt love the Lord thy God with all thy heart, and with all thy soul, and with all thy mind. This is the first and great commandment. And the second is like unto it, Thou shalt love thy neighbour as thyself. On these two commandments hang all the law and the prophets." (Matthew 22:37-40.) This doesn't allow much space for any double loyalties. By our disobedience to God's law and the increase in our participation in crime, sin, disorder, and the ugliness that stems from Satan, we surrender our allegiance to the Creator and submit to an alien.

It is interesting how clearly this period of alienation of affections was foreseen over nineteen hundred years ago. Jesus said, ". . . as the days of Noe were, so shall also the coming of the Son of man be." (Matthew 24:37.) And the apostle Paul says:

This know also, that in the last days perilous times shall come.

For men shall be lovers of their own selves, covetous, boasters, proud, blasphemers, disobedient to parents, unthankful, unholy.

Without natural affection, trucebreakers, false accusers, incontinent, fierce, despisers of those that are good.

Traitors, heady, highminded, lovers of pleasure more than lovers of God;

Having a form of godliness, but denying the power thereof: from such turn away.

For of this sort are they which creep into houses, and lead captive silly women laden with sins, led away with divers lusts,

Ever learning, and never able to come to the knowledge of the truth.

Now as Jannes and Jambres withstood Moses, so do these also resist the truth: men of corrupt minds, reprobate concerning the faith. (2 Timothy 3:1-8.)

But if we go over to Satan and continue beyond the point of no return, we will then be required to live with him. Now is the time for us to make some decisions about what kind of ideologies we want to be in love with. We might make our citizenship more secure by taking a good, solid, permanent, unyielding pledge of allegiance to that nation which God himself established for our benefit.

We should also take a pledge of allegiance to our wives and

our families and to all those principles of righteousness on which our success and happiness are based. We might also make our own personal covenant to serve God and keep every one of his commandments. If our commitment is firm enough, and we are dedicated enough, then no matter how much we are courted by evil, we will remain true to righteousness.

We can't very well ride two horses in the same race. We can't look up and down simultaneously. We can't serve both God and Satan. When we break any of the laws of God, to that extent we go over to the enemy. With every sin we transfer some of our loyalties and break some of our natural attachments. With every sin a part of us is defecting to the enemy and causing an estrangement from God. But we are also transferring our blessings away from ourselves. How disappointed we may sometime be if we have to look to Satan for our blessings and our happiness.

Satan is an alien. The Communists are aliens; sin is an alien; crime is an alien; and slavery is an alien. Our own errors and weaknesses are aliens, and they are robbing us of our blessings. However, God is our friend. He is our eternal Heavenly Father. If we love him with all our hearts and serve him with all our strength, then we are safe. Our wives and families are to be with us throughout eternity. We must be loyal to them in the best meaning of that word. Righteousness is our only means for eternal happiness. Therefore we must avoid the alienation of our own affections and learn to be loyal citizens of God's kingdom.

All Mixed Up

RECENTLY I had the interesting though frustrating experience of losing my sense of direction. I started out to find an address in an area with a number of winding roads and some "afterthought" streets placed in the middle of the blocks. I thought I knew where I was going and how I was going to get there, but after following a street with a lot of turns in it, the direction-finder in my brain seemed to get stuck, somehow, so that it no longer registered my directional changes. I have had a similar experience on an airplane. As soon as I get on the plane, I usually get out a book that I have been anticipating reading, and because I pay very little attention, the airplane can make many turns while I continue facing in the direction that I was when I lost myself in my book.

I suppose that subconsciously I had been turning off my direction-finder too much, and when I had to be my own navigator I began having trouble. Then my mixed-up sense of direction told me that I was going north when I knew I was actually going east. Before I was aware of what was happening, I had gotten several blocks off course. In trying to get myself back on the right track, I stopped my car and tried to correctly orient myself. However, when one is badly mixed up, this is not an easy thing to do. My mental compass could be compared to a compass giving wrong directions because of the influence of some magnetized ore body close by. The occasional street markers were hard for me to understand. They were saying one thing, and my mixed-up brain was saying something else. The things that seemed true to. my brain were denied by other evidences, and vice versa.

Finally I took the easy way out and asked a passerby if he would direct me to my address. He said, "If you will follow me, I will take you there." Then as I drove along behind him, I thought how many other important goals are placed within our reach if we have a dependable guide to follow.

In my life I have had some other confusing experiences. Once in a while I have a dream in which I can't remember where I parked my automobile. I don't seem to have the slightest recollection whether I left it in New York or London or Mexico City. In my dream it is tremendously important that I find my car, and my agitation over my loss fights with my confusion until I am almost exhausted mentally. At other times I have dreamed that I am an actor about to go on the stage, but for the life of me I can't remember my lines. Or I may be a student about to take a final examination for which I am completely unprepared. After one of these frustrating experiences, I wake up in a very disturbed mental state.

Then I feel a great sympathy for some of those troubled people to whom I listen occasionally who, in trying to solve life's important problems, say, "I am all mixed up." I can solve my frustrations merely by waking up, but some people are unable to arouse themselves and so must live with these frustrations and confusions twenty-four hours a day. My mind can be swung back to normal in a few minutes, but some people must live with this imbalance and frustration for the rest of their lives. I am sure that it seemed a very simple thing for my friend to lead me to my destination. Likewise, the moral, mental, social, and occupational mixups of others often seem very simple to me. But they just can't seem to get rid of that conflicting body of magnetized ore that is drawing them off their course and making it impossible to distinguish between north and east, right and wrong, or the causes of happiness and misery.

I suppose that I would not have become mixed up in the first place if I had paid more attention to where I was going. Or I probably could have saved myself from being confused if I had been a little better prepared with a street map, a compass, or just a better set of mental directions. Perhaps I could have solved my problems merely by centering my attention on what I was doing. The Bible speaks of double-minded men. I suppose that these are men who think double. Sometimes we set our minds on the wrong things; sometimes we think by a crooked process, and sometimes we don't think at all.

There are several things that I might do to help me remember where I parked my automobile. I could pay more attention or I could write myself a note and put it in my pocket. It has been said that a good file and a poor memory are a lot better than a good memory and a poor file. It may be that my mind punishes me occasionally in my dreams because I needlessly confuse and agitate it by asking it to remember too much.

Sometimes I make office appointments over the telephone while I am at home or verbally when I am on the street. If I try to carry them all in my mind, I am likely to forget some of them. This gives my mind a feeling of agitation and unrest for fear that it may fall down on its job. I am sure that my brain would appreciate it if I were a little more businesslike and wrote myself a memorandum so that it would be relieved of some of these unnecessary responsibilities. I might also decrease the possibility of confusion and frustration by more thoroughly making up my mind about standards and preparation. Then my brain would have no occasion to worry over either a bad performance or my lack of being prepared.

Anyway, after I had found my address and had attended to my business, I got back into the territory with which I was more familiar. Then my brain made a correction in its compass setting, and immediately everything was all right again, and I knew with perfect assurance which was north, which was east, where I was going, and how I was going to get there. Then my brain was in perfect agreement with the markings on the street corners. If there had been no markings, I still would have known where I was and what the street markings should have been. Then I felt that very satisfying feeling of peace and harmony that comes from the assurance of knowing the score. This feeling of peace and self-confidence furnishes a striking contrast to the frustration and frenzy that comes from feeling half lost.

Again I thought of the troubled people who complain of being mixed up. Some of them have a moral or social or spiritual compass that won't work. They sometimes get lost in their purposes. They are unable to trust themselves in any responsibility involving right and wrong. They don't always pay attention to the signboards that life and success have erected for their guidance, or they erect street markers to suit their own desires, without reference to where they will be taken. They frequently can't trust themselves or their abilities. Then they sometimes go in the wrong direction or do the wrong things when they actually don't mean to do so.

When I got back to my office, I got out my dictionary and looked up the meaning of this important word *confusion*. It said that for one to be confused was to be thrown into a condition of disorder. It said that confusion meant to be mixed up or to have things jumbled together so that one couldn't be distinguished from another. It is bad enough for one to be mixed up in his physical directions, but it is far more serious to be confused about one's cultural or moral values. It can be pretty serious when one gets mixed up in the objectives by which his life's successes are determined.

There are many kinds of confusion, making it difficult to discriminate between right and wrong, and we actually make many false identifications and false judgments because we haven't properly set up our standards or made up our minds about our own programs. One does a lot of things when he is intoxicated that he would not do while he is sober, and he is a lot more likely to do wrong things while he is angry or has a hateful attitude. Cain killed his brother Abel only after he had made an unacceptable offering to the Lord. As a result, his countenance had fallen and he was jealous and envious. Cain was confused, and under these circumstances, killing his brother probably seemed to him to be the best thing to do. Then he tried to avoid punishment by lying. Cain's circumstances were wrong, which only helped him to get the wrong result. The unprofitable servant who made the mistake of hiding his talent in the ground gave his reason by saying, "I was afraid." Fear often confuses us so that we don't know whether to listen to our conscience or to our fears.

Sin and lust and disease can also throw us off our course. A little prejudice or a little hate or a little sin will throw our minds out of balance and make them almost completely undependable.

I got mixed up because I was unprepared and insufficiently thoughtful. But there are many kinds of ignorance, indecision, indifference, sin, and conflict that cause confusion. There are people who take part of the direction for their moral lives from the instructions in the scriptures and part from their own appetites. Frequently these two do not agree, and they get about as badly mixed up as when the rays of force of some magnetized ore are in conflict with the normal lines of the earth's magnetism. When these conflicting forces begin contending in human lives, the mix-up frequently causes confusions that are serious enough to bring on nervous breakdowns or several kinds of mental disease. Someone has said that you never get stomach ulcers from what you eat —you get stomach ulcers from what is eating you.

The experience of getting lost reminds me of the experience of those people who were working on the tower of Babel. What a mix-up it must have caused when their languages were confounded so that no one could get his ideas over to anyone else. But confusion causes even more problems in our individual lives when we are willing to believe our own ideas instead of the holy scriptures. We frequently move to the other side of the road, ignoring that yellow line which is supposed to run between good and evil. Or sometimes we erase it altogether, which causes the error factor in our judgment, our fairness, and our morality to be greatly increased.

When we say that God is dead, or that we are not responsible for what we do, or that our behavior doesn't matter very much one way or another, a little self-induced confusion makes us unable to distinguish between God's morality and the so-called new morality (or immorality). We are also likely to believe that happiness can come from sin and evil indulgence. Without a dependable moral compass, we may think that strikes, racial strife, and wars are the best ways to settle our disputes. It is because we are all mixed up on so many questions in our own day that our world is teetering on the very edge of chaos. Chaos suggests the ultimate limit of confusion, in which things become hopelessly mixed up. We can actually go so far that no hope remains for ever getting ourselves untangled.

There are a number of situations wherein the physical body can get confused. Sometimes one loses his sense of physical balance, and he becomes unable to stand upright without support. Sometimes one's eyes get out of focus, and things are so blurred that he can't distinguish them clearly. One may also get some false standards in his mind that will prevent him from reasoning clearly. It can be a very simple matter for a person to get all mixed up in his attitudes, his personality, his faith, and his spirit.

Sometime ago I talked with a man who was mixed up in his morals. Instead of being capable of logically solving some of the little problems arising in his marriage, he began invoking sanctions against his wife. In trying to justify himself, he invented a new brand of morality all his own, which was in direct conflict with his teachings and his sense of right and wrong. As a result of the conflicts within himself and with other people, a sore began to grow. As he began picking at the wound, it began to fester. It became infected, inflamed, and finally became malignant, so to speak. In trying to justify his evil, he not only lost his mental balance and his sense of spiritual direction; he now believes that north is east. He has made enemies of his family, many of his friends, and his employer. He has largely lost contact with God and with his own better self, and he has these terribly dismal feelings of being all mixed up. His confusion causes him to be depressed and despondent, and it is pretty difficult to reach any successful destination while following two conflicting sets of directions.

Our conflicting nations can't get along because they go by different sets of standards and interests. Husbands and wives have conflicts for the same reason. It is pretty hard to support any standard merely because it seems right to one of the contestants. But one of our greatest benefits came into the world when the Son of God came here and organized his church, set us an example in righteousness, and then said to us, "Follow me." How simple it would be to find our eternal address if we would follow him.

In following the standards set by Jesus, we have an unchanging, unfailing, unerring standard that is fair for all and in which everyone can have confidence. If we could only learn to follow him, we could get rid of all of our confusion, our failure, and our unhappiness. We would then be successful in preventing ourselves from being mixed up and in keeping all sin and confusion out of our lives.

Among My Souvenirs

ONE OF the interesting customs of our day is the use that we make of symbols. Someone has said that a thing is important not only for itself alone, but sometimes it is even more important for what it stands for or what it is a sign of or what it makes us think about.

An American flag may be just an ordinary piece of cotton bunting with a particular pattern of stars and stripes, and yet to many people it represents freedom, opportunity, and a new start in life, free from the tyrannies of a despotic old world. To millions, the American flag represents the best that has ever been known, not only of freedom but of many other things.

An ordinary light in the window may have no particular significance by itself, and yet where a loved one is far away from home, that light in the window may symbolize all of the hopes, dreams, and longings of an eternity to the one who waits for the loved one's return. We have many other things that serve us as signs, symbols, and emblems to represent the most important things. The lion is the symbol of courage; the cross is the emblem of Christianity. The American eagle stands for the power and majesty of a great nation. Witches, broomsticks, cats, and pumpkins give us the feeling of Halloween. Christmas trees, Christmas carols, colored lights, wise men, and presents in Christmas colors add to our festive Christmas spirit. The blind goddess with her scales stands for justice, blind-fairness, and righteousness.

Then we have some special personal kinds of emblems or symbols that we refer to as souvenirs. We collect mementoes, pictures, letters, books, and other reminders that represent some special experience, person, occasion, memory, or place.

For a very good reason, everyone was given a collector's instinct by the Creator to begin with, and it lives and grows in the recipient from the time he is born. To test this natural endowment, suppose you take any small boy by the ankles and turn him upside down. Then if you will shake him a little, you will probably discover that out of his pockets there will drop a great assortment of accumulated treasures, including chalk, string, colored glass, and probably a chicken's foot, each of which has some special value to him. As the collector gets older, the items in his collection are upgraded first to fishing rods, skis, and guns, and then to stocks and bonds, real estate, and insurance policies. If the collector is a female, she will have a hope chest loaded with the treasures of handkerchiefs, pillow cases, negligees, and other pretty and useful things. There are some people who collect stamps, some collect butterflies, some collect art pieces, stationery, and beautiful tapestries.

Because of this God-given instinct, we fill hope chests and safety deposit boxes, as well as our minds, our emotions, and our hearts. What would anyone do without his memories and the tokens that remind him of them! We sing a song in which we say, "Memories, memories, dreams of long ago. O'er the seas of memories, I come sailing back to you. Childhood days, wildwood days, among the birds and bees. You left me alone but still you're my own, in my beautiful memories."

I recently heard a man and his wife tell of their honeymoon in a foreign land where they had many interesting experiences that they wanted to remember. Since that time, they have frequently rerun these events through their minds as they relive those special experiences of love and happiness that are so sacred to each of them. Each of us does something similar every day. All of our lives are spent on an accumulative basis. We don't just live from day to day, because as each day comes along, it finds us one day richer or poorer because of the experiences that we have had in the meantime. The attitudes and pleasures of today are at least partly made up by carrying over those things that we did yesterday. We should get more out of our senior year at school than we did out of our sophomore year because we have a larger accumulation of experiences to work with and to enjoy it with. A workman with greater experience is usually a more valuable man because he now has more to think with, which gives him a choice of a greater combination of successes. In our school years we fill our rooms with pennants and other special reminders of important things. We take innumerable pictures of people, places, and events. We save programs and reminders. We gather mementoes of the interesting places we visit and the interesting things that we do. And we fill our memories with philosophies made up of symbols, parables, and emblems.

We store up all kinds of joys and sorrows for a rerun in the future. Souvenirs not only help us to remember, but they help us live with more pleasure, and they endow life itself with greater meaning. It is for this purpose that we keep journals, memorize poems, and write down our own biographies. A good accumulation of souvenirs gives an upward swing to life and makes the end better than the beginning. The poet Robert Browning said: "Grow old along with me! The best is yet to be, the last of life, for which the first was made."

Each year we set apart the 30th day in May as Memorial Day. This began as a special time set apart on which to remember our soldier dead. However, it has come to have a much broader significance. It actually works out that every day is Memorial Day.

The first part of life is set apart to accumulate as many great experiences as possible, and "the last of life" is the time when we get the most from remembering. Of course, the greatest adventure that anyone ever has in the journey of life is life itself. Just to live is our greatest accomplishment, and to live well keeps us interested, ambitious, and successful as we go along. It also gives us something pleasant to look back upon as we contemplate the end of the journey. How fortunate we are that we have our agency enabling us to choose the greatest experiences, generate the most stimulating successes, and store up the greatest love of life. By way of contrast we might think of those who in the end of their lives have only mistakes, weaknesses, and sins to remember life by. Think what a depression might come to one who had only the unhappiness, failure, and degradation that he has caused to look back upon. A song apparently written by a disappointed lover says:

Among My Souvenirs

There's nothing left for me of days that used to be,
I live in memory among my souvenirs.
Some letters tied with blue, a photograph or two,
I see a rose from you among my souvenirs.

A few more tokens rest within my treasure chest
And though they do their best to give me consolation,
I count them all apart and as the teardrops start,
I find a broken heart among my souvenirs.

Others have found an even more disappointing collection in a distorted mind, a ruined reputation, a lung cancer, a damaged soul, and a hopeless prospect for a happy eternal life. Even in eternity it may be pretty hard to forget those we have led astray with our bad example or those whom we have seduced by our immorality. Sometimes souvenirs lose their value because those whom they call to mind have proven unworthy. William Shakespeare said: "To the noble mind rich gifts wax poor when givers prove unkind."

Our present friendly partners who participate in our sins may someday feel very resentful toward us when they are asked to pay a heavy price because of our evil influence. I know of a man who shot himself because he induced a friend to put a lot of money in a worthless investment that he believed to be good. He intended to do his friend a favor, but he could not overlook the fact that his friend went bankrupt as a result of his recommendation.

How much worse it would be to knowingly or unknowingly influence one to make a worthless investment in life that would leave him bankrupt. That everyone will be held accountable for his influence and his leadership is an awful responsibility. Down the broad way of life, no one walks alone. Each one stands at the head of some kind of caravan. One of the best ways to get a good collection of souvenirs in life is through our service in helping to lift people up and make them better.

The poet has said:

> Success when you sum it all up isn't gold
> Nor is it in doing some deed that is bold,
> For the money we make and the houses we build
> Mean nothing the moment the voice has been stilled,
> But he has succeeded who when he is gone
> In the heart of another is still living on.

A squirrel stores up acorns to his heart's content. To about the same end Whistler once painted a tiny picture of a spray of roses. The artistry involved was magnificent. Never before, it seemed, had the art of man been able to execute quite so deftly a reproduction of the art of nature. The picture was the envy of the artists who saw it, the despair of the collectors who yearned to buy it for their collections. But Whistler steadfastly refused to sell it for, said he, "Whenever I feel that my hand has lost its cunning, whenever I doubt my ability, I look at the little picture of the spray of roses and say to myself, 'Whistler, you painted that. Your hand drew it, your imagination conceived the colors, your skill put the roses on the canvas.' " Then said he, "I know that what I have done I can do again." Then he gave us a thrilling philosophy of success. He said: "Hang on the walls of your mind the memory of your successes. Take counsel of your strengths, not your weaknesses. Think of the good jobs you have done, think of the times when you rose above your average level of performance and carried out an idea or a dream or a desire for which you had deeply longed. Hang these pictures on the walls of your mind and think of them as you travel the roadway of life."

The number and quality of our mementoes will be greatly increased by keeping our lives in closer touch with the source of all good. The scripture says: "But the Comforter, which is the Holy Ghost, whom the Father will send in my name, he shall teach you all things, and bring all things to your remembrance, whatsoever I have said unto you." (John 14:26.)

The word of the Lord tells us a lot of things that we should store up in our minds so that we can clearly remember them. When Jesus instituted the holy sacrament, he said, ". . . this do in remembrance of me." (Luke 22:19.) He said, "Remember the sabbath day to keep it holy." (Exodus 20:8.) Paul said, "Wherefore I put thee in remembrance that thou stir up the gift of God, which is in thee by the putting on of my hands." (2 Timothy 1:6.)

If we remember our covenants, if we remember to do good works, and if we remember the kind of destiny that we would like to have, we will sometime have a lot of wonderful souvenirs in our memories.

Without the holy scriptures to keep us reminded of great ideals, and without our great literature to stimulate our activity, we would have long ago plunged ourselves into a period of dark ages. But the word of the Lord and the records of the great experiences of others has accumulated for us the necessary ideals and ambitions to fill our treasure chest. We should get some benefit and some memento from every great experience that we can make our own either by birth or adoption. The greatest ideas are all prepared to give us something. We have a song that says, "Please give me something to remember you by when you are far away from me." That is a good philosophy to apply to the world's great literature as well as the holy scriptures.

Someone once asked a little girl if she knew what was in the Bible. She said that she did. She said, "There are some pressed violets in it. There is a lock of baby's hair in it, and some of sister's love letters are in it." But there are a lot of other things in the Bible. There is a divine plan for our eternal salvation in it. There are some great biographies in it. There are some stimulating ideals in it. There are some stern commands from God in it as well as some love letters from him to help us to remember our duties. There are some other wonderful ideas available out of which we may build greater ambitions, higher ideals, and a happier, eternal life for ourselves. In exercising our collector's instinct, we may gather the greatest experiences to motivate us. We may fill our pockets with money and our minds with the mementoes of our trip through life. And someday, we will also find that the evidences of our own righteous obedience will be among our finest souvenirs.

Anti-Art

O NE OF the important facts of life is its constant change. Since the world began we have been asked to choose between the extremes of good and evil, right and wrong, success and failure. With some resemblance to the moon, our lives themselves sometimes have a dark side and a light side. And, like the moon, our attitudes, ambitions, and accomplishments often wax and wane. Sometimes we find our success riding the crest of a full tide, and sometimes we discover that the tide has gone out and left us stuck in the mud.

I know of a very fine woman who married a man when all of his indicators pointed toward a successful career. But he made a change for the worse that left her unhappily floundering in the shallows of the low tide that his life had caused. Another woman might marry a man without much promise while the marriage computer is flashing nothing but danger signals. But later this man's ships may come in loaded with many of the good things of life.

From time to time over the years we hear of certain people thinking about some kind of trial marriage or other experimental device by the help of which prospective marriage partners hope to discover an ideal spouse. And while anyone contemplating marriage should know a great deal about his prospective mate, yet no amount of experimentation can guarantee any permanent success. I know of one couple who were very happy during the first ten years of their union but who have been very miserable with each other since. Trying out marriage is like trying out the practice of medicine. Success in medicine or in life or in marriage is not achieved just in finding the right person; it is also in being the right person. Life doesn't give enough time for very many kinds of experiments. King David was called a man after God's own heart in his youth. Then he tried out adultery and murder. Instead of helping him, his new experience made his life much more difficult. Solomon was king of Israel when he was a teenager. He was blessed with greater wisdom than anyone who had ever lived up to that time, and he saw God twice, but he tried out some disobedience to God, and he died an idolator, very much out of God's favor.

In the present day some people have done away with the moral restrictions between the sexes and have provided for a much wider field of sexual experience. But we are now finding out that instead of making marriage adjustments easier, they are being made much more difficult, and instead of learning we are piling up such a large number of stumbling blocks that success and happiness sometimes become impossible.

It is not very wise to attempt to get happiness from those experiences that God has forbidden. Our experience in doing as we please is now loudly proclaiming that man is still not a very good judge of right and wrong or of what is in his own best interests. Recently an evolutionist who had grown up with the idea that man has climbed upward from some simple form of life expressed the opinion that something must have gone wrong, as the growth process seems to have been thrown into reverse, and a condition of worsening now seems to be carrying us back in the other direction.

It is certain that our respect for law has recently been diminished whereas our crimes are increasing by leaps and bounds. We appear to be less capable of getting along with each other now than we were even in the Dark Ages. The divine objective of peace on earth, goodwill toward men is also running in reverse. There are many people who feel that the idea of righteousness itself is not realistic in our day. A moral recession has threatened the very existence of the home, the family, the country, and the church. When such depressing movements as the hippies and the yippies can flourish in our soil without any logical reason or intelligent effort, something must be seriously wrong. Our increased appetite for dope, alcoholism, and nicotine addiction shows that we are losing a lot of ground.

It is no wonder that a voice is heard from the bowels of the earth saying, "Wo, wo is me, the mother of men; I am pained, I am weary, because of the wickedness of my children. When shall I rest, and be cleansed from the filthiness which is gone out of me? When will my Creator sanctify me, that I may rest, and righteousness for a season abide upon my face?" (Moses 7:48.)

However, among all of our many recently developed problems, it seems that one of the most unfortunate is the tendency of so many to rebel against beauty as well as to fight against goodness. In large measure many people have become anti-art. God intended to stimulate our finest appreciation when he made the earth such a beautiful place. Think of the tremendous artistic fascination of earth's oceans, its skies, its sunsets, its landscapes, and its flowers. God put all kinds of magnificent colors, fragrance, beauty, and riches into the earth. However, he reserved his greatest beauty for his own children. When God created us in his own image, he included a love of truth, a godly character, a miraculous personality, and a tremendous artistic sense.

The dictionary says that art is the systematic application of knowledge, skill, and taste. Our artistic sense was intended to produce such objects as beautiful painting, inspiring music, and harmonious sculpture. The fine arts are primarily concerned with the objects of our imagination. They include those subjects that we appreciate for their beauty, taste, and inspiration rather than for their actual utility. We refer to such things as painting, drawing, architecture, and sculpture as the fine arts of design. Other artistic studies include poetry, music, dancing, and the dramatic arts. The liberal arts include grammar, logic, rhetoric, astronomy, philosophy, and history. We might compare the fine arts to fine gold or fine people.

Fine gold might be described as gold that has been fully refined. It has been finished and brought to its perfection by being freed from its impurities. A fine man is also one who is refined, who is complete. He was formed in God's image. He is well fashioned and has a noble appearance. If he follows God's program, his impurities are removed, and fine personality and godly character traits develop within him. This gives him a fine tone, makes him fine spirited, and great beauty forms in his soul.

Art forms an important part of every great life. In fact, the most important art is the art of living successfully. One may be an artist as a musician, or as a painter, or as a sculptor, but the finest art is that which is displayed when one puts good taste, good judgment, and righteousness into his life and makes it beautiful and happy. Then it is harmonious with all that is beautiful, true, and good.

The dictionary represents some of the antonyms of art by such words as inferior, gross, heavy, coarse, blunt, dull, and awkward. What a great tragedy for our world when large groups of people rebel against beauty, order, righteousness, cleanliness, fineness, and good taste. Our present-day rebellion against art has taken many forms. We have the plotless movie, the painting that does not inspire, the music that carries us back to the jungle, the philosophy that makes us more coarse, the drama that debases our characters, and the speech that depresses our souls.

All art should have a happy ending, and drama is more inspiring if the hero has a haircut and does noble things. The purpose of art is to inspire, to refine, to instruct, to uplift, and to make us better and more complete than we were. The values are lost when our drama fills us with violence, when our philosophy teaches us sedition, when our literature motivates failure and glamorizes immorality. In many cases we have taken away from our art and literature that which is spiritual, patriotic, and moral. We sometimes say that the good is something that is theoretical and unrealistic, and to promote the religious may be against the public interest. Even realism has a positive and a negative side, but the realism of our modern rebellion seeks to center our attention primarily in the negative.

In some periods when people have gone to college, they have dressed themselves in their best clothes and worn their finest mental attitudes. They have been anxious to put their best foot forward, and it is considered a great honor to get good grades. However, there are now some who feel that anyone trying to appear at his best is not telling it as it is, and therefore many people prefer to display themselves at their worst.

Formerly in educational institutions we used to house scholarly students in inexpensive buildings. But now this situation is also changing. We levy high taxes and erect elegant buildings as a base for many who don't take a bath or get a haircut to launch a rebellion against the administration. A great general once said that he would rather have iron men in wooden boats than to have wooden men in iron boats. And a scholar who says his prayers, has his hair cut, takes a bath, and does some studying may reach higher goals housed in makeshift buildings than makeshift, drug-addicted students who use marble halls as a place in which to argue about repealing the Ten Commandments in favor of their own version of the new morality. The beauty of the coeds of yesteryear furnishes a striking contrast to some of their modern sisters who now patronize institutions of higher learning with uncombed hair, and faces, attitudes, and morals to match.

Some university students of a few years ago were an inspiration to behold, and there is still a great art in appropriate dress, good grades, high morality, immaculate cleanliness, and willingness to pay the price demanded for real character. Both on and off the campus, many women now wear a strange kind of apparel that could belong to either sex, and the general tolerance of a sloppy, uncared-for appearance has been greatly increased among us. A member of a hippie group recently referred to the outlandish garb of his own clan members as "casual dress." Proper attire and interested care for one's own person are more than ordinarily important, as there is a very close relationship existing between beauty on the outside and beauty on the inside. Schlegel says, "There is no more potent antidote for a low sensuality than the adoration of beauty." Aristotle said, "Beauty purifies the thoughts as suffering purifies the passions." Through a proper appreciation of the beauty of nature, we may put ourselves in tune with the infinite. On the other hand, when we surround ourselves with the sordid, the unclean, and the rebellious, they tend to get into our minds, our hearts, and our personalities.

Beauty in our landscapes, or in our homes, or in our music, or in our literature has an uplifting effect upon us. However, there is an ebb and flow in nature. We have a high tide and a low tide. The moon waxes and wanes. There is also an ebb and flow in life. We are not always faithful. All of our trends are not forward. Sometimes it is too easy for our minds to slip into a reverse gear and allow rebellion, negative thinking, and evil to take over. Our situation is made more serious when we tolerate this awful perversion of always wanting to appear at our worst.

This trend manifesting itself in our modern art was recently illustrated by a calendar showing twelve prize-winning drawings. As subjects the artists had chosen to paint such things as abandoned shacks that were surrounded by disorder and weeds. These were places where no self-respecting person would think of actually living. And yet we allow this spirit to live in our minds. Other pictures displayed other situations shown at their worst. It seemed that in these so-called art pieces, the artist's primary concern was to show dilapidation, deterioration, confusion, and decay, and call it realism.

We do something similar in our writing. We distribute millions of books each day picturing the base things of life. We take interest in actual horror movies and those that deal in hate and violence, and we glamorize crime and sin.

By the perversion of our anti-art, we are committing the great sin of degrading ourselves, whereas the greatest art is that which is the most uplifting. The greatest music is that which most stirs our souls and lifts us up to a higher level in life. All reading and all art and all philosophy should be constructive and elevating. Daniel Webster was speaking as an artist when he said, "The greatest thought that has ever entered my mind is the consciousness of my individual responsibility to God."

This is not an art that is written or drawn or acted out on the stage. It is that which we live. It is that which is used to inspire our minds and fill our lives with good works. Emerson once said that "beauty is the mark that God sets on virtue." The greatest virtue is finally the most beautiful. And the highest inspiration is to know that God lives, that righteousness is good, and that death is not the end of life. One has a great artistic sense when he understands that order is the first law of heaven and that cleanliness is next to godliness. How very helpful it also is to know that as a man thinketh in his heart so is he. May we so develop our artistic powers that we will love beauty, truth, and righteousness.

Bewitched

A<small>N INTERESTING</small> story is told of a captain sailing his ship through the south seas. At one of his stops he picked up an unusual-looking stone, which he took on board and placed in the captain's cabin. A few days later when he again set sail, he discovered that, for some reason, the ship's compass was acting very strangely, and he decided that the ship was bewitched. The unusual stone was a piece of magnetized iron ore, and only after it had been thrown overboard was the compass again able to accurately guide the ship.

This is an interesting story, but it is much more than that. People also sometimes get bewitched when they take contrary influences on board in their lives. The apostle Paul cites one manifestation of this kind of confusion that took place among the members of the church. He said to them: "O foolish Galatians, who hath bewitched you, that ye should not obey the truth. . . ." (Galatians 3:1.) Luke describes a similar situation when he says: "There was a certain man, called Simon, which beforetime in the same city used sorcery, and bewitched the people of Samaria, giving out that himself was some great one: . . . And to him they had regard, because that of long time he had bewitched them with sorceries." (Acts 8:9, 11.)

The dictionary says that a witch is one who practices the black art of magic. A witch is regarded as possessing supernatural or magic powers gotten from evil spirits. The dictionary points out that witches and sorcerers are people who deny God and renounce both God and his grace. Witches are people who have made a league with the devil and have given themselves over to him body and soul, and by his influence they injure and destroy other people.

In our literature we have many accounts in both fact and fiction where someone has been bewitched. Saul, king of ancient Israel, was dismissed as king for this reason. The prophet Samuel said to him: "For rebellion is as the sin of witchcraft, and stubbornness is as iniquity and idolatry. Because thou hast rejected

the word of the Lord, he hath also rejected thee from being king."
(1 Samuel 15:23.)

The scripture also tells about Cain, who was influenced by
evil spirits. The record says that he loved Satan more than God,
and he made a covenant to serve Satan. Others have done and
are still doing very similar things, and as a consequence many
people are still being bewitched by bewitching people. Certainly
in our day we see a lot of those who are bewitched with rebellion,
immorality, and irresponsibility.

Twenty-nine centuries ago the blind Greek poet Homer
wrote the great travel story called the *Odyssey*. This is an account of Odysseus, sometimes called Ulysses, who was king of the
little Greek state of Ithaca. He and his soldiers had fought in
the battle of Troy. The chief interest of the *Odyssey* is centered
in the adventures of their ten-year journey homeward across three
hundred miles of island-dotted sea. Once a raging wind blew them
off their course, and they landed on the island of the lotus-eaters.
It was said that when men ate the magic fruit of the lotus tree
they were bewitched into forgetting about their families and their
responsibilities, and they lived in a dreamy forgetfulness and in-
dolent enjoyment. Only when Odysseus dragged his sailors back
aboard their ships were they able to recover enough of their ambition to continue their journey homeward. There are many
people who have these same kinds of problems who never do recover their senses.

One of the greatest adventures came to Odysseus and his
men when they landed on the island domain of the bewitching en-
chantress Circe. While there, some of the men fell into her hands,
and she turned them into swine. It was only with great difficulty
that Odysseus was able to break her spell and force her to set his
men free. This experience delayed Odysseus and his men for a full
year on Circe's enchanted island. In one way or another many
men are still being turned into swine by the enchantments of evil.

In the course of the journey of these Grecian soldiers, they
were required to pass an island where other bewitching sirens
lived. It was already known to Odysseus that in times past the
song of these sirens had lured many sailors to their deaths. He
had been warned in advance about the hazards of listening to the
music of these fascinating, dangerous creatures. When he came
near to their islands, fearing that his men would not be able to
withstand the temptation, he had all of the members of his crew

fill their ears with wax so that they would not be able to hear the sirens' song.

Odysseus himself was overcome by curiosity and did not put wax in his own ears. But not quite trusting his own strength, he protected himself against his own weakness by having his men bind him to the mast. He gave them strict orders that no matter what might happen, they must not release him until they were past the island and out of range of the temptation. When they came within the hypnotic sound of the sirens' song, Odysseus weakened and ordered his men to pull their ship up to the shore. But the ears of his men were full of wax, and they could not hear his orders. The caution of Odysseus saved the day, and they rowed on past the temptation without succumbing to it.

In writing the *Odyssey*, Homer was making some comparisons with that more important journey which we sometimes refer to as the odyssey of our own lives. He certainly anticipated our day of rebellion with its seductive enchantments of evil. In an effort to seduce others and turn men and women into swine, one of the most prominent, Jerry Rubin, the revolutionaries' yippie spokesman says in his pornographic book *Do It,* "We have combined youth, music, sex, drugs, and rebellion with treason, and that is a combination that is hard to beat." Many of our day are being more badly bewitched by this evil combination than those who lived in the days of King Saul or Homer. Like Cain, there are many who have made covenants to love evil instead of righteousness, and only the devil could inspire such absolute satanism as that exhibited by some of the evil men of our day.

The power of music, both for good and evil, was recognized long before Homer. Aldous Huxley's book *Brave New World,* in attempting to appraise the evils of our day, says: "New and previously undreamed of devices for exciting mobs have recently been invented. The radio has enormously extended the range of the demagogue's raucous yelling. The loudspeaker amplifies the heady music of class hatred and the destructiveness of militant [minorities]." This book points out that an assembled mob of men and women who have previously been conditioned by reading the daily accounts of evil can be reduced in almost no time at all by loud, wild band music, bright lights, and the oratory of an evil person to a state of almost mindless subhumanity. Never before have so few been able to make fools, maniacs, or criminals out of so many in so short a time.

According to the Midszenty Report, Dr. William Sargent, a leading scientific authority on the human nervous system, reports that under stress of loud percussion music and bright lights, people can be brainwashed to believe almost anything.

Dr. Sargent says that "electrical recordings of the human brain show that it is particularly sensitive, among other things, to the rhythmic stimulation by percussion, bright lights, and drugs. And certain rates of rhythm can build up recordable abnormalities of brain function and explosive states of tension sufficient even to produce convulsive fits in predisposed subjects. In such a situation," he adds, "belief can be effectively implanted in people after brain function has been sufficiently disturbed by accidentally or deliberately induced fear, anger, or excitement. . . ."

In an address to the Royal Society of Medicine in 1965, Dr. Sargent elaborated by saying, "Adolf Hitler, the Beatles, and the African witch doctors all practiced a similar type of brainwashing. . . ." People can be brainwashed and bewitched to believe almost anything. The tragic thing about being bewitched is that evil, sin, and nonsense may all become palatable. The loud rhythmic music, dope, and emotional dancing are all effective ways of getting at the nervous system. When Adolf Hitler got people into a high state of excitement by yelling and loud noises, his evil schemes seemed all right to them. Hitler used this system of bewitchment to kill twenty million people, including himself. In his book *The Riot Makers,* Eugene H. Methvin provides facts on the scientific aspects of certain kinds of music as a weapon for psychological warfare.

Vice President Spiro Agnew has charged that America's youth are being brainwashed into drug use, largely promoted and spread by rock music via the communications media.

And Art Linkletter, the TV personality, whose daughter died as a result of a drug "trip," agrees.

Bob Dylan, one of the undisputed forefathers of today's so-called acid-rock music, is quoted by an undergound New York newspaper as saying: "If parents knew what I was saying in my songs, they would break the records." One of Bob Dylan's earliest recordings, "Mr. Tambourine Man," is about a trip away from the worries of the world. Trip is slang for the effects one experiences on LSD and other hallucinatory drugs. This first song to combine drugs with music was a tremendous success.

Hundreds of other drug-rock compositions, with the added ingredient of sex, have followed. And many millions of copies have been sold to young people.

Jesse Kornbluth, a devotee of acid-rock, explained in his music review column in the *New York Times:* "Rock, drugs and sex—the foundations of the so-called New Culture—have been around long enough so that they are subliminal in our lives. . . ."

The word *subliminal* is used by psychologists to describe something that exists or occurs in one's subconsciousness. When something evil has been sublimated in our subconscious mind, it can sometimes bewitch our lives without our knowledge.

Many evil men get out on the stage, dressed in ludicrous clothing, where they writhe, reel, stagger, and frequently look like someone on a bad trip who has been driven insane by nightmares that possess them but that they cannot understand. Thousands of young people have been lured by acid-rock bands, the promise of cheap pot and dreams of free love and sex to many so-called rock festivals around the country. Most publicized was the Woodstock Festival. It was Communist-inspired, and it was the place where our enemies served the first free dope in America. They said that this festival was "three days of music and peace."

The Altamount Festival, held at Altamount Speedway in Alameda County, California, attracted approximately 300,000 young people who watched as four of their number were brutally murdered, one of them stabbed to death by a member of the Hell's Angels motorcycle gang directly in front of the stage where Mick Jagger and the Rolling Stones were screaming their particular brand of music.

The rock festival phenomenon, as many youthful participants will quickly point out, represents the new generation "doing its own thing." Their explanation goes something like this: "We are tired of war, poverty, discrimination, and capitalist exploitation. We are turning to love, music, communal living, and sharing. We totally reject the rules and regulations of the establishment and are creating a new life style."

The truth of the matter is that many young people today are unaware that they are being victimized by exploiters. The Powder Ridge Pop Festival, held July 31 to August 2, 1970, near Middlefield, Connecticut, serves as a good example:

Although covered by television and the press, no mention was made that: (1) the co-owner of Powder Ridge is closely linked with numerous radical leftist movements and, in 1962, initiated a legal suit against Secretary of State Dean Rusk over the denial of a passport allowing him to visit Communist Cuba, and (2) Powder Ridge has, in the past, been used as a meeting place for pro-Communist organizations and personalities.

It comes as no surprise to discover links between gangsters, pro-Communists, and the booming acid-rock business. They are aware that the youth market is wide open for exploitation with unlimited possibilities.

And so we might ask ourselves, "O foolish Galatians, who hath bewitched you, that ye should not obey the truth . . . ?" And when we understand the close relationship between rock music, promiscuous sex, drug abuse, rebellion, and all evil things, then we may be able to throw them overboard in order to unbewitch ourselves. Then we will be able to sail a straight course in righteousness.

Blind Obedience

A NUMBER OF years ago we had a family living in our neighborhood in which the father seemed to take great pride in his oft-repeated declaration that he didn't want his children to blindly follow the Church. He said that he wanted them to do some thinking of their own, to break some new trails, and to follow their own ideas. He agreed that this might involve them in some mistakes, but he felt that they would come out of it stronger people if they always stood on their own feet and did their own thinking.

Certainly there is far too little real thinking being done in the world, but it is thought that our greatest single idea is to know where we are going. We must also know the most effective procedures for getting there. With some definiteness we need to know from the highest authority what the real purpose of life is. We also need a dependable star to steer by and a reliable compass to keep us on our course. It takes constant steering to keep an automobile going in a straight line, and everyone needs some divine help to keep him thinking straight.

When we have no higher intelligence than our own to direct us, we frequently get lost, and no one can afford to make very many of the great mistakes personally. There are some serious disadvantages in breaking too many new trails on our own. When we put ourselves on a trial and error basis, we frequently find ourselves hopelessly bogged down in the quagmire of our own mistakes. The Lord expressed an opinion on this point when he said: ". . . cursed is he that putteth his trust in the arm of flesh." (2 Nephi 4:34.) Among other disadvantages, it is very expensive to live endlessly by our own untested opinions. This is especially true when, as is usually the case, our own opinions are so highly mixed with prejudices, false information, and unholy desires. Entire cultures and civilizations frequently go astray when living after their own opinions. In a very large number of cases self-directed individuals are almost always wrong.

For a counter plan there is a great scripture that says, "Trust in the Lord with all thine heart; and lean not unto thine own understanding. In all thy ways acknowledge him, and he shall direct thy paths." (Proverbs 3:5-6.) And that proposal embodies a wonderful way of life. God is the source of all good. He has all knowledge, he has all power, and he is all-wise. He knows the end from the beginning. He has told us that crime, sin, ignorance, ugliness, and sloth are wrong. We can know without a question of a doubt that he is right and that it would give us a great advantage if we would take him at his word and strictly follow him. And yet for some mysterious reason we don't seem to like any of those terms that indicate any measure of blind obedience.

Recently I rode through a storm with an aviator in a little one-engine airplane. I was very anxious for him to be blindly obedient to his radar beam and to the instructions that came from the man in the radio control tower. With our lives in his hands, we would not want the pilot to be breaking any new trails through a black thundercloud. It would be a lot safer for him to forget about thinking for himself and to obey the man in the control tower, who knew more about the boundaries and intensities of the storm, the location of the mountain peaks, and where the runway was. How strange, then, that we are so willing to trust our eternal lives to those unknown combinations of ignorance, fear, lust, hate, and prejudice that cause so many crackups among us.

We sometimes become so obsessed with the idea of doing our own thing that we swing away from a safe, blind obedience to a disastrous blind disobedience. Recently, after a young man had his hair cut, the barber said to him, "Your mother will like that haircut." The young man said, "Well, if she does, I won't." This contrary streak of blind disobedience decreases the ability of parents to help their children because they become afraid to counsel them frankly.

A father recently had some very important information that he dared not give his son because he was afraid the son would do the exact opposite. The father thought that there would be less danger in the son's ignorance than in his perverseness.

Much of the rebellion of our day comes from our tendency toward blind disobedience. We see the wholesale phenomenon of children rebelling against their parents. This rebellion is not just against bad parents or poor parents or unwise parents. It is probable that there is about as much rebellion going on against good parents and rich parents and wise parents. Many ministers' children go astray by turning against the instruction of their fathers. The children of educators are sometimes dead-set against education. And the children of hard-working, self-supporting parents often turn themselves into human derelicts and idlers. Some people who have taken great pride in doing more than they get paid for have children who enjoy living from the labor of someone else.

However, the greatest rebellions and the most serious cases of blind disobedience are those that we direct against God. God has said, "Thou shalt not commit adultery" (Exodus 20:14), and so evil people rig up all kinds of schemes to foster the new morality on a wholesale basis. Some great industries are growing up for the purpose of manufacturing birth control gadgets, practicing abortion, treating venereal disease, and dealing with the awful problems of divorce, broken homes, unhappy parents, and unstable children. We could relieve ourselves of the need for all of these if we would merely obey God.

God said, "Thou shalt not steal" (Exodus 20:15), and so we turn ourselves into kleptomaniacs. We steal money, automobiles, and merchandise. We rob the government, our employers, each other, and God. Think what a paradise our earth could become if all of us practiced a blind obedience to those great laws of God known as the Ten Commandments. Blind obedience in its best meaning is a great success idea.

On one occasion an angel came to Adam and asked him why he offered sacrifice. He said, "I know not, save the Lord commanded me." (Moses 5:6.) What better reason could anyone ever have? How could one better reach the highest goals than by two or three kinds of blind obedience? For too many people even the suggestion of this idea would be very offensive. However, if we objected to obedience on this basis, we could still effectively solve our problems by so studying the program of the Lord that we would know the importance of all of his laws for ourselves.

One man said that he didn't just obey God—he agreed with him. But just suppose that we didn't always agree with God; then what? There are many people who actually make themselves think that they believe in adultery and in stealing and in sloth. There are many people who believe that murder, arson, and treason can promote some kind of a benefit for them. And yet think of the chaos that would exist in the world and in our lives if everyone followed the policy of endlessly doing what seemed good to him. Even now it is not our own convictions about righteousness but our police and military forces that are largely maintaining our civilization.

What a great idea it would be if, instead of depending on the police to hold our society together, we were fully obedient to God and to law and to righteousness because we wanted to be. No matter whether it was blind obedience or an obedience that was fully understanding, any kind of righteous, whole-souled obedience would transform our lives for good. In the midst of his afflictions, the great old prophet Job demonstrated the value of blind obedience when he said, "Though he slay me, yet will I trust in him." (Job 13:15.) There is no other program that will bring such outstanding success in life as obedience—obedience to the laws of God, obedience to the laws of nature, and obedience to our powers of reason. Nothing else can take the place of obedience. Obedience is the first law of heaven.

The most educated people sometimes get about as far off the track of success as those who are less learned. Science can't solve our problems, because action must usually be taken before there is time to make a full and complete investigation of the facts. The prophet Samuel said to King Saul, ". . . to obey is better than sacrifice." (1 Samuel 15:22.) And to obey is also better than to rationalize or to alibi or to philosophize or to rebel.

The Lord himself has said that "as the heavens are higher than the earth, so are my ways higher than your ways. . . ." (Isaiah 55:9.) We show our greatest intelligence when we follow God. We may follow him blindly or otherwise, but we should follow him. When the Lord said to Peter, "Will ye also go away?" Peter said, "Lord, to whom shall we go?" (John 6:67-68.) And that is still our most important question. Whom can we trust? We can't trust the Communists, and we can't trust the arm of flesh. We can't always trust ourselves. We might make a list of those times when we have seriously disappointed ourselves by following our own opinions.

Mostly we can't even understand ourselves, let alone trust ourselves. Certainly we can't afford to leave the welfare of our immortal souls exclusively in our own hands. There is a great line in scripture that says: "Yet man is born unto trouble, as the sparks fly upward." (Job 5:7.)

When we break our own trails, we make a percentage of mistakes that is much too high for us to tolerate. This is unnecessary when we can easily figure out for ourselves that God is always right. We know with an absolute certainty that God is always right. We know with an absolute certainty that those who keep the Sabbath day holy will be a different people from those who do not. We have seen enough broken, twisted, distorted lives to know that "Thou shalt not commit adultery" is a good law and should be followed. Absolute obedience is good because morality is much harder to understand when we are the ones being driven by lust than it is when the adulterer has one of our daughters in his sights.

Everyone except the violators knows that we would be much better off if we strictly obeyed the Word of Wisdom and every other commandment.

Recently over the radio I heard a very prominent minister teaching people that it was not necessary for anyone to be baptized. Where did he get the authority to contradict the word of the Lord? As Jesus stood on the mount about ready to ascend into heaven, he said: "Go ye therefore, and teach all nations, baptizing them in the name of the Father, and of the Son, and of the Holy Ghost." (Matthew 28:19.)

"He that believeth and is baptized shall be saved; but he that believeth not shall be damned." (Mark 16:16.)

This minister is going to get into a lot of trouble putting his puny logic up against the word of the Lord. The Lord has been pretty harsh with ministers of religion who teach their own doctrines in his name, for this has caused almost all of our world's problems. Isaiah said: "The earth also is defiled under the inhabitants thereof; because they have transgressed the laws, changed the ordinance, broken the everlasting covenant." (Isaiah 24:5.)

In our own day the Lord has said that those churches teaching man-made doctrines are an abomination in his sight and that their professors are all corrupt. He said: ". . . they draw near to me with their lips, but their hearts are far from me, they teach for doctrines the commandments of men, having a form of godliness, but they deny the power thereof." (Joseph Smith 2:19.)

This statement used to bother me some, since I have known many ministers who were intelligent, gentle men who desired to be as helpful as possible. But Jesus himself said: "Whosoever therefore shall break one of these least commandments, and shall teach men so, he shall be called the least in the kingdom of heaven. . . ." (Matthew 5:19.)

Suppose we tried to imagine what the worst sin could be. If I committed the unpardonable sin and became a son of perdition, only one person might be hurt as a consequence. If I became a murderer or stole an automobile, as heinous as those sins are, yet the damage might be confined to a very narrow area. But when, like this great minister, I teach a million people to disobey the word of the Lord, the area covered by the sin is greatly extended and the sin is intensified.

The wise man Solomon concluded his book of Ecclesiastes by saying: "Let us hear the conclusion of the whole matter: Fear God, and keep his commandments: for this is the whole duty of man." (Ecclesiastes 12:13.)

This is not only the whole duty of man; it is also the wisest course. Whether it is blind obedience or some other kind is far less important than whether it is obedience or disobedience. There are some people who seem not a bit ashamed to put their own untried wisdom up against the wisdom of the holy scriptures, and there are some who do not hesitate to disobey or even ignore the great God who created heaven and earth and placed us here, fashioned in his own image. It is certain that the greatest good in our lives would be a full-determined obedience.

The Book of Instructions

W E HAVE developed a number of interesting procedures to assist us in solving some of the complexities of our present-day affairs. To help us with some of the problems incident to our knowledge explosion, the people who manufacture our appliances now send along with their product a book of instructions for their use.

For example, our family recently came into possession of a color television set. This miraculous instrument is one of the wonders of our day. It has taken our world nearly six thousand years to produce it, and it might take another six thousand years for some of us to learn to operate it if we first had to understand it. It performs miracles that, if I didn't actually see, I wouldn't believe. The sights and sounds of the world's scenery, music, gunfire, and tornadoes are all hurled through the air in every direction by a hundred telecasting stations. But they all find their way to quietly assemble in my living room. The book of instructions that came with the television set tells me which knobs to pull and which dials to turn to get any program onto my television screen in the right shade of color with sound effects to my heart's content.

Because of this modern-day wonder, our family has been able to watch astronauts land on the moon. I don't even try to understand how it is that these identical pictures and sounds are in ten billion other locations on every part of the earth's surface at the same time. Once when we tired of waiting for action on the moon, we turned the television knob and watched some elephants stampede in Africa. When that was over we paid a short visit to Queen Elizabeth in Buckingham Palace and then went back to finish our program on the moon.

The thing that impresses me most is the fact that in order to benefit from all of these miracles I don't even need to understand them. Neither do I need to pay for any part of the billions of dollars worth of scientific equipment necessary to produce them. All I need to do is to read my book of instructions. Then by pulling the right knobs and turning the proper dials, I can bring into my living room the finest symphonies, the greatest stage plays, the most constructive movies, the biggest tidal waves, the hottest wars, and all of the other wonders that make up our age.

But we are the beneficiaries of a lot of other miraculous events. I have a daily newspaper laid on my front porch that tells me what is going on in every part of the world during every hour of the day and night. I could not gather the news and print my single paper for a million dollars, and yet I get the news gathered, the paper printed, and the delivery made for less than the cost of the paper used. I don't need to become a reporter or a printer or a news analyst to get all of these facts with the most expert opinions about them. Nor do I need to understand the millions of other miracles in order to receive their blessings. I can attend school in my own home, or go sightseeing in Europe, or fly over the North Pole, or do a million other wonderful things merely by keeping on good terms with my book of instructions.

Our family recently transacted some business with General Motors and as a result we acquired an automobile. It will go fast or slow, uphill or downhill, backward or forward as I manipulate the gadgets. I can have almost any desired temperature inside the car no matter what the climate may be on the outside. If I pull the right buttons, even on the darkest night, two giant head-lamps throw great beams of light down the roadway ahead of me. This car has some little mechanical "hands" that keep the snow wiped off the windshield. Other devices will wash the front window, tell me the time of day, how warm the engine is, or how much gasoline remains in the gas tank. My automobile has puncture-proof tires, push-button windows, six directional seats, turn blinkers, tail lights, radio, and power-steering. With a little pressure from my right foot the 350-horses under the hood will fly across the earth at 70 miles an hour and keep up the pace day after day, without complaining about being tired. As long as I follow the book of instructions, everything performs miraculously whether I understand how or not.

However, the most complicated of all of our machines is the human machine. In great admiration David explained, ". . . I am fearfully and wonderfully made." (Psalm 139:14.) And certainly we can all say that again! For example, I have a personal fuel tank called a stomach. Into it I can put all sorts of herbs, grains, meats, sweets, and liquids, and the most fantastic of all manufacturing devices will turn them into energy, vision, heat, light, and understanding. This digestive system can take proteins, carbohydrates, and fats and turn them into flesh and blood, bones and tissues, brains and personality. I also have a wonderful pair of lungs. They automatically draw into themselves a mysterious substance called air that I can't see or understand. My lungs not only understand what they are doing, but they are fully automatic. They work while I am asleep or awake, sick or well, and while I am running or standing still. In the field of their activity my lungs are far more intelligent than I am. But every other organ of my body also has an intelligence that far surpasses mine with regard to its function.

My bloodstream contains trillions of microscopic red corpuscles that carry oxygen and nutrition to every part of my system. I have other trillions of white corpuscles that serve my body as its medical men. My white corpuscles fight disease, kill infection, and keep me in good health without my knowing what is happening. Billions of these wonderful little corpuscles are automatically manufactured in the marrow of my bones every day. Yet if I had all of the intelligence of the wisest combination of medical men, I would not know how to manufacture even one red corpuscle, and I wouldn't have the slightest guess about how to supply the oxygen to nourish even one brain cell. I know very little about estimating the needs of my liver, thyroid gland, or spirit. I don't even know where the self-starter is located that enables me to get myself going every morning. Every human being has some wonderful abilities to move and speak and laugh and think without knowing how it is done. There are millions of ideas filed away in my brain, any one of which can be flashed upon an invisible screen by pushing the right mental buttons. I also have an inaudible voice speaking to me that I have never heard, and yet it is telling me things every minute of every day in a language that is clearer than any audible voice. It lets me know when I am hungry or tired or cold or when I feel guilty or inferior or lazy.

The other day someone asked me to give them my opinion about two possible book covers. After I had looked at each one for a few seconds, something told me several reasons why I liked one very much and why I liked the other one not at all. In this interesting combination that I call myself, I have many aptitudes and abilities that are as mysterious to me and even more wonderful than those miracles on my television set. If I touch the right buttons I can laugh, love, think, repent, breath, sleep, eat, work, and worship. If I turn the dial to the right place, an unmistakable voice will tell me when I am doing wrong and when I am being unwise. I have some tremendous assets that even my television or automobile doesn't have. Somewhere within myself I have a wonderful thing called life, which is the most valuable of all commodities. I also have a brain, a personality, and a will. I have a marvelous physical body equipped with a lot of helpful emotions. I also have a spirit, and while no one, including me, knows very much about it, yet I wouldn't sell it for a trillion dollars. It is an interesting fact that I have never so much as even seen my own spirit, and yet it is very close to me. I live with it every day. I can feel its presence, and I can recognize some of its abilities and attitudes.

I also have a whole collection of miraculous instincts, abilities, character traits, and ambitions. I have a conscience, a voice, a will, a set of emotions, and access to the use of the still small voice. But probably my greatest good fortune is that the omnipotent Creator, who is the manufacturer and the inventor of all of these wonderful installations, has prepared some instructions as to how I should most effectively operate myself.

Some 3400 years ago God came down onto the top of Mount Sinai and to the accompaniment of the lightning and thunder of that holy mountain gave us some important rules to make us function more effectively. As a safeguard against ruining ourselves, he gave us some stern "thou shalt nots." The first step toward any success is to get clearly in mind and make some decisions about those things that we must not do. From the top of Mount Sinai God placed these flashing red lights of warning on such things as murder, adultery, dishonesty, profanity, Sabbath day violations, and the practice of identifying with false gods.

In 1832 the Lord placed some "thou shalt not" signs on alcohol, nicotine, and caffeine to emphatically warn us against them. Then in January 1964 the Surgeon General of the United States gave us a kind of progress report picturing the devastation that was taking place in our magnificent human machinery because we were not following instructions but were taking poisonous substances into our lungs, tissues, and bloodstream.

A prominent doctor recently attended the birth of a baby whose mother was a user of morphine. When the baby was born it looked more like a tiny Egyptian mummy than that proverbial bouncing baby described in the book of instructions. The baby's skin was an unhealthy blue-gray color, and within a few moments after birth he began to twitch and jerk with an increasing violence. The doctor knew that the baby was responding to his mother's craving for dope. He also knew that unless the baby received an immediate injection of morphine, he would have a convulsion from which he might never recover. The doctor injected the dope, which produced only a very short tranquillity. In less than an hour the baby was again twitching his way toward a convulsion. The nurse said, "The poor little guy is hooked just like his mom." She said, "What did he ever do to deserve a rotten deal like this?" When the mother was questioned about her habit she said, "Okay, okay, I am on the needle, so what? That is nobody's business but my own." The doctor said to her, "You don't believe that any more than I do." Then he went on to comment on the tragic life this poor little human being has to look forward to living with a mother who is out of control of herself and who is trying to make herself believe that what she does is nobody's business but her own. When she saw the pathetic-looking little son that she had produced, she closed her eyes and began to cry. What a tragedy that she didn't give her son the kind of start in life that he would have had if she had followed the Lord's book of instructions. From it we learn that our immoralities, our venereal diseases, our venereal attitudes, our atheisms, and our crimes can have devastating effects, and they are the business of a lot of other people, including God.

I might claim that my automobile belongs to me, but it is still the business of a lot of other people if I drive it down the wrong side of the street at a hundred miles per hour. But whom are we ourselves responsible to?

The apostle Paul says, ". . . ye are not your own. For ye are bought with a price." (1 Corinthians 7:19-20.) Christ redeemed us from death by sacrificing his own life. Even the earth on which we live belongs to him, and only by his grace are we permitted to live here and to work out our eternal salvation. The most important part of our success is to pay particular attention to the direction given in our book of instructions. It says that we should take maximum care of our bodies, our minds, our spirits, and our personalities. We start out our lives here with a father's blessing given under the power of the priesthood.

We are directed that at the age of accountability we should

be baptized, receive the gift of the Holy Ghost, and join the Church. At that time we are asked to make some covenants of faithfulness and not to take poisonous ideas into our minds. Then as we develop our abilities we may receive the priesthood, and by the quality of our service and obedience we may demonstrate our worthiness for increased blessings. We are instructed to be married in the temple, where the sacred family relationships are formed for eternity. The book of instructions says that these covenants must be kept. We are privileged to take upon ourselves the name of Christ and live by every word that proceedeth forth from the mouth of an all-wise Heavenly Father. And one of his greatest commands has to do with having children and rearing them according to his rules. But the correct answer to every problem in our lives is found in these great books of instruction that God has caused to be written to teach us how to live. Our primary responsibility in life is to follow them.

The Colors of Life

ONE OF the very interesting facts about our world is its colors. I have often wondered how many billions of buckets of paint the Lord must have used to paint the oceans, the skies, the landscapes, and the sunsets in glorious color. It would be difficult for one to be in a beautiful flower garden with all its patterns and various shades of design without realizing that God is a great lover of color and beauty. This artistry carries over into every area of life. Someone with less imagination than the God of creation might have designed our food in one package, but God added great interest and color when he gave us red apples, black cherries, blue plums, purple grapes, with a dazzling array of blackberries, green gooseberries, oranges, and lemons.

Recently I reread the story of Solomon's temple. The building specifications were written by God and the building was one of the wonders of the ancient world. Many millions of dollars worth of fine gold was used in its construction. But besides the gold, the scripture also mentions the fine twined linens and other materials used in its furnishings. The striking colors of scarlet, gold, and purple added greatly to the beauty and attractiveness of this house of God. In fact, the color probably added as much to the temple's magnificence as did the gold. Since that time, we have increased the glory of our colors so that we now have paints, fabrics, enamels, and appliances in hundreds of stimulating shades and hues. We decorate our homes in Tahiti blue, delphinium, deep bronze, turquoise, rose, emerald, raspberry, old gold, and mace. Color is in the very air we breathe and in the sunlight that gives us life and strength.

The scripture says that Christ "is in the sun, and the light of the sun, and the power thereof by which it was made." It says that this "light which shineth, which giveth you light, is through him who enlighteneth your eyes, which is the same light that quickeneth your understandings; Which light proceedeth forth from the presence of God to fill the immensity of space—The light which is in all things, . . . even the power of God who sitteth upon his throne, who is in the bosom of eternity, who is in the midst of all things." (D&C 88:7, 11-13.)

This wonderful sunshine that comes from God contains the many mysterious elements necessary for life. In addition to lighting up our lives, this wonder of sunshine is what gets into our watermelons to make them grow and gives them color. It vitalizes our vegetables and makes the fruits so delicious to our taste. It is interesting to remember that we do not live on an independent earth. If this colorful light of the sun's rays were turned off for just a few hours, no life would remain upon our earth.

The sun's rays themselves perform great miracles. They come through the frigid pitch-blackness of outer space without giving off their light or heat or color until they reach our atmosphere. Then the sunshine unloads its warmth and distributes its store of vitamins and health to sustain and energize our lives. This beautiful white light is occasionally broken up by the rain to show us God's great rainbow of color, but whether we see them or not, sunshine is always made up of many colors, and they serve many purposes.

We have also learned to make some rainbows of our own. When a scientist passes an ordinary beam of sunlight through a crystal prism, it comes out the other side separated into its various colors of red, blue, yellow, violet, orange, green, and purple with all of the other hues and tints that belong to God's brilliant color spectrum. And then we sometimes apply these rainbow colors to represent those particular traits, colors, and abilities in us.

Since 1893, American universities have used a rainbow color code to represent the different branches of higher learning. At commencement the white tassels on the caps of some graduates indicate that they have graduated from the school of arts and letters, blue stands for philosophy, scarlet is for theology, green is for medicine, purple is for law, golden yellow is for science, orange is for engineering, and pink is for music.

We also take these colors from God's spectrum and apply them to represent certain personality traits in us individually. When we are angry we say that we see red. We sometimes describe the character quality of a person as being true blue. When some people develop a yellow streak, it is an indication that they are suffering from a lack of courage. Under some circumstances, one may be green with envy or white with fear. We use color to describe either those who have a dark past or a rosy future. When we are at our best, we say we are in the pink of condition.

Life itself is a kind of prism through which we filter the sunshine to make the particular spectrum we desire for our own lives. In the spectrum of life, white stands for light, wisdom, purity, joy, and glory. Red stands for courage and valor. Blue, the color of the sky and the ocean, is the most common color. It is also the symbol of heaven. Blue stands for truth, piety, and sincerity. Gold stands for honor and loyalty. We have this quality of genuineness in mind when we frequently describe someone as pure gold. Silver stands for faith. Green is for youth and hope. The darkest and most somber of all of the colors is black. It stands for grief, sorrow, and death. Black is also a malicious, threatening, slanderous, deadly color. It stands for evil and malignancy. We represent blackmail, blackball, and a blackened reputation by this dark, evil color. Of course, our greatest concern should be to keep our souls off life's blacklist by a careful selection of the colors that we use in our own spectrum of living.

We need to include a lot of purple in the arrangement of our life's color scheme. Purple is the royal color and denotes high rank and great nobility. Orange is for continued strength and endurance. But this beautiful white light that comes from God is a composite of all of the colors in God's spectrum. Sometimes we refer to someone as a sunbeam or a ray of sunshine. That is a pretty good idea, and each of us should be filled with the warm sunshine of friendliness and goodwill. Enough of the right colors in our activity will also guarantee our eternal success.

It is, of course, very important that we give the best colors the most dominating positions. On one occasion someone said to an invalid, "My, how sickness does color life." The invalid replied, "It surely does, and so far as I am concerned, I intend to select my own colors." What a great privilege it is that we may take whatever colors we desire from God's spectrum and breed into ourselves individually those traits which they represent.

The other evening I was one of those invited to visit in the newly furnished home of a wealthy friend. No expense had been spared to make his house a model of utility and comfort. It was a showplace of beauty, and all the colors of the rainbow were attractively included. The building itself was of the finest quality, and the designing and decorating left nothing to be desired. It was a little bit difficult, even in imagination, to conceive of anything more attractive, harmonious, beautiful, pleasant, or comfortable. But what was even more important, the occupants themselves radiated an even more satisfying spectrum with those great human qualities which they had built into themselves. Included among the many desirable virtues that stood out in their lives was an aura of love, the warm feeling of friendliness, and the soul of honor.

They exemplified those great maxims that say, An honest man is the noblest work of God; order is the first law of heaven; cleanliness is next to godliness. How beautiful to see great convictions of truth shining like valuable gems in one's life. Their lives had an intelligent purpose. They were filled with joy and enthusiasm. Then, above all of these, is that great quality of godliness that so greatly brightens life. The house in which they lived was very valuable, the furnishings added color, harmony, and beauty, but it was the people who lived there who gave it its greatest importance and meaning.

While enjoying the good dinner, the fine company, the pleasant conversation, and the general beauty in our friend's home, I tried to imagine what the mansions in heaven would be like that were mentioned by Jesus. Someone has said:

> If God hath made this world so fair
> Where sin and death abound,
> How beautiful beyond compare
> Will paradise be found.

Jesus said: "In my Father's house are many mansions: if it were not so, I would have told you. I go to prepare a place for you. And if I go and prepare a place for you, I will come again, and receive you unto myself; that where I am, there ye may be also." (John 14:2-3.)

On one occasion the apostle Paul indicated that he had once been caught up into paradise, which he refers to as the third heaven, where he "heard unspeakable words, which it is not lawful for a man to utter." (2 Corinthians 12:2-4.) And Paul must have known something about what was meant when he quoted the prophet Isaiah and said: "Eye hath not seen, nor ear heard, neither have entered into the heart of man, the things which God hath prepared for them that love him." (1 Corinthians 2:9.)

We can imagine beauty, luxury, and elegance that would cost billions of dollars, but Paul says that it has never even entered into man's heart the things that God has prepared for those who love him. And while we cannot imagine the glories of heaven, yet I think that we ought to try. We should also try to imagine what kind of people will live there. The scriptures speak of God's glory. We are told that the magnificence of his presence is so great that a man in his natural state cannot live in his presence. I am sure that the heaven where God dwells will not resemble a hippie camp, nor will that be the kind of people who dwell there. The people who inhabit God's mansions will be godly people. And by using God's own standards that we should judge a tree by its fruits, we can be perfectly sure that God loves beauty, cleanliness, morality, order, and righteousness. We also know that he has great ability as a designer, and that he loves harmony, color, and fragrance. We also know that God loves truth, honor, goodwill, and has in mind an eternal happiness for us; otherwise he would not have gone to such great lengths in recommending that we adopt these traits in our lives. In fact, God has included in us a natural, inborn quest for excellence on an instinctive basis, so that it gives us great joy when these qualities are made a part of our lives and activities.

Of course, we think that our earth, even in its present state, is a very beautiful, wonderful place, but this earth presently exists in its fallen condition. It is still under the curse placed upon it at the transgression of Adam. But some day the earth will be celestialized and become beautiful beyond our present imagination. In that inspired tenth Article of Faith we say, "We believe . . . that Zion will be built upon this [the American] continent; that Christ will reign personally upon the earth; and, that the earth will be renewed and receive its paradisiacal glory." But the glory of the earth will be exceeded by those children of God who dwell upon it.

The ultimate destiny of man is to become a celestial being and qualify for that eternal order to which God himself belongs. The earth will eventually become a celestial sphere and be made a fit place for the Creator's presence. Certainly the glory and majesty of God would not fit very well in a telestial environment. I don't think that he would like to live in a place filled with stifling tobacco smoke or the stale, nauseating smell of liquor. I do not think that he will people the celestial kingdom with those who are out of their minds with some kind of dope addiction or given to sex orgies. I am sure that he would not care to spend his time listening to degrading stories, profane oaths, and seeing acts of violence, or share the spiritual depression of drunken people reveling in crime. Certainly dishonesty, cheating, and selfishness are not a part of God's activity spectrum.

God himself has said that he "cannot look upon sin with the least degree of allowance" (D&C 1:31) and no evil will ever be permitted in his presence. And if we would sometime like to enjoy the beauty and luxury of his eternal mansions and their appropriate environment, then we must exclude all ugliness and blackness from our lives or it will cause us to be excluded from the celestial kingdom. We should also leave all inharmonies and untruths behind. What a thrill it ought to be that a genuine repentance can purge out those colors of sin and death and help us to develop to the full those colors that come from God's spectrum, made up as it is of that rainbow of virtues that come from him. The light from his presence will kill the germs of every evil and purify our lives that we might qualify for eternal life in that place which Paul describes as the "glory of the sun." (1 Corinthians 15:41.)

The Distortion in Definitions

ONE OF the biggest problems of our world is the trouble we have in communicating our ideas because of changed word meanings. When Dante, the Italian poet, wrote his great literary masterpiece *The Divine Comedy,* a comedy was not something that was funny. It was something that had a happy ending. A more understandable title for our day would be *A Divine Journey* or *A Divine Experience.*

The Bible admonition to fear God may not give the exact shade of meaning today that was originally intended. Our dictionary sometimes gives as many as forty different meanings for the same word. For example, the word *foot* may refer to a member of one's body or to a twelve-inch measurement. It may indicate one's position at the foot of his class. The foot of the bed is not the same as the presser foot of a sewing machine. A foot may be a group of syllables constituting a metrical unit of verse, or a measure of music. There are also some figurative meanings, such as "he jumped in with both feet," or "he put his foot down," or "he put his foot into it."

However, we have probably made more changes in our language in the past few years than in many preceding centuries all put together. And as our sins have become worse, and our crime rates have increased, we have so degraded our words and corrupted our speech that we resemble those people who poison their own drinking water. With a more easy acceptance of the so-called new morality, extensive use is made of those slimy, dirty words to give expression to our ideas. Whereas some of our noble, inspiring, wonderful words of the past have been degraded, at the same time they have been robbed of much of their dignity and beauty.

For example, since time began we have had a magnificent word called *freedom.* To millions of people it has had a sacred tradition with a holy meaning. It has stood for a liberation from slavery and a release from those evil influences which previously held us bound. To some, freedom has also meant the absence of error, evil, weakness, sin, and disease.

On January 6, 1941, President Franklin D. Roosevelt gave a speech about such great American freedoms as the freedom from want and the freedom from fear. Other important traditional freedoms are the freedom of speech, the freedom of religion, and the freedom of assembly. But many evil people are now hiding behind this beautiful and exalted word as they claim a freedom to promote vulgar, disloyal, profane thoughts, causing increases in crime, the degradation of sex, and the multiplication of violence.

The Communists claim validity for such false freedoms as their claimed freedom to enslave such weaker nations as Hungary, Poland, Czechoslovakia, and East Germany. They want freedom to bury the United States and to subjugate all nations and bleed them of their material wealth and human resources. They have banished God so as to be free from any religious restraints that would be imposed by an allegiance to any power but their own. We have had a great uprising of people in our own land who claim such false freedoms as the freedom to break the Ten Commandments and the freedom to disbelieve in God.

Many want to be free to enslave themselves with drugs, immorality, and sin. There are many people with problems of immorality, drunkenness, and dope addiction who say: "What I do with my life is nobody's business, but my own." But when their sins result in unstable children and venereal attitudes in others, everyone knows that their sins must be the business of someone else. Some claim the counterfeit freedoms to riot, burn, kill, break the law, shout obscenities at the police, destroy the establishment, and cause anarchy in their own society. Some use this word *freedom* to cover up verbal filth, pornography, nudity, and the most mini-standards of morality.

Twenty-five hundred years ago Socrates went around ancient Athens saying to people, "Define your terms." Before he engaged in any discussions, he wanted to know what his friends were talking about. It would be a pretty good idea for our own day if we would honor our speech and not degrade our beautiful, honorable words by associating them with debasing, dishonorable practices. Because of our self-granted freedoms to practice the new morality and indulge our criminal tendencies, our entire society has been thrown for a serious moral less.

In the days of Noah the Lord sent a flood to destroy their version of the new morality and wipe out their crime wave. But soon after the flood, sin again began to raise its ugly head in the hearts and in the language of the people. And so from the Tower of Babel the Lord scattered the people abroad over the earth and he confounded their language to make it more difficult for them to contaminate each other. We could greatly upgrade our own society if we would abandon the use of those dirty, disloyal, faith-destroying, degrading words that are inseparably connected with evil activities.

A few years ago the Egyptian armies marched on Jerusalem with the publicly announced intention of subjugating the Israeli people. They distorted their own speech to make their project appear entirely proper to themselves. However, when the Israeli armies fought back and drove the invaders out to a safer distance, the Egyptians accused the Israelis of being the worst kind of aggressors. Nations are sometimes like criminals who attack a community and then cry police brutality when officers of the law try to prevent the destruction the criminals are attempting.

In the past we have had a fine word called *reality* or *realism*. It means that we should recognize all facts as they are. That is a fine idea. But the members of some rebellious, angry groups who are trying to overthrow the government, destroy the establishment, ridicule religion, and discredit our finest traditions have now picked up this word and have radically changed its meaning as well as its spirit.

They have invented a battle cry around it which says, "Tell it as it is." With their attitude of destruction, they insist that everything be told as it is at its worst without recognizing any good. They don't want things discussed as they could be or ought to be. Their idea is to talk only about the corruption in government, the hypocrites in society, the crooks in business, and the brutality used in trying to save lives. By distorting the meaning of good words, they try to show that slavery is better than freedom, that anarchy is better than law and order, that those dictators trying to enslave others are more to be desired than the self-government of free, God-fearing men. To them anyone who sees anything good in the establishment is being unrealistic.

The term *the new morality* in many cases actually means *immorality*. Jesus was certainly speaking of our new morality when he looked forward to our day and compared our wickedness to Noah's day.

When the great words *love* and *peace* are scrawled on the propaganda placards of a hippie camp, they do not have the same meaning that they had when Jesus used them. To these strange human beings, love frequently means the worst kind of a free and promiscuous association of the sexes, and peace may indicate their desire to be excused from any effort or responsibility. One of this new breed said: "We are tired of war, poverty, discrimination, and capitalistic exploitation. We are turning to love, music, communal living, and sharing. We totally reject the rules and regulations of the establishment and are creating a new life style."

When some of the nations objected to the German madman Hitler, who was enslaving the smaller nations, he shouted back in injured anger, "Let us alone. We want peace." He wanted peace so that he could enslave the world. Hippies also want peace; they don't want any of their evil plans regulated. They want to carry on their immorality, dope addiction, and sin in peace.

To describe *drug addiction,* some of its devotees use such terms as mind expansion rather than soul destruction.

That great Christian word *tolerance* is now being used as a direct tool of Satan. To some, tolerance means that everything goes, that nothing should be placed out of bounds. With enough tolerance we can make an easy adjustment to every sin. Many years ago Alexander Pope wrote about one kind of tolerance when he said:

> Vice is a monster of so frightful mien
> As to be hated needs but to be seen;
> Yet seen too oft, familiar with her face,
> We first endure, then pity, then embrace.

The word *high* once meant *up* or *elevated* or *exalted.* To many it now refers to one who is under the influence of drugs and living in an unnatural world of make-believe and unreality.

The word *festival* used to indicate a festive, joyous, happy occasion. It described a day of civil or religious feasting and celebration. Shakespeare once referred to a festival as "a blessed day." But now a festival might refer to a rock music festival, which may also include a drug festival, a sex festival, and a rebellion festival thrown in.

There is a practice of deliberately changing word meanings in order to produce evil, bring about antagonisms, and destroy good. By this process people may be confused and led away from God. The prophet Isaiah could have been speaking of our day when he said:

Woe unto them that call evil good, and good evil; that put darkness for light, and light for darkness; that put bitter for sweet, and sweet for bitter!

Woe unto them that are wise in their own eyes, and prudent in their own sight!

Woe unto them that are mighty to drink wine, and men of strength to mingle strong drink:

Which justify the wicked for reward, and take away the righteousness of the righteous from him! (Isaiah 5:20-23.)

The scriptures announce several serious curses because of these deceptions. In the book of Deuteronomy it is said: "Cursed be he that removeth his neighbour's landmark. . . . Cursed be he that perverteth the judgment of the stranger. . . . Cursed be he that confirmeth not all of the words of this law to do them." (Deuteronomy 27:17, 19, 26.)

Jeremiah said: ". . . for every man's word shall be his burden; for ye have perverted the words of the living God." (Jeremiah 23:36.)

We also distort the meanings of the commandments by our disobedience. The other day on the street I passed a group of young girls who were probably fifteen to seventeen years of age, and even in this age of degenerate sights, I was shocked to see them. They looked like a vicious pack of prowling wild animals. Conforming to a spirit so common in our day, they seemed to have made their inappropriate boys' clothing about as dirty and unattractive as possible. Their long hair was uncombed and their persons uncared for. Their attitudes and expressions were the outward indications of what I am certain was going on inside of them. It was evident that these young female human beings had long since abandoned their parents, their homes, and their interest in the Ten Commandments.

They were perverting the ways of the Lord by the sin that was corroding away their resemblance to that Divine Being in whose image they had been created. Certainly they were missing their high destiny of being the most beautiful part of God's great creation. Neither were they qualifying to be the holy inspiration for God's man-creation, nor were they producing the purity of life required to be the mothers of those spirits that God desires to send into the world through their instrumentality. Certainly they were missing the commandment which God had said to them: "Be ye clean that bear the vessels of the Lord." (D&C 38:42.)

I shuddered as I thought about what the ultimate end might finally be for these young women. The outward signs indicated an overwhelming possibility of drug-addiction, immorality, and many other kinds of evil. The sex patterns of our day clearly point out what will happen as these females make their contacts with their male counterparts. And what chance will their children have for a good life when they are born and molded under such unfavorable circumstances?

How far some of us are missing the high mark set by the Lord when he said, "Verily I say unto you all: Arise and shine forth that thy light may be a standard for the nations." (D&C 115:5.) Again he said: "For Zion must increase in beauty, and in holiness, her borders must be enlarged; her stakes must be strengthened; yea, verily I say unto you, Zion must arise and put on her beautiful garments." (D&C 82:14.)

The most beautiful creations of God are his children, and in many ways the most favored of his children are those designated to bear and rear children. Certainly they should strive to be beautiful even as God is beautiful. There can be no question about the fact that God is a lover of beauty. The Bible says God made everything beautiful. (Ecclesiastes 3:11.) Order is the first law of heaven and cleanliness is next to godliness. God dresses in beautiful clothing. When Jesus took Peter, James, and John up onto a high mountain and was transfigured in the presence of Moses and Elias, the record says: ". . . and his face did shine as the sun, and his raiment was white as the light." (Matthew 17:2.)

May we use our greatest power in maintaining the meaning of our noble words and also in making our lives and actions beautiful.

A Dog's Life

Recently from my hotel room very early in the morning I heard a dog barking down on the street, and as I was lying there in my bed listening to him bark, I had a number of interesting thoughts about him. I calculated that there was a rather large number of other people whom the dog had awakened, and like me, they were now listening to him. My first thought was to wonder why this dog's owner had given him so much freedom to break up the slumbers of so many people. However, I was mostly concerned with the dog himself, and I thought how interesting it would be to understand what his life would be like and how it would be to see the world from a dog's point of view. Ordinarily dogs are very intelligent animals, and many of them have been closely associated with human beings. They have some senses more highly developed than our own. That is, they have a better sense of direction, a keener sense of smell, and an ability to hear that is far superior to ours.

I wondered what kind of ideas dogs had about life and how they felt about people. I wondered if they were ever discouraged with their dog's life or if they ever envied us or if they ever made any comparisons with us as I was now doing with them. Although he had awakened me a little early, I didn't feel too bad about it, as I was very comfortable in my bed. I felt a little sorry that in all probability he never had a bed better than a cold doorstep. Because this dog seemed to enjoy his barking, I wondered just what he was getting out of it. As far as I know, barking and wagging his tail are about the only means of communication or expression that a dog has. If this dog was trying to say anything, he seemed to have only one phrase, for he kept repeating the same bark over and over again. It seemed to me quite unlikely that this dog believed that he was doing any essential service by his barking. He probably was not trying to extend a morning greeting or sound an alarm or do any entertaining. Apparently he was not trying to communicate with any other dog. I wondered if those dogs that were watch dogs or sheep dogs or human companions or pets felt that they were profitably employed. In any event, it never seemed to occur to them to go on a strike, incite a rebellion, or even object to being underfed or mistreated.

In my earlier years, I had some very pleasant relationships with some faithful, devoted dogs. I don't know how I could have felt a greater personal loss than I did when one of my faithful dogs was run over by an automobile after I had raised him from a pup. I will always remember the look of love and pain in his eyes as I nursed him through his dying hours. And even after many years have passed, he still seems to be an important part of my memories. Even now I felt a kind of friendly fellowship with this dog barking outside the hotel. However, I found myself being grateful that I didn't have to change places with him, as I greatly preferred the better comfort, wider range of activities, and more effective means of expression that the Creator had granted to me as a human being. It would seem to me to be a very serious limitation if I couldn't read, write, laugh, talk, work, and do the thousand other interesting things that people do while dogs just bark, lie on the doorstep, and wait for some opportunity to be with and serve their masters.

Then I thought of the restricted means of expression that is given to all of God's other nonhuman creatures. The primary means of vocal expression for the rooster is to crow, and he crows in the same key and hits the same notes that roosters have been hitting for thousands of years. And none of the others seem to be any better off. Hens cackle, frogs croak, cows bellow, horses neigh, birds sing, pigs grunt, sheep bleat, goats blat, snakes hiss and rattle, bears growl, and lions roar. A bee sets up a series of buzzes as he makes his rounds of thousands of miles gathering his honey and storing it in the same quality hexagon-shaped honeycomb cell in which bees have stored their honey for thousands of years. The cells of the present-day honeycomb are exactly the same dimensions as those found in Egypt manufactured by the bees of thousands of years ago. Apparently the honey then had the same quality, the same taste, and the same appearance as now. It seems that none of the animal creations are ever permitted to learn a single thing from any previous generation.

However, we are almost overwhelmed by this vast array of life. Many of God's animal creations have talents far surpassing our own. For example, on an average, a turtle lives longer, a rabbit runs faster, an eagle sees farther, a horse has a better sense of direction, a dog has a keener scent, and yet they have these severe limits placed upon them beyond which they cannot go, so that all animals must do their thing exactly as they have done it for thousands of years. As far as we can see, they have no future growth prospects in sight. Even with their keen senses and their alertness, all of their limitations seem definitely and unchangeably fixed.

It is interesting to read in the Bible the account of God's creation in which animals play such an important part. Sometime ago someone complained that the Bible contradicted itself with two accounts of the creation, but the Bible clearly tells of *two* different creations, not just one as is sometimes believed. The account of the creation given in the first chapter of Genesis is a spiritual creation. The one recorded in the second chapter is an earthly, physical creation. The Bible also makes clear that animals and plants, as well as people, were a part of the spiritual creation in heaven before they were made to grow physically upon the earth. Of the fifth day of creation the book of Genesis looks forward to an earthly creation and says:

"And God said, Let the waters bring forth abundantly the moving creature that hath life, and the fowl that may fly above the earth in the open firmament of heaven.

"And God created great whales, and every living creature that moveth, which the waters brought forth abundantly, after their kind, and every winged fowl after his kind: and God saw that it was good.

"And God blessed them, saying, Be fruitful, and multiply, and fill the waters in the seas, and let fowl multiply in the earth.

"And the evening and the morning were the fifth day.

"And God said, Let the earth bring forth the living creature after his kind, cattle, and creeping thing, and beast of the earth after his kind: and it was so.

"And God made the beast of the earth after his kind, and cattle after their kind, and every thing that creepeth upon the earth after his kind: and God saw that it was good.

"And God said, Let us make man in our image, after our likeness: and let them have dominion over the fish of the sea, and over the fowl of the air, and over the cattle, and over all the earth, and over every creeping thing that creepeth upon the earth.

"So God created man in his own image, in the image of God created he him; male and female created he them.

And God blessed them, and God said unto them, Be fruitful, and multiply, and replenish the earth, and subdue it: and have dominion over the fish of the sea, and over the fowl of the air, and over every living thing that moveth upon the earth." (Genesis 1:20-28.)

Then in the second chapter of Genesis everything is in readiness for an earthly creation, and the record says:

"These are the generations of the heavens and of the earth when they were created, in the day that the Lord God made the earth and the heavens,

"And every plant of the field before it was in the earth, and every herb of the field before it grew: for the Lord God had not caused it to rain upon the earth, and there was not a man to till the ground.

"But there went up a mist from the earth, and watered the whole face of the ground.

"And the Lord God formed man of the dust of the ground, and breathed into his nostrils the breath of life; and man became a living soul.

"And the Lord God planted a garden eastward in Eden; and there he put the man whom he had formed.

"And out of the ground made the Lord God to grow every tree that is pleasant to the sight, and good for food; the tree of life also in the midst of the garden, and the tree of knowledge of good and evil.

"And the Lord God said, It is not good that the man should be alone; I will make him an help meet for him.

"And out of the ground the Lord God formed every beast of the field, and every fowl of the air. . . ." (Genesis 2:4-9, 18-19.)

The Lord said, ". . . nevertheless, all things were before created; but spiritually were they created and made according to my word." (Moses 3:7.) That is, plants, animals including my canine friend at the hotel, and people all lived in heaven before they were physically placed upon the earth. Certainly animals have spirits the same as humans do. They will also have a resurrection and an immortality. I am confident that if we understood the entire program of God we would be more than ever delighted with the benefits of our own lives. I am so grateful that God has lavished so many blessings upon his own children. First he gave us the most noble identity when he created us in his own image. He gave us the form of angels. The beast was put down on all fours and thus his vision was cast upon the ground, but man was created upright in the image of his Maker that he might look up to God and to righteousness and to progress and to his destiny, which is to become like his eternal heavenly parents. We have a Father in heaven. We also have a mother in heaven, as certainly no one ever had a Father in heaven or on the earth without also having a mother. And we were given our godly powers of expression so that we could laugh and sing and love and think and feel happiness and be thrilled with joy.

It is very interesting to me to try to imagine what a dog's life is like, but the most exciting idea that I can think of in the world is to think about what it may someday be like to know first-hand what God's life is like.

It seems quite unlikely that a rather ugly caterpillar ever even imagines that he may someday be a beautiful butterfly. But one of the great blessings of our lives is that we may know in advance that it is our destiny to become like God. Among our other great endowments, God has given us the most wonderful language possibility, enabling us to enjoy a happy and meaningful communication with God and with others of our kind. The animals are unable to read or write even the most simple speech, and it has been pointed out that anyone is unable to think effectively until he has a language to think with. Beautiful poetry, eloquent prose, and stimulating experiences can all be used in forming beautiful words, pleasant emotions, and the most noble, exciting thoughts.

The psalmist said: "How sweet are thy words unto my taste! yea, sweeter than honey to my mouth! Through thy precepts I get understanding: . . . Thy word is a lamp unto my feet, and a light unto my path." (Psalm 119:103-105.) And the writer of Proverbs says, "Pleasant words are as an honeycomb, sweet to the soul, and health to the bones." (Proverbs 16:24.)

How grateful we should be that God did not limit us to barks, growls, bleats, and hisses. As our means of expression, he gave us words, and we may sing, pray, laugh, and worship. Contemplating our marvelous human creation, the psalmist said:

"When I consider thy heavens, the work of thy fingers, the moon and the stars, which thou hast ordained;

"What is man, that thou art mindful of him? and the son of man, that thou visitest him?

"For thou hast made him a little lower than the angels, and hast crowned him with glory and honour.

"Thou madest him to have dominion over the works of thy hands; thou hast put all things under his feet." (Psalm 8:3-6.)

One translation of this scripture says: "Thou hast made him for a little while lower than the angels." When we have made the most of our situation, then God will exalt us on high. Then we will know something about life in its most pleasant form, and we may understand the scripture which says, "O Lord our Lord, how excellent is thy name in all the earth! . . ." (Psalm 8:1.) What an exciting idea to contemplate that God, angels, spirits, and men are all of the same species in various degrees of righteousness and in different stages of development. The only restrictions that are placed on us now or in eternity are those that we place upon ourselves.

It should be our primary objective in life to do all of those important things necessary to qualify.

An Epitaph

THE MOST valuable commodity in the universe is life, and two of the most important events in life are birth and death. Everything depends upon being born, but death is equally important as it is our entrance into immortality. The two important events of birth and death have an interesting relationship to each other, as we live to die and then we die to live. Most of life is preparation. We prepare for school; we prepare for marriage; we prepare for our life's work; we prepare for death. In the antemortal existence we prepared for this life; in this life we prepare for eternal life. The event that gives life most of its importance and urgency is death; and the more effectively we have lived, the more satisfactorily we may die.

Everything depends on what we do in between these two dates.

The thing that everybody wants to know about a basketball game is the score. At a horse race, people congregate at the tape to see how the horses finish. That is also the most interesting thing about the race of life. Jesus was anticipating our final score when he said, ". . . he that endureth to the end shall be saved." (Matthew 10:22.)

A lot of people have made wonderful starts but poor finishes. Others start poorly and finish like champions. Some with championship possibilities become dropouts and never reach the finish line. The greatest preparation for death is to make the most of our life, and the billing slip of every birth points to that time when we will be laid away in the cemetery. As usual farewell procedures, our friends get together and conduct a memorial service in our honor where eulogies are said and someone writes a final epitaph to go on our tombstone. These last words serve as a kind of summary of our life. The word *epitaph* comes from the Greek words *epi,* which means "upon," and *taphos,* which means "tomb." Therefore an epitaph is an inscription on one's tomb, which is usually made as full of praise as possible to represent all of our final score, including all of our hopes and eulogies.

Sir Christopher Wren was the builder of St. Paul's Cathedral and many other famous buildings in and around London. When he died they buried him in the cathedral that he had built. On the wall above his grave were inscribed these words; "Here is laid to rest the builder of the Church and the City. If you seek his monument look around you."

The science of criminology says that no one can pass through a room without leaving some evidence of his having been there. It may be only a footprint or a fallen hair or a scent, and yet to some extent everyone modifies his environment. Our epitaph will sum up the evidence that we leave of how successfully we have lived our lives. Christopher Wren left behind him a great cathedral in which thousands could worship God. Others leave dens of vice, where thousands bring eternal damnation upon themselves as well as lead other people to ruin. Some have taught false doctrines and destroyed people's faith in God.

Some have walked at the head of a caravan going down that broad road toward eternal death and have left their epitaphs written in the immorality that they have left blossoming along the way. The apostle Paul left thousands of devoted Christians who had obtained their faith through his personal teachings. He also left many uplifting letters that for nineteen centuries have been inspiring people toward righteousness. Paul wrote his own epitaph, saying, "I have fought a good fight, I have finished my course, I have kept the faith." (2 Timothy 4:7.)

Thomas Jefferson also wrote a summary of his own mortal existence. In it he called attention to the fact that he was the author of the Declaration of Independence and the president of the University of Virginia. He did not mention that he had also been the President of the United States for two terms, bought Florida from Spain, made the Louisiana Territory a part of the United States, and had been a member of Congress, Vice President of the United States, and Governor of Virginia.

On the tomb of Robert Burns a friend inscribed the following:

> An honest man here lies at rest,
> As e'er God with His image blest;
> A friend of man, a friend of truth,
> A friend of age, and a guide of youth.
> Few hearts like this with virtue warm'd,

Few heads with knowledge so inform'd.
If there's another world, he lives in bliss;
If there's none, he made the best of this.

On a tombstone in Aberdeen Churchyard is written:

Here lie I, Martin Elginbrodde;
Have mercy on my soul, Lord God,
As I would have were I Lord God,
And ye were Martin Elginbrodde.

David Gray wrote:

Below lies one whose name was traced in sand;
He died not knowing what it was to live.

Robert Burns wrote the epitaph for his father as follows:

O ye, whose cheek the tear of pity stains,
Draw near with pious rev'rence and attend!
Here lie the loving husband's dear remains,
The tender father, and the gen'rous friend.
The pitying heart that felt for human woe,
The dauntless mind that fear'd no human pride,
The friend of man—to vice alone a foe,
For even his failings lean'd to virtue's side.

And Mark Twain wrote on his daughter's tomb:

Warm summer sun,
Shine kindly here.
Warm southern wind,
Blow softly here.

Green sod above,
Lie light, Lie light,
Good night, dear heart,
Good night, good night.

Edwin Markham wrote an interesting epitaph for himself.
He said:

Let us not think of our departed dead
As caught and cumbered in these graves of earth,
But think of death as of another birth—
As a new freedom for the wings outspread,
A new adventure waiting on ahead,
As a new joy of more ethereal mirth,
As a new world with friends of nobler worth,
Where all may taste a more immortal bread.

So comrades if you pass my grave sometime,
Pause long enough to breathe this little rhyme;
Here now the dust of Edwin Markham lies,
But lo, he is not here, he is afar
On life's great errands under brighter skies,
And pressing on toward some more melodious star.

It might be a very worthwhile project to undertake to write an epitaph that would fit our own lives. Or as an alternative, suppose that we were going to invite God to give the eulogy at our funeral. It would be stimulating to plan what we would hope that he would say of us on that occasion. Actually, we are the ones that will determine what is said and written, and we have a lifetime to furnish the evidence from which the inscriptions on our monuments will be taken. Our funeral service is the last and one of the most important sessions that we will ever attend. It will be the only one where our final life's score will be calculated.

At our funeral many important things may be said. That will be the time when God and our friends will be standing at the finish line. That will also be the time when they will sum up our lives and write our score in the Lord's book of life and carve our epitaphs on our tombstone and in their hearts. They will also send us on our way by giving some loving eulogies and singing a few sacred hopeful songs of farewell at our departure. There is a sacred song sung at many funerals called "The Christian's Good Night," in which we sing:

Good night, beloved,
Sleep and take thy rest.
Oh, lay thy head
Upon my weary breast.
We love thee well,
But Jesus loves thee best,
Good night, Good night, Good night.

There is another hopeful, comforting hymn that might make up a part of the spirit of our final epitaph, and by which we may be encouraged to look forward to our destiny. It is called "Beyond the Sunset."

Beyond the sunset, oh blissful morning,
When with our Savior, heaven is begun.
Earth's toiling ended—oh glorious dawning,
Beyond the sunset when day is done.

Beyond the sunset, no clouds will gather,
No storms will threaten, no fears annoy.
Oh day of gladness, oh day unending,
Beyond the sunset, eternal joy.

Beyond the sunset, oh glad reunion
With our dear loved ones, who've gone before.
In that fair homeland, we'll know no parting,
Beyond the sunset, for ever more.

We can't all make our entrance upon the stage of life at the same time. We were sent ahead of our children to prepare the way, to get an education, to learn to make a living, and to provide a home for them. Some must also leave this life ahead of others for similar reasons. The following lines may help us during this time of separation.

Should you go first and I remain
To walk the road alone,
I'll live in memory's garden, dear,
With happy days we've known.

In spring I'll wait for roses red
When fades the lilac blue,
In early fall when brown leaves call
I'll catch a glimpse of you.

Should you go first and I remain
For battles to be fought,
Each thing you've touched along the way
Will be a hallowed spot.

I'll hear your voice,
I'll see your smile,
Though blindly I may grope.
The memory of your helping hand
Will buoy me up with hope.

Should you go first and I remain
To finish with the scroll,
No lengthening shadows shall creep in
To make this life seem droll.

We've known so much of happiness;
We've had our cup of joy.
And memory is the gift of God
That death cannot destroy.

Should you go first and I remain,
One thing I'd have you do:
Walk slowly down that long lone path,
For soon I'll follow you.

I'll want to know each step you take
That I may walk the same,
For someday down the lonely road,
You'll hear me call your name.

And so we return again to the idea that all of life is a preparation, and what a tremendous experience we expect to have when we cross the borders of this life! Then we will have that happiness and glory promised by the Lord, discussed at our funerals, and written in our hearts. Then we will know love, beauty, happiness, and a feeling of worthwhileness that we have never yet imagined. Therefore, with these important dates of our birth behind us and our death ahead of us, we might muster our greatest efforts to make the most of what is immediately before us.

Ergophobia

SOMEONE RECENTLY wrote to the question and answer section of a newspaper and asked the writer of the column to explain to her the nature of a disease called ergophobia. The inquirer had a relative who had been diagnosed as suffering from this particular malady, and she wanted to know the symptoms and what the percentages of fatalities were. The newspaper representative explained that ergophobia was an aversion to work or a fear of work. He went on to say that while an intense dislike for work was not necessarily fatal, yet it could be and in a great many cases it actually has been.

We do not always understand the widespread devastation caused by this plague that makes it one of the most dreadful of all human diseases. Of course, a less imposing name for ergophobia is just plain laziness. On many occasions Jesus referred to this destructive malady as sloth, and so far as is known, the most stinging rebuke ever heaped upon the head of anyone by him was upon the unprofitable servant whose fear made him bury his talent in the ground. Jesus was kind to the repentant adulteress. He had a sympathetic interest in the thief on the cross who wanted to do better, but he said to the lazy man: "Thou wicked and slothful servant." (Matthew 25:26.) Then he said to those who were with him: "Take therefore the talent from him, and give it unto him which hath ten talents. . . . And cast ye the unprofitable servant into outer darkness: there shall be weeping and gnashing of teeth." (Matthew 25:28, 30.) Jesus came into the world calling for workers. He was pleased with people who were willing to do their share. He spoke of that eternal law that even faith without works is dead. It is always true that when we take away the works, the faith dies. You can't keep faith in cold storage. There is no such thing as preserved faith, and there is no excellence without labor.

The dictionary says that a sloth is a sluggish, slow-moving, tree-dwelling mammal with long front legs and curved claws that enable him to hang from tree limbs while he eats its leaves. How-

ever, the dictionary also explains that sloth is an inclination to in-
action and indolence in people. It is a disinclination to labor, an
allergy to service with an attendant lack of growth. How our society would be improved if in one of our knowledge explosions we
could find a cure for sloth with its kindred ailments of lethargy,
indifference, and apathy. The idler is a sloth, the ignoramus is a
sloth. The one who steals to avoid work is a sloth. Some drug
addicts will steal or kill to get dope, but few of them will do constructive work. Disloyal draft dodgers have ergophobia. Hippies
have ergophobia. Some of the so-called Jesus people, participating
in the new craze, will sing, march, and shout slogans, if someone
else will support them. As a result of our scientific medical research, some of our most deadly physical diseases have been prac-
tically eliminated. The once dread diseases of tuberculosis, diph-
theria, polio, and spinal meningitis have now almost disappeared.
In 1886 smallpox killed over 120,000 people in the United States,
but so far as is known, in recent years smallpox has not killed a
single person. But ergophobia is now with us in its most exag-
gerated form. An idle mind is the devil's workshop. An idle body
causes all kinds of weakness, degeneration, nervous breakdowns,
and death. When the real business of this planet began, God first
closed down the Garden of Eden paradise, and his very first law
had to do with the development of our industry. He said: "In the
sweat of thy face shalt thou eat bread. . . ." (Genesis 3:19.)

This is not a command of punishment; it is a command of
opportunity. This is not just the way that we get our bread; it is
also the way that we develop our characters, build our bodies,
and improve our personalities. This is also the way that we provide for ourselves and our families and do almost every other
worthwhile thing in the world. Later this law was supplemented
out of the fires and smoke from the top of Mount Sinai when God
said: "Six days shalt thou labour, and do all thy work." (Exodus
20:9.) Mostly we don't work six days anymore. We have greatly
reduced not only the days and the hours, but also the work. We
declare many extra holidays. We have many long and frequent
vacations. We fill our shortening days with rest periods and coffee
breaks. Unemployment insurance has induced many people to
spend a large part of their lives in paid idleness.

We have had some government programs that have paid
people for not growing crops. With our government subsidies and
relief, we pay a large part of our population for their sloth. The

government gets its money for handouts by raising the taxes and increasing the national debt rather than the old-fashioned way that says that the idler "shall not eat the bread nor wear the garments of the laborer." (D&C 42:42.) Instead of commemorating Labor Day with a good demonstration of labor, we even spend our Labor Days in idleness, and many people are now looking forward to a four-day week with a three-hour day.

We have disregarded the instruction of Jesus about being doers of the word and not hearers only. Christianity itself is not just a collection of ideas; it is a set of activities. Scientists can now repair damaged hearts and successfully remove parts of diseased stomachs, but when one gets this crippling disease of ergophobia, he is beyond the reach of doctors and is in serious trouble all over. His income is reduced; his enthusiasm for life goes down; his education deteriorates. His nervous system suffers, and he tends to lose his moral, mental, and spiritual, as well as his financial, health.

Dr. Alexus Carrol once wrote a great book entitled *Man, the Unknown.* He says that men and women were built for struggle. It was intended that they should subdue the elements, suffer fatigue and hunger, and fight with wild beasts. Now we sleep in heated bedrooms, ride to work in heated automobiles, eat soft food, and get our tissues shot through with ergophobia. In the beginning God said: ". . . cursed is the ground for thy sake; . . . Thorns also and thistles shall it bring forth to thee." (Genesis 3: 17-18.) This extra work is good for us. But now most of our mental, as well as our physical, work is done for us by machines. The result is that we weaken ourselves. It seems that every power that we summon to our aid makes us weaker. When we walk with crutches, our leg muscles deteriorate. Not only does faith die without works, but almost every other thing dies as well. When the mole quit using his eyes, nature took away his eyesight. When we stop using the muscles in our arms or our brains or our personality, they first get flabby and then disappear.

Recently I reread the story of Mark Anthony, the friend and successor of Julius Caesar. He made himself the master of the world and then died of ergophobia. After Caesar's assassination, the world was divided into two great war camps. One was led by the conspirators under Brutus, the other by Octavius Caesar and Mark Anthony. During the long hard war that followed, Mark Anthony distinguished himself as the greatest general in the world. How did he do it? The primary part of his success was industry, and his awful fate came because of his idleness.

Someone has described his rise and fall as follows:

"Armed with his tireless industry, his convincing speech, the power of his logic, the courage of his leadership, and his own self-discipline, he swept everything before him. He took upon himself the hardest tasks with the most wondrous good cheer. He lived for weeks on a diet of insects and the bark of trees. This dedication and ability soon won the unquestioned loyalty of his men, the acclaim of the people, the support of Octavius and his own self-confidence.

"Opposed by such power, the enemy generals began dropping out of the fight one by one and finally when the war was won Mark Anthony stood where the great Julius Caesar had once stood, as the unquestioned master of the world."

But when the need for struggle was past, Mark Anthony became idle. Probably the greatest error that anyone ever makes is to quit, to become inactive, to give up, to surrender himself to indolence.

Mark Anthony fell in love with the bewitching Queen Cleopatra of Egypt. He became victim of the soft luxury, perfumed elegance, and immorality of the Egyptian court. His great mind became clouded by the fumes of wine, and as he abandoned his better self, his magnificent personality began to disintegrate. Then he soon lost the loyalty of his men, the acclaim of the people, the support of Octavius, and his own self-respect. Finally a guard of soldiers was sent from headquarters to take Anthony into custody and bring him back to Rome in chains. It did not now require an army to take Mark Anthony. A mere handful of the most ordinary soldiers was now all that was needed.

Anthony avoided arrest by thrusting a dagger into his own heart. As he lay dying, he recounted to Cleopatra that there had been no power in the world sufficient to overthrow him except his own power. He said, "Only Anthony could conquer Anthony." Then contemplating the arrival of the soldiers and the great disgrace that he had brought upon his nation, his associates, his family, and his friends, he made his last speech, which William Haynes Little has translated into verse:

Let not Caesar's servile minions
Mock the lion thus laid low.
'Twas no foeman's arm that felled him.
'Twas his own hand struck the blow.

He who pillowed on thy bosom
Turned aside from glory's way;
When made drunk with thy caresses,
Madly threw the world away.

Mark Anthony had held securely in his hands the control of the entire world, and there had been no power on the earth sufficient to take it away from him except his own power. "Only Anthony could conquer Anthony." Then because of his own idleness and evil he threw away an entire world. But each of us holds in his hands a world that is far more valuable than that which belonged to Mark Anthony. There is no power in the world that can stand between us and the celestial kingdom of God except our own power, but by a little idleness, a little sin, a little thoughtlessness, and a little sloth each of us may throw away every blessing.

George S. Benson, nationally known educator, author, lecturer, columnist, and fighter for private enterprise, tells the story of the seagulls of Conch Island, Florida, just off the waterfront of St. Augustine. Some years back, their pitiful plight made news all over the nation. The Conch Island gulls were the pride of the Atlantic; powerful of wing and keen of eye, they were flashing, slashing, diving fishermen. For years they would fly each morning far out to sea, search out their small fish prey schools, and dive among them to eat their fill.

Then the shrimp fleet moved into St. Augustine. In the late evening of each day, the fleet would come in from the shrimp grounds, and at dockside, clean thousands of pounds of shrimp. The water was littered with bits of culled shrimp. The Conch Island gulls quickly recognized their bonanza. Naturally there was no longer any need for them to fly for hundreds of miles out over the ocean looking for food. The tide brought the shrimp right up on their Conch Island beaches. To the seagulls it was like having their supper served in bed.

For three years the shrimp fleet stayed at St. Augustine. Then it moved far around the coast. The Conch Island gulls waited in vain for their food to be served to them. After a few days they began starving. Their shrimp handout had ended. The St. Augustine residents heard the gulls' mounting screams. When they investigated, they found that the older gulls had lost their ability to hunt and fish for themselves, and the new generation of gulls had never learned at all. Whether we are talking about the animal kingdom or the members of our human society, the handout program is the most dangerous, the most self-defeating, and, in the end, the cruelest policy that anyone can adopt.

A great welfare program where handouts are given to citizens and nations soon makes them become like the Conch Island gulls, unable and uninterested in taking care of themselves. When people need help, our natural tendency is to rush to their aid. Our love for someone, or our money, or our abundance can easily get in the way of wisdom and destroy the receiver.

Recently I talked with a young man who for a few years had been a partial practitioner of the philosophy of one variety of hippie-ism. Now he wanted to do better, but it was difficult for him as he was just plain lazy. His skin was a kind of death color. He had little to show for muscles, where his chest should have been he had a depression, and it seemed as though he didn't have enough strength to work up a sweat. He was another victim of this world plague of ergophobia.

If God answered all of our prayers for peace and plenty, we would all soon destroy ourselves. Emerson says that mostly we are parlor soldiers. We like to dine nicely and sleep warm, but we shun the vigorous battle of life where strength is born. A far better prayer is for us to help God, and as it has been said, "The hands that help are holier than the lips that merely pray." Someone prayed a great prayer, saying:

> I ask no heaven till earth be thine,
> No glorious crown till all thy work be done;
> When earth shall shine among the stars,
> Her sins wiped out, her captives free,
> When all men live gloriously unto thee,
> Then for my crown, more work give thou unto me.

Fool's Gold

O NE OF the most important substances in our world is its gold. It
has been widely sought after since time began. Many prospectors
have given their lives in finding it, and numerous wars have been
fought for its possession. The discovery of gold at Sutter's Fort
in 1848 initiated a kind of human stampede when people from
every part of the country headed for California.

Gold is prominently mentioned in the history books and
in the Bible itself. It has been used to erect temples and idols. A
tradition suggests that even the streets of heaven may be paved
with gold. The ancient Greek deity Dionysus granted King Midas
his fondest wish so that everything he touched would be turned
into gold. But in one way or another, there are many people who
are still trying to make this golden dream come true. Some people
have married for gold, some have labored for it, and others have
stolen it. Stories have been written about the goose that laid
golden eggs and the Garden of Hesperides, where grew the golden
apples that were guarded by nymphs and a sleepless dragon. We
also remember Jason and the golden fleece and Edgar Allen Poe's
story of the "Gold Bug." But we are all still on the alert for buried treasures, and we are constantly being bitten by various gold
bugs or hit with gold bricks.

Gold is also one of our most important commercial articles.
We use gold for ornaments, for jewelry, and for filling our teeth.
Before it was against the law we also carried golden coins in our
pockets. But because gold is so important to our national trade
and credit, the government has now taken over primary possession of it. Instead of having it guarded by sleepless dragons, we
have now buried it at Fort Knox and have it guarded by some
sleepless machine guns. But even though it is buried it is still
very important. Gold has a specific gravity of 19-3/10, which
means that it is nineteen times heavier than water. Because pure
gold is too soft for ordinary use, it is hardened by alloying it with
some other metals. Then its purity is measured in carats. A carat
is 1/24th; hence an alloy containing 14/24th gold is said to be a

14 carats fine; 18/24ths would be 18 carats fine; and pure gold is 24 carats. The price of pure gold was set by legislation on January 31, 1934, at $35.00 per ounce. We use this as a measuring stick for other values. We sometimes try to compliment someone by saying that he is worth his weight in gold. If you have a 120-pound wife worth her weight in gold, her value would be $50,000. If she were turned into 120 pounds of gold, she would be about 1/19 of her present size, whereas if she were turned into gold and her size kept constant, her weight would increase to a total of 2,280 pounds.

For a hundred years prior to 1934, gold was the primary support of our monetary system. We referred to this system as the gold standard. Under it, creditors could expect that all debts would be paid in gold. This gave everyone the confidence of a secure foundation and a value that could be depended upon. However, after the first World War, some of the nations were unable to pay their debts in gold, and one by one they abandoned the gold standard and adopted in its place a kind of managed currency. Under this new arrangement, certain government officials are supposed to use their personal opinions to determine what our money should be worth. But at about this same time, we also began to abandon some of our symbolic gold standards. We began substituting our own personal opinions for what had previously been unchangeable. For centuries, the Ten Commandments and the Sermon on the Mount had served as a kind of gold standard of conduct. These fundamental codes were built on the word of God, who is "the same yesterday, to day, and for ever." (Hebrews 13:8.) In our day, he has the same standards of honesty, reverence, faith, and morality that he has had since time began.

However, in some way, we his children have largely abandoned many of the time-honored standards of truth, and in their place we have come to depend on personal opinions, frequently based on satisfying our own individual convenience. In place of our time-honored gold standard, a kind of new morality has arisen among us by which we measure our conduct by a new yardstick. In this new code, there are no harsh authoritative "thou shalt not's" such as are found in the Ten Commandments. This new standard places very little if any conduct out of bounds. Our new code sometimes says that God is dead and that what one believes doesn't matter very much. It proclaims that we are the products of our environments so that no one is to blame for what he does. With this process of reasoning, we can use a lot of cheap substitutes instead of insisting on the genuine article.

According to the kind of alloy that is used, one may have yellow gold, white gold, or green gold. We can have 10-carat gold, 14-carat gold, 18-carat gold, or 24-carat gold. But it is an interesting fact that nature has also fashioned some cheap gold counterfeits in the form of iron pyrites that are called fool's gold, and although they are only worthless counterfeits, many people have thought of them as genuine.

I suppose that one of the hardest of life's lessons is to learn that all is not gold that glitters. Even in the ten-cent stores, we may buy the most wonderful collection of gold rings and bracelets, set with giant diamonds. We also have some gold rushes of our own in which we strike out for some of those symbolic forms of fool's gold. And although these imitations sometimes seem very impressive, they are only counterfeits of the genuine article. For just as diamonds can be made out of glass, and worthless twenty-dollar bills can be made to look real, so we can develop counterfeit character traits, imitation religions, and moral standards made of fool's gold. Emerson once said that our greatest sin is pretense. He said that most of us were like pennies trying to pass ourselves off for half dollars. Many of us live in a kind of fool's paradise and indulge in fool's reasoning and enjoy a fool's happiness. But when these imitations are tested in the fire or examined in the light of God's truths, they are often found to be worse than worthless.

The dictionary says that a fool is one who is deficient in judgment or who so lacks discretion that he acts absurdly or stupidly. It is interesting that very few people fail in life because they lack intelligence or can't develop sufficient ability. Too frequently we are simply fooled or misinformed or careless or disinterested. Because our judgment can never be any better than our information, we frequently fail to reach our goals primarily because of our foolishness. Even the scriptures make more references to fools than to sinners. Penitentiaries, reform schools, and mental hospitals also contain more victims of error and weakness than of intentional sin. Almost everyone wants to do right and to be successful and happy. But sometimes we never quite reach our goals merely because we do the wrong things. We allow ourselves to be influenced by the wrong people and develop the wrong objectives and attitudes.

So far as we are informed, the rich man mentioned in the scriptures who died while his barns were bulging with goods that he couldn't use was not an evil man. Jesus didn't say that he was dishonest, immoral, or lazy. Certainly, he appears to have been very successful in his occupation. He must have been an intelligent and industrious worker to have accumulated such a great amount of wealth. The Lord didn't call him a sinner; he merely said he was a fool. Apparently, this man had misunderstood the real objectives of life and was therefore unprepared for death. With his wealth stacked around him he heard the Lord say, "Thou fool, this night thy soul shall be required of thee." (Luke 12:20.) Certainly anyone is foolish who exhausts his energy on those things that can never bring him any benefit, and yet this is exactly what so many people do. Our testing is being given in a world of opposites where we see the contrasts of good and evil, success and failure, right and wrong side by side. The wheat and the tares are frequently allowed to grow together until harvest time. These contrasts can help us to develop our judgment and our righteousness. However, we should be aware that every genuine article has a counterfeit that we must learn to recognize. It has been pointed out that even God has no temple where Satan does not soon locate some den of vice close by.

Jesus established the gospel of Jesus Christ upon the earth and taught those divine principles which, if practiced, would enable us to qualify for God's highest kingdom. But immediately a flood of counterfeits were introduced. As the scripture says, the people had "transgressed the laws, changed the ordinance, and broken the everlasting covenant" (Isaiah 24:5) that Christ himself had established. In our own day of enlightenment, a dozen counterfeit doctrines are being proclaimed for every one that is genuine. In his own image God created male and female and gave them a miraculous power called procreation. This was part of the divine program wherein all of God's spirit children may receive a mortal body under the most favorable circumstances. It was ordained that this power of procreation should be exercised only within the sacred confines of the marriage relationship, where children could be loved, educated, and provided for. But this great power was soon being abused, and presently a vast group of moral counterfeiters are contending for premarital and extramarital sex relationships.

There is a kind of free love promiscuity that is painted with the glamour of fool's gold. However, because it ruins the lives of many people, it is far worse than counterfeit. There are other counterfeiters who prostitute the beauty and appeal of the human body in their attempts to sell booze or get people to buy cigarettes or do those other things that have a soul-destroying effect. All of the virtues, the character traits, and even the abilities are the targets of counterfeiters. To live on counterfeit money would be undesirable and unpleasant, but how much worse to live a counterfeit life and know that we ourselves are phonies instead of genuine human beings. Frequently, even one's ideas, ambitions, and ideals are counterfeit, and then his whole accomplishment usually turns out to be nothing more than fool's gold. Fool's gold may have a lot of glitter but it gives no real satisfaction. It would be disappointing to find that your valuable diamond ring was a worthless imitation from the ten-cent store. But how much worse to discover that your loves, friendships, or virtues had no real substance and were actually worse than worthless.

Recently the newspapers told of a group of young hoodlums who get their greatest happiness from glue sniffing and dope addiction. Dishonesty and sloth are the counterfeits of honor and industry, and they can easily set in motion those influences that can make one's life itself worthless. Instead of building quality and genuineness in oneself, there always seems to be a temptation to try to counterfeit happiness and to get our feelings of worthwhileness by merely taking off and getting drunk. But this false sense of elation soon wears off, and the resulting depression of spirit proclaims the harmfulness of such cheap counterfeits. The glittering fool's gold called alcohol always leaves one far worse off than he was before. Anyone is a fool who lives by fool's logic in a fool's world.

God himself has set up genuine happiness as the chief objective of life. Righteousness and doing good to others are always elevating to our minds and spirits. It is interesting that God has made some genuine happiness pills that are easily available to us. Even in small doses, good deeds and uplifting thoughts make us happy. Any real success always produces joy. To be genuinely worthwhile gives us genuine satisfaction, and there are no substitutes for happiness. But all imitations are useless, and every counterfeit is harmful. A depraved mind can never think anything but depraved, unhappy thoughts. Satan is miserable because he is evil. One who seeks happiness in wickedness is a fool, and every time one does any evil deed, large or small, he is lowering himself just that much and is putting a little more worthless fool's gold into his life's treasury. The teenage hoodlums who commit their vandalism for kicks should listen to the voice of the prophet who said: "Be not deceived; God is not mocked: for whatsoever a man soweth, that shall he also reap." (Galatians 6:7.) When it makes any human being feel good to destroy the property of someone else, or when a group of hoodlums can get a thrill out of beating an old man to death, they may be sure that their lives are being seriously perverted. Satan's program for spreading bloodshed, famine, ignorance, and misery over the earth is the counterfeit of God's plan for our eternal salvation, and it is up to us to be able to tell the difference. If we go about it right, God will help us to make our lives of pure gold.

Force

ONE OF the most devastating influences in our world is the evil philosophy of force. Force is one of the major sins of nations, societies, and individuals. One of the most common manifestations of this destructive power is seen when national dictatorships flourish. Our world has been set back a long way by the evil domination of the Napoleons, the Hitlers, and the Communists. While Joseph Stalin ruled Russia he also bathed his own country in the blood of millions of his countrymen. Those who have followed him have imposed their will upon the souls of other millions of human beings. We remember the malicious propaganda of Khrushchev with his bluffing, his vicious threat making, and his shoe rapping. His threat of "We'll bury you!" represents the longing of Communist ambition to dominate. And if they thought they could, the Communists would enslave the entire world without a second's hesitation. They devise systems of brainwashing and related pressures as a science to satisfy their satanical desire to control people's minds and emotions. It is a sickening thought that any human being would attempt to banish God and say he is dead and then seek to replace him by establishing himself as the supreme power in the world.

Our minds go back to another generation when in leading up to the first World War, the Kaiser of Germany commonly used the phrase "Me and Gott." This indicates how power-mad dictators frequently come to think. However, with the world's increase of ungodliness, present-day dictators leave off the "Gott" and use only the "Me." We have one of the most pitiful examples of this doctrine of force operating just a few miles off our southern shores.

Cuba is a small country of great beauty and rich natural resources. It came into the possession of the United States as a result of the Spanish-American War. It was given its independence in 1909 and for a number of years had a democratic government. In recent years dictators have held the people down and have wasted the national strength in their struggle for control.

That unhappy country is now ruled by an immoral, bigoted, be-whiskered, villainous dictator by the name of Fidel Castro, who dominates, demoralizes, and improverishes his own countrymen as he tries to please his own vanity. He also uses this island as a training center of evil as he threatens the peace and safety of a large group of human beings outside his own country.

God has always disapproved of force and of some men trying to dominate the minds, affairs, or property of other men. Dictators insist upon having their own way, and those who disagree with them are usually assassinated, and unhappiness and failure come to many people as a consequence. Dictators usually set themselves up to decide right and wrong, and frequently they use half-truths and misrepresentations to make their course seem right, whether it is or not.

In our own day God has said that it is wrong to exercise force or dominion or compulsion upon the lives and minds of men in any degree of unrighteousness. Human freedom is the cause to which God has given one of his most firm personal commitments. But in this connection it is very interesting to remember that national dictators are not the only ones who are guilty of using force unrighteously.

In a recent political meeting, called to discuss an important issue, a group of paid hireling agitators arose from their seats as the speaker was announced and stomped out of the meeting in an attempt to discredit the speaker and what he stood for. A more civilized group might have been expected to try to enlighten those whom they believed were in error. There are many nonlogical ways of creating social and individual pressures. Many large groups stage marches or carry signs or burn draft cards or try to cause someone embarrassment in order to secure some notoriety or benefit for themselves. Besides promoting crime and delinquency among ourselves, we have frequently abandoned reason and persuasion and substituted a kind of trial by frenzy or a trial by hysteria, to create social pressure. As in the case of Russia, the winner is sometimes the one who can make the most noise or cause the most trouble for someone else. In the old days, men frequently used to determine right and wrong in a trial by combat. Now we frequently try to see who can create the most pressures or be the most unfair. There are many groups who want recognition and benefits whether they are entitled to them or not. They threaten elected officers and embarrass, frighten, or humiliate others into compliance.

The great Christian message through the ages has been one of "peace on earth, good will toward men." The Communists completely reverse this program with many paid agitators specifically assigned to foment trouble and set one group of people against another. They seek to build up their own strength by tearing others down. Many people in our great, free, democratic America are following the dictator techniques by resorting to sub-reasonable methods to create unrighteous pressures. It was a related technique that sent the rabble-rousing mob to the palace of Pilate in the middle of the night crying, "Crucify him, crucify him!" The power that can be developed by this evil force is seen in the fact that even Pilate, the Roman governor, was persuaded against his will. In his personal examination of Jesus, he found no fault in him, yet he yielded to the mob's evil influence and permitted the death of the best man who ever lived.

Mobs of vandals and hoodlums are presently going about both by day and by night stealing and destroying and beating for what they call kicks. Recently such a gang of sub-moral gangsters, saturated with the philosophy of force, beat an old man to death. When questioned, they said they bore the old man no ill will; they merely wanted the thrill of killing someone. The human mind can be a deadly power when perverted by this awful philosophy of force. Almost unknown to us, this attitude is infiltrating many departments of our lives. William James once said, "Our minds are made up by what they feed upon." The mind, like the dyer's hand, is colored by what it holds. If I hold in my hand a sponge full of purple dye, my hand becomes purple, and if I hold in my mind ideas of hate, lust, strife, and force, my whole personality is changed accordingly. When we feed our minds upon the kind of passion, violence, greed, filth, and irresponsibility that fills our newspapers, movies, and magazines, it is natural that that is what our lives will become.

Recently for several days a woman paraded back and forth in front of a certain office building with a sign that didn't make the slightest sense to anyone; but she seemed to imagine that she was taking the part of some kind of a heroine. She had heard of others carrying signs, and she wanted to be in the act and to attract a little attention to herself. She had had some moral and personality problems, but now she was the center of attention. Sometimes logic or reason or right don't seem of great importance to people. Anyway, it is sometimes a little difficult to attract attention by doing good deeds, but anyone can easily and quickly get attention by starting a fight or doing something spectacular or harmful or evil.

Recently one of the long-haired, unshaven, unbathed kind of young men went around town trying to get someone to buy him a bicycle and then finance him on a transcontinental journey. He wanted to develop as much notoriety as he could and then ride on Washington, D. C., to induce the Congress to adopt a particular law that he had figured out. He was asked why he didn't write a letter to his congressman or to the President. But he figured that first he had to do something a little more shocking in order to get attention. This young man was a dropout from school, a dropout from church, certainly a dropout from cleanliness. He had no money, no job, and no interest in finding one. He was only interested in seeing that Congress did not overlook any of its responsibilities.

It was suggested to him that he might do a little better job with Congress if he would find out a little more about his proposition and then get a job and learn something about financing himself. It was thought that he might have a little more influence with Congress if his own mental, social, and financial affairs were put in a little better condition. But a kind of high pressure, exhibitionism, was the only way he seemed aware of to get things done. And while we are thinking about it, we might examine ourselves occasionally to discover how many subreasonable things we are trying to force upon other people. Many people are able to get their good friends to indulge in a few friendly drinks of liquor, a little immorality, or a little dishonesty, and whether we kill someone with a hammer or destroy him by a bad example, the end result may be about the same.

It is a startling thought to remember that God will hold each of us responsible for his influence. The improper use of his influence is probably the most serious sin of Satan himself. It was bad enough that he rebelled against God in the council of heaven, but it was a much greater sin when, by his influence as the light bearer, he led away one-third of all of the hosts of heaven after him. He not only fell himself, but he also destroyed the chances for eternal exaltation of a great multitude of his friends. By our influence or example or sometimes by actual physical force, we sometimes accomplish about the same thing.

A few evenings ago as a certain family was preparing to re-
tire, they heard the screams of a young girl coming from their
front lawn. They turned on the lights and ran to her assistance to
find five boys holding her so that she could be raped by the sixth.
Five other girls were looking on from three cars parked near by.
Apparently this girl had not been as quick to succumb to this
male immorality as her friends had been, and by a kind of general
agreement it had been decided to forcefully initiate her into their
club. If sexual sin stands next to murder in the catalog of crime,
what must God's opinion be of the enormity of a crime where
one's life and memory are soiled and violated by force? God has
said that he "cannot look upon sin with the least degree of allowance." (D&C 1:31.) He has firmly condemned immorality as one of
the greatest crimes, and he has vigorously forbidden the use of
force or compulsion in any of its physical, moral, or social forms.
This is one of our most serious world disorders, as so many people
prefer merely surrender to pressure rather than to have any
trouble or suffer any embarrassment.

Each of us is born into God's world holding a share of the
responsibility for its welfare. It is our duty to teach righteousness
and to set everyone else a good example. God himself has said,
"For behold, this is my work and my glory—to bring to pass the
immortality and eternal life of man" (Moses 1:34), but as God's
children, it also becomes our work and our glory to bring to pass
the immortality and eternal life of man. Jesus said, "Follow me."
And we are supposed to follow him in every particular. We are supposed to follow him in his good example and in his righteous influence and in promoting the freedom of other people. Every life
will finally be judged by how well it carries out that single direction.

The apostle Paul says we are not our own but that we have
been "bought with a price," and we are charged with an important
responsibility. We all know the kind of life that God would like
us to live. He has said to us that we may choose for ourselves,
but he doesn't want us to be forcing our will upon others. The
poet was speaking for Deity when he said:

> Know this, that every soul is free,
> To choose his life and what he'll be,
> For this eternal truth is given
> That God will force no man to heaven.

He'll call, persuade, direct aright,
Bless him with wisdom, love and light,
In many ways be good and kind,
But never force the human mind.

Freedom and reason make us men;
Take these away, what are we then—
Mere animals and just as well
The beasts may think of heaven or hell.

God is the greatest advocate of freedom, free agency, and righteousness. He is not a sign carrier nor a marcher seeking notoriety, nor does he try to dominate us nor influence us for evil, whereas Satan is the chief exemplar of force; and every time we think of using undue influence upon the minds and wills of other human beings, we may know that that one impulse is being dictated by evil, as there can be no other source. America is the world's greatest nation, and as a group we are the world's most privileged people, and we have a divine mission to keep freedom and righteousness alive in the world. What a tremendous influence we would have for good if we stopped the pressure we use in satanizing each other so that we could properly honor freedom and always keep righteousness alive in our hearts and help it take root in the lives of others.

God Bless the Establishment

A MONG THE most characteristic activities of our age are the large number of changes presently taking place in our society. In so many ways our world is making radical departures from that way of life that our fathers knew and cherished. In the past we have thought of our most constructive citizens as those who always put back into the community more than they took out, whereas now so many people want to get out more than they put in. In addition, we want to kill the goose that lays the golden eggs. By our propaganda, rebellion, race riots, and evil we tear down the source of our benefits. We want to belong to the club without paying our dues. We want to pick the fruit without planting the trees. We want to vote ourselves benefits that were produced by someone else, and we don't know how to exercise the privileges of dissent within the framework of law and order.

Many people are now in the process of abandoning their own personal standards of integrity and culture. Many have abandoned their loyalty to the flag, their allegiance to the means of production, and their belief in the Ten Commandments. Many are now discrediting the religion of Christ and the other great traditions on which so much of our civilization of the past has rested.

There has been a serious breakdown in our respect for authority. A sweeping socialism is making serious changes without much thought being given to analyzing the problems or producing satisfactory solutions. Sound principles have little importance in the face of some of our modern movements to abandon religion, our individual enterprise, and our good sense.

Many of our modern people do not understand the relationship of work to success and happiness. Because many now insist on seeing everything at its worst, there is a tendency to destroy religious faith, kill patriotism, belittle hero-worship, and even make self-confidence of small effect.

Many have converted their lives over to patterns of ugliness and idleness where they behave at their worst. They expect to live by the sweat of other men's faces. We adopt a philosophy of trial by marches or make our point by carrying propaganda slogans.

The large increase in stealing, killing, and intimidation indicates that the fundamental concepts of freedom, basic human rights, the sacredness of human life and property are no longer in good standing with many people. By congregating in large groups, these rebellious people can give themselves a feeling of authority by supporting each other in their evil. And because of the propaganda of their own large groups, the opposing opinions of righteous people and even of God become relatively unimportant to them. To some people the value of law and government also shrink in importance, as do our time-honored social customs.

One person obsessed with a major interest in drugs said, "Why worry about having friends when you can get pot?" Some of this large group that is fostering our raging epidemic of rebellion, crime, sin, destruction, and the rejection of standards are young and inexperienced; some are misguided; some want attention, and some are frustrated by their own failures. The evil of our time has given birth to a brand new breed of human beings with a philosophy of selfishness, hate, and force, which is sweeping across our world with its primary focus in the general objective to weaken, punish, and destroy the existing order that they refer to as the establishment.

One of their spokesmen said: "We totally reject the rules and regulations of the establishment and are creating a new life style."

The dictionary says that to establish is to make stable or firm. It means to confirm or to settle, to enact a decree, or to ordain a principle. Much of the establishment being opposed has been ordained by God himself. The scriptures point out that governments were instituted by God for the benefit of man. The primary purposes of the government are to promote peace, success, security, law, and order. As we pledge allegiance to the flag, we say, "One nation, under God, indivisible, with liberty and justice for all." Abraham Lincoln referred to our national authority as a "government of the people, by the people, and for the people."

But there are other important parts of our God-given establishment that are also under attack. In the meridian of time the Son of God established his church upon our earth, one purpose of which was to establish in each individual life those important virtues of righteousness, integrity, industry, and responsibility on an eternal basis. The great primary laws of free agency, honesty, morality, goodwill, and honor among men were originally ordained in heaven, and they have been transferred to us upon the earth. God himself made the Ten Commandments a part of the establishment.

In addition to governments and the church, God also established our occupations. The beginning of our great agriculture and horticulture industries began when he covered the earth with sixteen inches of topsoil. At a time long antedating our mortality, God himself planted a garden eastward in Eden. Then for the benefit of our agricultural establishment, he invented seeds, irrigation water, and the processes of cultivation. He started our livestock industry by creating the animals even before he created the men who would take care of them.

As God stored up in the earth the great treasures of coal, iron, gold, silver, oil, and uranium, he laid the foundations for our important mining and manufacturing industries. As he made coats of skins for Adam and Eve, he started our tailoring enterprises. Our great businesses embody the best ways that we have ever been able to discover of providing for ourselves. Business, law, agriculture, and medicine all administer to important human needs and each therefore must be considered as a divine calling. We might continue on indefinitely through the entire list of manufacturing, mining, transportation, merchandising, communication, and the professions. Naturally some of the involved people, organizations, and programs have weaknesses, but our mortality is supposed to involve us in many learning situations; some great improvements have been made, and many people, companies, and regulatory bodies are trying as hard as they can to educate and train us to serve each other more effectively.

I, for one, never cease to be grateful that I am permitted to live in this marvelous age of wonders, miracles, and enlightenment, which the apostle Paul looked forward to and described as the "dispensation of the fulness of times" when all things should be brought together in one. (Ephesians 1:10.) When I think of the miracles being performed by our great manufacturing industries, our wonderful transportation systems, our great organizations for banking and merchandising, the professions and the trades, I again thank God for the establishment. The establishment makes occupational specialization possible. It helps us to produce and refine the things that we need as human beings, and our institutions challenge us to produce more effectively and make ourselves stronger by our own toil and our constant striving for improvement. Most of the important branches of the establishment also maintain important research organizations in an attempt to uncover those other great natural laws that God has ordained for our use and that are as yet undiscovered by us.

What a great and sustained thrill we should get from the effects that this wonderful system of freedom and individual enterprise has in developing our imaginations, our initiative, our ambitions, and our capabilities! Improvement requires that we learn to cooperate together in our own interests. We must also learn to get along with each other. I am very grateful for the fact that God made all men and women gregarious by nature in order to encourage us to unite together as nations and as businesses and as families and as human beings in order to more effectively carry forward that part of the work of the world that we have chosen to do. What confusion and suffering would result if each ignored all others by going his own individual way and endlessly doing his own thing. Friendly and organized cooperation is the best way to supply our own physical, mental, spiritual, and social needs.

The establishment also includes our libraries, hospitals, reform schools, and penitentiaries, which are jointly provided for the good of those in need. We should be so grateful for our wonderful laws and social conventions. Someone has said that the greatest invention of all time took place 2500 years ago at Platea when an obscure Greek perfected the process of marching men in step. When it was discovered that a great group of people could be organized with their attention focused on a single objective and their minds motivated by a single command, that day civilization began.

Then how unfortunate it is when any group of people become unthankful, destructive, angry, and unreasonable as they dedicate themselves to tearing down that which is not theirs and that which others have worked so hard to build up. Instead of getting on the team and doing their best to improve, educate, and build, they insist on breaking the harmony, rocking the boat, threatening the safety, and reducing the standards of others.

One wrecking crew can destroy more than a hundred groups of builders can create. One criminal can do more harm than a hundred citizens can do good. One sailor can scuttle the ship by scoffing at ideals and ridiculing standards without the slightest idea of what will take their place. So many people develop within themselves the devilish and unholy desire to destroy. They spit on the government and call our qualified officers of the law by unsavory names.

Those who have themselves been most unsuccessful seem to feel perfectly qualified to pass judgment on those who have succeeded. One may get an evil distortion in his own vision so that to him everyone else looks like monsters. To such a one the most beautiful flowers may look like poisonous weeds, opportunities may appear to be obstacles, and great men resemble criminals.

Many of those men who operate the establishment are hardworking men of foresight who have organized and built up important businesses that have furnished jobs to thousands of other people and greatly expanded our general prosperity. They have also established great financial foundations in order to help others. They have paid vast sums in state and federal income taxes, and then at death the balance of what they have earned has gone to the government and to other people. It is impossible to lift oneself up by pulling someone else down.

In becoming a millionaire, Andrew Carnegie made thirty-eight other people millionaires. On one occasion he was visited by a socialist who ranted and raved over the idea that Mr. Carnegie should share his great wealth with others. Mr. Carnegie asked his secretary for a statement of the Carnegie holdings and the population figures. When the statistics were ready, Mr. Carnegie figured for a moment and then said to his secretary, "Give this gentleman sixteen cents. That would be his proper share if all of my wealth were equally distributed among everyone." But if the establishment were actually liquidated, no one would be benefited very much even temporarily, and our means of producing goods and services would be destroyed; the workers would be unemployed, and chaos would reign.

Our capitalistic free enterprise system is the most successful way of living that has ever been devised and it gives us the opportunity to learn from the philosophy and industry of our greatest men. We can also be stimulated by their skill, courage, and ambition. We should not be too impatient to write the rules before we know the facts or have had some actual successful experience. A young man was once asked whether or not he could play the saxophone. He said he didn't know because he had never tried. Dwayne Laws expresses this thought under the title of "Band Leaders." He says:

> Each man, at times, has dreams of power,
>   And hopes that someday, when
> His ship comes in, he will assume
>   The leadership of men.
> But, any man who has such dreams,
>   One fact must understand—
> One must learn to face the music
>   Before he can lead the band!

If we become better people, the establishment will be better automatically.

Half-Believers

ONE OF the first steps toward any accomplishment is to believe in it. Faith is the foundation on which every success is built. Fortunate is the man who has some good, solid, righteous convictions concerning the important issues of life. It is one of our greatest of all good fortunes to be able to believe in great things with a whole heart. We are inspired by such great patriots as Nathan Hale, whose love of his native land made it possible for him to say, "I regret that I have but one life to give for my country." And it was another inspiring belief that made Job say of his Creator, "Though he slay me, yet will I trust in him." (Job 13:15.)

There are many advantages in being a full believer. Ernie Pyle, the late war correspondent, pointed out that nine-tenths of morale comes from pride in your outfit and confidence in your leaders. What great joy and success is ours when we feel completely proud of our families, love our neighbors as ourselves, and have a vigorous, wholehearted, honest, well-earned belief in ourselves. The poet has said:

> Trust in thine own untried capacity
> As thou wouldst trust in God Himself.
> Thy soul is but an emanation from the whole;
> Thou dost not dream what forces be in thee,
> Vast and unfathomed as the grandest sea.

> No man can place a limit in thy strength.
> Such triumphs as no mortal ever dreamed may
>   yet be thine
> If thou canst but believe in thy Creator and
>   thyself.
> At length, some feet shall stand on heights now
>   unattained,
> Why not thine own? Press on, achieve, achieve.

It was the Master himself who said, "If thou canst believe, all things are possible. . . ." ((Mark 9:23.) And the apostle Paul was trying to build faith, encouragement, and a good example into the life of Timothy, a young man whom he called his son in the gospel, when he said:

"Let no man despise thy youth; but be thou an example of the believers, in word, in conversation, in charity, in spirit, in faith, and in purity.

"Till I come, give attendance to reading, to exhortation, to doctrine.

"Neglect not the gift that is in thee, which was given thee by prophecy, with the laying on of the hands of the presbytery.

"Meditate upon these things; give thyself wholly to them; that thy profiting may appear to all.

"Take heed unto thyself, and unto the doctrine; continue in them: for in doing this thou shalt both save thyself, and them that hear thee." (1 Timothy 4:12-16.)

Following this doctrine of a wholehearted belief and a full dedication puts us securely among the believers. It also greatly increases our strength and happiness. But unfortunately, everyone does not always earn the right to believe even in very important things. A famous Canadian athletic coach once said that most people in and out of athletics were holdouts. What he meant was that we usually don't invest ourselves fully in what we are doing. We are afflicted with too many doubts, and we have too many reservations about things. There are too many issues about which we lack the necessary information on which to make solid, intelligent, proper decisions. Consequently we go into life with our fingers crossed, so to speak.

One of our most unfortunate situations comes about when we become holdouts on life, for when we hold out on life, life holds out on us. And by holding back in our faith, we become holdouts on God and members of the unfortunate group that someone called "life's half-believers." They are those who believe just a part of the time, or they believe in just some of the issues. This makes us guilty of those great sins of fractional devotion and marginal morals, which produces a minimal performance.

Jesus said that he came that we might have life and have it more abundantly. But it is impossible to live at one's best when he is only a half-believer. The agnostic says, "I don't believe, and I don't disbelieve." With enough lethargy and indifference, one gets to where he just doesn't care. There are some who are impartial about right and wrong. There was a group of fractional believers living at Laodicea to whom the resurrected Jesus instructed John the Revelator to write as follows:

"I know thy works, that thou art neither cold nor hot: I would thou wert cold or hot.

"So then because thou art lukewarm, and neither cold nor hot, I will spue thee out of my mouth.

"Because thou sayest, I am rich, and increased with goods, and have need of nothing; and knowest not that thou art wretched, and miserable, and poor, and blind, and naked." (Revelation 3:15-17.)

This reminds us of the psychiatrist who once said to a mental patient, "Do you ever have any trouble making up your mind?" The mental patient said, "Well, yes and no." There are many people whose convictions are caught on dead center. What miserable lives we lead when we can't make up our minds between right and wrong, good and bad, obedience and disobedience, success and failure. Then much of the time we remain as if we were wallowing in the slime of the low tide. We are left straddling the fence, and our dim understanding leaves us uncertain as to which way we should go.

The other day I looked up in the dictionary a term that was unknown to me. I had heard this word a number of times, but its meaning had never been definitely registered in my mind. Before I opened the dictionary this word probably did not have more than a five percent meaning. But even after I had read the dictionary's definition over several times, its meaning was still very hazy. To me the dictionary explanation was almost as cloudy as the word that it was trying to throw its light upon. Then I asked a friend of mine to study the dictionary with me and give me several concrete examples as to how this word might be used. Finally the light began to break through the fog to where I probably had a 40 percent understanding, but I am still not at home with this word. That is frequently the way it is with life's concepts. We may understand some perfectly, some not at all. We may fully believe some things and believe in even more important things not at all. Therefore our belief averages out somewhere in the twilight zone of those gray areas of life. We are life's half-believers.

In this connection, I thought of what the apostle Paul said in his stimulating discussion on faith, hope, and love. He pointed the fact out that presently we see as "through a glass darkly." He said, "For we know in part, and we prophesy in part. But when that which is perfect is come, then that which is in part shall be done away." He tries to make his own meaning more clear by saying: "When I was a child, I spake as a child, I understood as a child, I thought as a child: but when I became a man, I put away childish things." (1 Corinthians 13:9-13.) Sometimes a parent or a teacher says to a child, "Now are you sure you fully understand that idea?"

All good ideas can be gone over again and again until they are fully understood. That is a pretty good procedure for developing our convictions. We should go over them again and again until we fully believe all good righteous ideas. Jesus said, "If any man will do his will, he shall know of the doctrine, whether it be of God, or whether I speak of myself." (John 7:17.) When we live on a 100 percent basis, then we will be able to get out of that misty, shadowy, half-light in which so many of us live so much of our lives.

Many of life's problems are caused because too frequently our belief is regulated by our moods instead of the facts. Sometimes when we get a little discouraged or lonesome, we may do things that we would not do if we were living at our best. There is an ebb and flow in our lives. We go up and down on the scale of excellence. We sin at night and hate ourselves in the morning. We frequently react to things not according to whether they are right or wrong but according to how we feel at the moment.

Many people have a kind of fair weather faith that disappears in the storm. The following expression is found in the book of Genesis:

"And Jacob vowed a vow, saying, If God will be with me, and will keep me in this way that I go, and will give me bread to eat, and raiment to put on,

"So that I come again to my father's house in peace; then shall the Lord be my God:

"And this stone, which I have set for a pillar, shall be God's house: and of all that thou shalt give me I will surely give the tenth unto thee." (Genesis 28:20-22.)

So many people are inclined to say, "If everything goes well, then I will believe and behave." Job's faith seems to be more effectively integrated with good as he said: "Though he slay me, yet will I trust in him." (John 13:15.)

Ralph Waldo Emerson once pointed out a typical problem of a half-believer when he said that his moods had difficulty in believing in each other. He said it was about as difficult for him to manage his attitudes as to manage thunderbolts. At times his brain would become a blank and leave his mind in a state of barrenness. Life often seemed to him like a flash of light followed by long periods of darkness. To give continuity to his work, he began keeping a journal. In his journal he wrote down every thought with every suggestion that he believed would be helpful. Each day he collected in his journal all of his disjointed dreams, his mental reveries, and the fragments of all of those ideas that his mind was capable of conceiving. He discovered that the act of writing an idea down improved the quality of both the idea and his mind. His journal became the hive in which he stored the honey of his mind as the bees of his brain distilled it. When once his ideas were written down, he could then review them again and again with the thought of making any needed improvements.

As he had daily visits with great ideas, he grew accustomed to their faces, and he was able to improve their dress, brighten their eyes, increase their muscle power, and join them together in a more effective marching order. When once Mr. Emerson had snared an idea, he never allowed it to get away. He immediately wrote it down and put it into his mental incubator. He knew that ideas have a natural tendency to propagate and that each of his thoughts had the possibilities for a large posterity.

Emerson worked incessantly. He said, "Of all the tonics, work is the most effective." There was a great inspiration for Mr. Emerson in every assertion of his will, and like every other person, he needed a mental generator to set industry in motion. He knew that faith without works is dead. You can't keep faith alive in isolation; there is no such thing as preserved faith. Therefore, memorizing, writing the right things down, and taking action can strengthen belief. A song or a phrase or a poem with a strong emotion attached has the power to keep our faith impulses strong and in motion. But when left in an indefinite condition or in some hit-and-miss kind of position, they soon fade and become dim, indistinct, and unusable.

Someone was once asked what he thought about a certain thing and he said, "I don't know, I haven't spoken on it yet." Before we speak on ideas or write them down, we must think them through and make decisions about them, and then if we get them definitely fixed in our minds and memorized, our power is increased. Like everything else, our faith grows by exercise. As we recount our blessings, we increase them; as we practice our loyalty, it grows. When we express our love, it becomes stronger. We must not only believe in God, our country, and our families, but we must earn the right for them to believe in us. There are many women who desperately want to have confidence in their husbands and to believe in their integrity, but they feel insecure and are afraid because of some weakness in them that lies too near the surface. For the same reason there are many people who don't dare trust themselves. To only half-believe in ourselves has made the inferiority complex the most widespread disease in the world. But with a sure knowledge of the facts, a strong conviction of right supported by some whole-souled decisions and some unwavering industry, we can make ourselves stronger than anything that can happen to us. The most important part of that faith that we should build into ourselves centers in the Creator. He is all-wise, all-powerful, and all-good. He is the only fixed center of truth in the universe.

What a thrill when we can really say, "We believe in God." That doesn't just mean that we believe that he exists and that we know the kind of being that he is; it also means that we believe in him. We trust him. We believe that he knows his business and that his teachings are all in our interests. Then we can get rid of the doubts, the hesitations, the reservations, the vacillations, and the half-light in which we sometimes live. We might pray for deliverance from half-belief by singing with the poet:

> I ask no dream, no prophet's ecstasy,
> No sudden rending of this veil of clay,
> No angel visitant, no opening skies,
> But take the dimness of my soul away.

The Hard Life

IN OUR day we hear many complaints about how difficult life is. So many people feel burdened down with unpleasant problems and bothersome temptations. Our taxes are high, and we have the threat of the atom constantly hanging over us. Our difficulties are further increased by the crime, vandalism, and delinquency with which we have to contend. There is also a lot of sin in the wrong places and enough political malfeasance to give us serious concern.

However, it was never intended that life should be a downhill roller coaster ride. Actually it is one of our greatest good fortunes that life is difficult. Charles Kingsley once said that we should "thank God every morning when we get up that we have something to do that day that must be done whether we like it or not. For," said he, "being forced to work and forced to do our best will breed in us faith, virtue, temperance, self-control, and a thousand different virtues that the idle never know." Solving a lot of good hard problems can also keep us from feeling too sorry for ourselves.

One of the things that bothers me more than almost any other thing as I go about a little bit is the large number of people, particularly young people, who get discouraged. A discouraged person is always a weak person. I think it doesn't matter very much whether or not there is just cause for the discouragement. Whenever we start getting discouraged we start losing our strength, and weak people do all kinds of unprofitable things. Discouragement destroys our faith, our enthusiasm, and our enjoyment. It causes us to lose interest in life. When we lose interest in life, we lose many of the blessings that go with it. Most of our difficulties are actually blessings in disguise. Someone has put this philosophy in verse under the title of "Adversity." He says:

> The tree that never had to fight
> For the sun and sky and air and light,
> That stood out in an open plain
> And always got its share of rain,
> Never became a forest king
> But lived and died a scrubby thing.

The man who never had to toil to live,
Who never had to win his share
Of sun and sky and light and air,
Never became a manly man,
But lived and died as he began.

Good timber does not grow in ease,
The stronger wind, the stronger trees,
The further sky, the greater length,
The more the storm, the more the strength.

The sun and cold, by rain and snow,
In tree and man good timbers grow;
Where thickest is the forest growth
We find the patriarchs of both.

And they hold council with the stars,
Whose broken branches show the scars
Of many winds and much of strife.
That is the common law of life.

These laws relating to adversity make up a very important part of our success. The reason that we sometimes lose confidence in prayer is that so often we cannot identify the answers that we receive.

We ask for strength, and God sends us the difficulties which make us strong.

We pray for wisdom, and God sends us problems, the solutions of which develop wisdom.

We plead for prosperity, and God gives us brain and brawn to work.

We plead for courage, and God gives us dangers to overcome.

We ask for favors, and God gives us opportunities.

Oscar Wilde once said that if God wished to punish us, all he would need to do would be to answer our prayers. If all of our prayers were answered, then no one would ever die, no one would ever get sick. We would never make a mistake. We would always get our own way. Then no wisdom would be generated and no strength would be developed.

Frequently we want God to do our work, prepare our speeches, select our occupation, tell us whom to marry and where to invest our money, without our becoming very heavily involved. We all like to be inspired and noted for our wisdom without having to develop it. We want to always say and do exactly the right things. In a way that we don't always understand, God has already provided a very effective means by which we may do exactly that. That is, that we should throw in a lot of study and hard work with which our prayers can be supported. Even if we made a mistake once in a while, it is still true that self-effort, the courage of our convictions, and a lot of thoughtful activity are still the finest instruments of growth. We generate fears while we sit; we overcome them while we work. If we always had someone to do our thinking for us, solve our problems for us, and pay for our mistakes for us, then we would resemble hothouse plants, and we would actually become weaklings.

Emerson says that mostly we are parlor soldiers. We like to dine nicely and sleep warm but we shun the vigorous battle of life where strength is born. We sleep in heated bedrooms, ride to work in heated automobiles, eat soft food, live soft lives, and consequently become soft. However, man was built for vigorous activity. It was intended that he should struggle with the elements, control the thorns and thistles, produce his own food, fight the wild beasts, and suffer hunger and fatigue. These are those blessings in disguise that give us strength, endurance, and resourcefulness. They keep us lean, hungry, and ambitious. We need to get more industry into ourselves, and we need more outside difficulties to overcome.

It was a great prayer when someone said, "Lord, send me something hard to do today." We can only learn to handle difficult challenges effectively by first handling a lot of smaller challenges effectively. In ancient Greece, Pericles said, "No one should be appointed to a big office until he has first filled several smaller offices well." One of the purposes of life itself is to be tested and proved and tried and strengthened. We do not always remember that it takes a lot of hard pounding to make good steel. The dross and impurities of life can be more readily burned out of us when the furnace is made seven times hot. Most great people owe their greatness to the problems they have solved.

The early Sandwich Islander believed that the strength of every enemy that he overcame became a part of his own strength. That is still exactly what happens. With this great law in mind, someone prayed a great prayer, saying, "If trouble comes, let it be in my day." If there is something hard to do, let me do it. Don't send it to Bill or Henry or Jim; it might upset them or cause them to be over-discouraged. Frequently, in contrast to this attitude of strength, we like to think about the good old days when we had everything to our liking. This may have been in our youth when we had strong parents to do most of the work as well as to carry most of the responsibility. But parents are usually not doing us a favor when they are making it too soft for us.

At one time Adam and Eve lived in a paradise where everything necessary for their welfare had been provided. Then they had no temptations and no worries about good and evil. They had no government problems, no taxes, no education, no children, and no parents. They had no problems with clothing, food, housing, transportation, sickness, or death. Then mortality came into the world, but it did not come by accident. This was provided for from before the foundations of the world. It was God himself who provided that all men and women should have these wonderful earthly experiences. We needed some actual problems to cope with on our own.

Therefore, God closed down the Garden of Eden and put Adam and Eve out into a lone and dreary world that produced weeds more readily than good plants. This was a place where, even without any cultivation, thorns and thistles grew luxuriously. Then they had to contend with deserts, crop failures, and wild animals. Sickness, death, and evil were introduced into the world. On top of all of this it was said to man, "By the sweat of thy face shalt thou eat bread." (Moses 4:25.) But that is not a command of punishment; that is a command of opportunity. That is not just the way we get our bread; it is also the way we build our characters, develop our personalities, overcome our evil, and do almost every other worthwhile thing in life. One good way to judge anyone's ability might be to measure the size of the problems with which he is able to cope successfully.

Someone has said that a man can be judged by the size of the thing that gets his goat. Isn't it interesting that even the devil himself is put among us in our own interests? That is, God could destroy Satan at any instant he desired, and we might ask, "Then why doesn't he?" And he himself has given us the answer. He has said, "And it must needs be that the devil should tempt the children of men, or they could not be agents unto themselves; for if they never should have bitter they could not know the sweet." (D&C 29:39.) In one of the greatest lines in all sacred literature, Paul gave us this same kind of advice when he said, ". . . all things work together for good to them that love God."

(Romans 8:28.) That is, if we love God, if we think right, if we have the right attitude, if we do the right things, then everything works out in our interests.

Many years ago I had a friend who had a drunken ne'er-do-well father. But this young man loved God. He always did the right thing, and nothing could have been a more potent teacher of righteousness for this young man than his drunken, unrighteous father.

Charles Dickens, in his great book *A Tale of Two Cities,* tries to describe the period of the French Revolution of a couple of hundred years ago by saying: "It was the best of times, it was the worst of times, it was the age of wisdom, it was the age of foolishness, it was the epoch of belief, it was the epoch of incredulity, it was the season of Light, it was the season of Darkness, it was the spring of hope, it was the winter of despair, we had everything before us, we had nothing before us, we were going direct to Heaven, we were going direct the other way."

These opposites with an increase of intensity are still with us. This is the greatest age of miracles, wonders, scientific marvels, and opportunities ever known. But the balance is maintained by the fact that this is also the worst age of evil that has ever been known. As a good banker goes up the financial scale, he always keeps his assets and liabilities equal, and so it is with us: the greater the prize, the more the risk so that the balance may be maintained.

In Tokyo Bay, General Douglas MacArthur said, "It is of the spirit if we are to save the flesh." All good military leaders understand that every victory must first take place in the mind of the conqueror. The greatest of all conquests is that conquest over ourselves. David said, "He that is slow to anger is better than the mighty; and he that ruleth his spirit than he that taketh a city." (Proverbs 16:32.)

Recently a man was telling about an experience that had taken place in his early youth. He was aware of a moral transgression committed by one of his friends. He talked this matter over with his mother. She pointed out to him several reasons why such activities were wrong. This young man not only loved his mother, but he also had great confidence in what she said. And because he loved God and his attitude was one of complete obedience to right, he made up his mind that immorality would be forever excluded from his activities. His mind was made up so solidly that no temptation has ever had a chance since. The strength of his mother became a part of his own character. Definite decisions about righteousness can give enough strength to make any hard life easy. We may have all of the advantages that we elect and none of the disadvantages that we reject.

A seminary class was once having a debate about whether it was hard or easy to get into the celestial kingdom. They finally decided that it was hard to get into the celestial kingdom if you worked at it easy, and it is easy if you worked at it hard. It's awfully hard to do the things you don't want to do. It's awfully difficult for a chain smoker not to smoke. It's almost impossible for an alcoholic not to drink. It's very difficult for a dishonest man to tell the truth, but it is just as easy for an honest man to be honest as it is for a dishonest man to be dishonest.

If you want to have an easy life, then you should learn how to work hard at good things. We should learn how to make up a water-tight mind so that our decisions never leak any evil. Recently I saw a long list of the chief battles of World War II. Some of those long to be remembered engagements were: the Battle of Bataan, the Battle of the Coral Sea, the Battle of Guadalcanal, the Battle of Iwo Jima, and the Battle of Okinawa. Then I wondered what it would like if we made up a list of life's battles. We can win the battle of faith, the battle of morality, and every other battle of life if we just learn to keep a water-tight mind and then fight as hard as we can, having a great appreciation of our opportunities. Then God will continue to answer all our prayers for strength.

Honor

SOMEONE HAS said that before anyone can think effectively he must
have a language to think with. We endow our words, phrases, and
symbols with power, and they change our lives either for better or
for worse. Without words, life would largely lose its meaning.
Through our language we train ourselves to love art, enjoy music,
and appreciate great literature.

I have just finished reading the biography of the man who,
so far as I know, is the greatest salesman in the world. Some
meaningful success stories placed in contrast to the hardships
of his youth had put a great hunger in his heart that became the
basis for a fantastic personal accomplishment. It is pretty difficult
to separate words from emotions and ambitions. The right words
can give people an understanding of religion, an appreciation
of beauty, the feelings of happiness, and the attitudes of success.

Dale Carnegie once wrote a book entitled *How to Win
Friends and Influence People.* If we effectively run these ideas
through our minds enough times, a change soon takes place in our
conduct. But we can also make friends with the greatest accomplishments by getting intimately acquainted with the words that
represent them. One of the words that can produce the finest
motivations and ambitions is a majestic word called *honor.* This
word not only stands for some of the finest things in life, but it
also helps to produce them. In our own interests we need to set
this word up on a pedestal where we can pay it our constant
homage and receive from it its strength.

The great Boy Scout program is centered in the noble word
honor. The entire movement revolves around an oath taken by
each boy as he qualifies for membership; and frequently thereafter, he raises his right arm to the square, extends his three middle fingers to make the Scout sign, and then makes a solemn covenant in which he says, "On my honor I will do my best to do my
duty to God and my country and to obey the Scout Law; to help
other people at all times, to keep myself physically strong, mentally awake and morally straight." That oath represents one of
our world's greatest concepts, and this is a commitment to life
that everyone should take.

One's honor is his greatest possession, and to enshrine this word in his heart will help to hold him firm against the pressures of dishonor. What tremendous wealth is developed in oneself when honor is the chief ingredient of his ambition.

Some thirty-four centuries ago, the God of the universe came down onto the top of Mount Sinai and said: "Honour thy father and thy mother." (Exodus 20:12.) Obedience to this one idea alone would soon transform our world. The quality of our religion is determined by how well we honor God, and we could transform this earth into God's paradise if we properly honored ourselves. Shakespeare gave us a thrilling line when he said: ". . . to thine own self be true, and it must follow, as the night the day, thou canst not then be false to any man."

To speak of a woman's honor may mean her chastity, her purity, and her righteous dependability. As a sign of respect and admiration, we refer to certain high office-holders, such as the mayor and the judge, by their chief characteristic when we say, "Your Honor." President Dwight D. Eisenhower said that in America our national administration should have such honor at home as to always insure the highest respect for our nation abroad. Honor represents the highest standards of justice and responsibility. Josiah Gilbert Holland wrote an inspiring prayer in which he said:

> God give us men! A time like this demands
> Strong minds, great hearts, true faith, and
> ready hands;
> Men whom the lust of office does not kill;
> Men whom the spoils of office cannot buy;
> Men who possess opinions and a will;
> Men who have honor—men who will not lie.

And Annette Wynn's poem entitled "Memorial Day" indicates that each of us should cultivate his own honor and not depend on that which belongs to someone else. She says:

> Is it enough to think today
> Of all our brave, then put away
> The thought until a year has sped?
> Is this full honor for our dead?
>
> Is it enough to sing a song
> And deck a grave; then all year long
> Forget the brave who died that we
> Might keep our great land proud and free?

Full service needs a greater toll—
That we who live give heart and soul
To keep the land they died to save,
And be ourselves, in turn, the brave!

We honor great men most highly when we ourselves are honorable. Honor is something that each of us can and must develop for himself. A boy underwrites his Scout oath by obeying all of the Scout laws. If any Scout or any king or any apostle can learn to keep those great laws of honor concerned with being trustworthy, loyal, helpful, friendly, courteous, kind, obedient, cheerful, thrifty, brave, clean, and reverent, then his honor is safe.

In the days of Jesus a ceremony was instituted involving the washing of feet. In addition to the religious significance of this ordinance, it must have also been very pleasant after a long hot day's journey to be refreshed by having one's feet washed. But Jesus instituted an even greater and more pleasant law of refreshing when he gave us the fundamental laws of repentance and complete baptism as the primary means for cleansing our lives. As a part of the honor code, the Lord has said to everyone: ". . . be ye clean, that bear the vessels of the Lord." (Isaiah 52:11.)

One of the most uplifting of the philosophies of Jesus was built around the concept of that straight and narrow way leading to eternal life. This idea requires that we rule as out of bounds all inharmonious things. Certainly the path of honor is also a straight and narrow road and all dishonor should be forbidden.

Everyone understands that no airplane can keep losing its altitude for a very long period without having a crackup. And just so, no one can for long tamper with his honor without destroying it. When one loses his honor, most of his happiness also goes down the drain. Just as there are not many people who ever die without first getting sick, so there are not many people who get off that straight and narrow way at right angles. We lose our blessings a little bit at a time. People do not usually become dropouts from education, or excellence, or morality all in one drop. Big drops begin with little slips. Just as death follows a deterioration of one's health, so also one's honor usually starts developing some leaks before the major tragedy takes place.

When a believer develops a leak in his faith or when his airplane runs out of gas, he still doesn't usually fall in a vertical line.

With a 5,000-foot altitude and a 200-mile-an-hour velocity, an airplane can soar for fourteen miles before the crackup. Those who become involved in sin or failure usually do not hit the ground at the first offense. Very generously life usually gives us some intermediary time for repentance. With a quick reformation we may restore our honor and avoid a crackup, but we must not ignore a descending altimeter for very long.

I know a man who, during the past few years, has held and lost several jobs, and one of the reasons is that he doesn't see the danger in losing altitude until he is confronted with the crackup. This man is a very capable, fine-looking, intelligent person. However, this defect of permitting weakness in himself has made him a quitter. He starts out on each job with the assurance that his ability, aptitude, and I.Q. are capable of producing a fine success. But he lets too much failure get into his work.

Because he is not as strict as he should be in following the laws of success, he usually flies at treetop level. He does what he feels like instead of doing what is right. He is much too friendly with sloth and entertains some serious touches of irresponsibility. All success is like the old Model T Ford—when you turn off the engine the lights go out. This man doesn't seem to understand that in order to maintain a proper altitude the engines must be kept running.

To become a success, one must think and work like a success. One of the characteristics of failure is that those involved always dislike what they are doing. Because this man works like a failure, he soon begins developing dislikes for what he is doing and disharmony with the people with whom he is associated. It is perfectly natural, therefore, that the thermometer of his enthusiasm as well as his altimeter soon begin to fall, and of course his income always follows.

Some people don't seem able to tell that they are getting off the straight and narrow way until they find themselves completely out of bounds, and some people don't know that they are failing until they actually find themselves in the crash. There are some who never find out that crime and sin are unprofitable until they are asked to start paying the penalties. And so it was that in the early stages of each of this man's employments, when people tried to tell him that he was on his way out of the business, he thought that they were being ridiculous. Then finally, when the inevitable came, he couldn't understand how it had happened. He usually tried to explain his failure by rationalizing. He felt that he was the victim of circumstances. Either business was poor, the national economy was unsound, or he made a mistake when he selected this particular job in the first place. He could never realize that his failure was completely of his own making.

Many people try to explain the success of others on the basis of some natural ability. They rationalize their own poor showing by saying: "I wasn't cut out for this kind of work." However, if you ask them what kind of work they were cut out for, they won't know. Shakespeare came closer to the truth when he said, "The fault, dear Brutus, is not in our stars, but in ourselves, that we are underlings."

In accounting for any success, we should remember that everyone has two personalities. He has the one that he was born with and the one that he acquires after he is born. It is our acquired personality that we make a living with and live an honorable and successful life with. Such great instruments of success as industry, courage, positive mental attitude, enthusiasm, faith, and honor are not free gifts, but they can all be limitlessly developed. Abraham Lincoln once said that we are about as happy as we make up our minds to be. And we are about as successful and as honorable and as faithful as we make up our minds to be.

One of the tricky things about success and failure is that we are not always aware of which we are cultivating. Frequently we are actually making our own success impossible by tolerating too many defects among our virtues. Then we are unable to identify the reasons for our disinterest, our dishonor, or why our dislike for what we are doing. Primarily it is not the kind of work that makes us unhappy and unsuccessful; far more frequently it is the way we do it and our attitude about it. Poor quality in our work always causes us unhappiness and tends to make us quitters. In the same way, it is the poor way that we carry out our marital responsibilities that causes our family problems and eventually sends us to the divorce court.

In fact, many people start getting a divorce even before they apply for their marriage license. Every single wrong thing that we do sends the marriage thermometer down by exactly that much. Unless we do a lot of those things that lift us up, we soon have a crackup. And so it is with life. We fail or succeed by each individual act. Success isn't in New York or in London or in jobs or in conditions or in circumstances; it is in us.

When we start doing the wrong things, a feeling is set up in our conscience that tells us to stop. If we don't obey, then instead of doing what is right, we try to rationalize and justify ourselves in our sins. Then we stop going to church and we stop saying our prayers. When we allow unresolved problems to fester in our lives, a mechanism is usually set in motion, and we start lashing out at our wives or becoming bitter toward the church or antagonistic toward God. The people did not crucify Jesus because of any evil he had done to them; they crucified him because of what they had done to him.

It is so easy to get some of these problems lodged in ourselves, and then almost before we know it, we are in serious trouble. The greatest safety and the finest success is brought about when we always maintain the finest standards of honor in everything that we do. We need to fly high in all of our duties, and then we will be highly honorable.

"Honour Thy Father and Thy Mother"

ONE OF the greatest ideas ever given in our world came down from Mount Sinai 3400 years ago when God said: "Honour thy father and thy mother." (Exodus 20:12.) This direction is closely related to that first and most important commandment that came out of the fires of Sinai wherein the Creator said: "Thou shalt have no other gods before me." (Exodus 20:3.) God is our eternal Heavenly Father. He is our greatest benefactor. He is our wisest teacher. By doing as he directs we may reach any state of accomplishment. But then standing next to God in our lineup of benefactors are our parents.

It has been said that because God could not be everywhere present, he made mothers. Mothers and fathers do much of the work of human upbringing and betterment that otherwise could only be effectively done by God. Napoleon was once asked what was the greatest need of France and he gave his one-word answer: "Mothers." And what a tremendous good fortune it is to have a godly set of parents. Good parents are the greatest need of nations and of individuals. No matter how capable or how loving or how thoughtful one parent may be, a single parent cannot do the job alone.

What a fortunate situation exists when a wonderful mother is supported, protected, provided for, and loved by a faithful, devoted, honest, God-fearing, hard-working husband who is the father of her children. And how favored is any man who has a devoted, inspiring, pleasant, spiritual wife who is the mother.

These two very special people were appointed by God to create our physical bodies, to mold our attitudes, and to care for our needs, particularly during our early, formative, dependent years. From our parents we learned to walk, talk, and think. They help to build our attitudes and form our habits. They teach us the fundamentals of religion and assist us in laying a solid foundation for our characters. What we will ultimately be will very largely depend upon God, our parents, and ourselves.

To honor our fathers and our mothers means to believe in them, to trust them, to obey them, and to live the kind of righteous, exemplary life that will make them proud of us. Of course the parents must be assisted by the children. It has been said that as every inspired book needs an inspired reader, so inspired parents need inspired children.

I once heard a famous sales manager give some very good counsel to a picky, hard-to-please, rebellious person who was trying to learn to be a good salesman. When the sales manager tried to correct the salesman, the salesman would frequently get angry if what was said didn't strike him just right. The salesman did not hesitate to put his own opinion up against that of his sales manager. Everyone had to put on his kid gloves when dealing with this salesman. Finally, the sales manager laid it on the line and told the salesman that he must either get down off his high horse or find himself a job elsewhere.

This sales manager knew that it was useless for anyone to try to help someone that he was afraid of. If every time the salesman was corrected his feelings would be hurt, or if he took a nose-dive into some kind of emotional depression, most of the good would be lost. The sales manager said, "I have more important things to do than to waste my time begging and coaxing and trying to pamper and to bribe you into being successful." This sales manager was one of the best men in the business. He knew his job backward and forward and upside down and standing on his head. It would have been very profitable for any intelligent salesman who wanted to be somebody to pay this man thousands of dollars to handle his training. But instead of listening, some salesmen insist on telling an experienced, highly successful sales manager how they want to be trained.

Everyone has blind spots and needs someone on the sidelines to give him directions, and if this sales manager had a friendly, obedient, appreciative salesman and if the sales manager felt perfectly free with the salesman, he could, with absolute certainty, quadruple the salesman's income, prestige, and job satisfaction. But if the sales manager is always running the risk of arguments, sulkiness, and unpleasantness, it doesn't matter much how capable he may be. And if the salesman does not have great confidence and love for the sales manager, the salesman will always be the loser.

When Job was having some trouble he said about God, who might represent his sales manager, "Though he slay me, yet will I trust in him." (Job 13:15.) And we might say hurrah for Job! With that kind of an attitude he just about had it made.

If one wanted to be a great soldier, what a privilege it would be to have a great general to teach him. Or how fortunate a young singer would be to be able to work under the direction of a master. It is possible to get a great coach or a great businessman or a great doctor who could almost guarantee the success of a friendly, devoted, obedient student who studies hard and works diligently and knows how to take direction.

There are some unwise children who depreciate, criticize, accuse, and dislike their parents. Some children think it smart to have their parents afraid of the unpleasantness that they can cause if any parental restrictions are imposed, whether they are right or wrong. One who wants to be a good salesman had better love, honor, and obey the sales manager and like it. Anyone pays an awful price when his sales manager or his parents are afraid of him.

One of the greatest of all success laws is that we should believe in God. But next to God we should believe in and obey and honor our parents, who, because of their special interest and love, have an extra ability to help us that no one else has.

When Aaron was appointed to be the mouthpiece for his brother Moses, God said to Moses:

"[Aaron] shall be thy spokesman unto the people: and he shall . . . be to thee instead of a mouth, and thou shalt be to him instead of God.

"And thou shalt speak unto him, and put words in his mouth: and I will be with thy mouth, and with his mouth, and will teach you what ye shall do." (Exodus 4:16, 15.)

And God made a similar arrangement when he commissioned our parents. In several very real ways they should be as God to us. Lincoln said: "All that I am or ever hope to be I owe to my angel mother." Because Abe honored, trusted, loved, and obeyed his mother, he received a tremendous benefit from her influence.

God gives every parent some godly powers that reach far beyond their natural human endowments. Someone reminisces about his mother as follows:

Your hair has faded, mother dear,
From gold to silvery gray,
Yet, in your eyes, that little spark
Of love, I see today.

It means that you are proud of me;
You're glad for what you've done,
And in your heart I never see
A shame for me, your son.

Oh, I remember very well
When first I learned to pray,
Each night beside my little bed
You taught me how to say—

God bless my mother that she may
Protect and care for me,
And guide me right with truth each day
An honest man to be.

The days flew by; the years came on.
You led me all the while and
Through the trials that break with dawn
You held me with your smile.

The waves are strong that tempted me
To plunder wrongfully,
But with your love I could not go
Adrift far out to sea.

The darker ways that beckoned me
To lie, to steal, to cheat,
I might have gone, could you not see
My life lay at your feet.

And all through life you toiled away
And struggled just for me
To make me what I am today,
And what I'm proud to be.

Then God, it seems, has answered them,
Those prayers we used to say,
And in my heart that mighty theme
An honest man will stay.

And when alone at times, dear heart,
You ponder o'er the past
And wonder will I think of you
As long as life shall last—

Remember that I love you still.
You linger ever near,
And in my heart and soul I pray
God bless you, mother dear.

The power and intensity of a mother's love is one of the wonders of the world. And even though parents may sometimes make some mistakes or even do some wrong things themselves, yet they do not want their children to do wrong things. This great invention of mother love reaches all the way down through the animal kingdom. Many animal, as well as human, mothers have willingly given up their lives for their offspring.

The story is told of a farmer whose barn caught on fire. The farmer led the cow out of the burning building and tied her to a tree out of the reach of the fire. He believed that all of the other animals had been rescued, but the cow knew that her calf was still in the barn. She tried to communicate that idea by bellowing and making as much noise as possible, but when she was unable to get her message over, she mustered all of her strength, broke the rope, and, completely disregarding her own welfare, rushed into the blazing inferno in a desperate attempt to save her offspring. The result was that both perished in the flames.

Human parents have been endowed on a much higher plane. They were created in God's own image, and they have been endowed with a set of his attributes and potentialities, and thrice blessed is he who receives the full benefits of keeping that great command saying "Honour thy father and thy mother." Because the beast was put down on all fours, his vision is cast upon the ground. But man was created upright in the image of his Maker that he might look up to God and to his parents and to truth and to honor and to progress.

In an attempt to make the most of the fifth commandment, we have set apart the second Sunday in May as Mother's Day and the third Sunday in June as Father's Day. On these occasions we give special attention to this divine law of the fifth commandment. When we exalt our parents in our minds and love them in our hearts and honor them by living a godly life, we lift ourselves up, for we always develop those qualities that we magnify in our hearts.

The apostle John indicated some of the great joys that come from honor when he wrote to a young man whom he thought of as his son in the gospel. He said:

"Beloved, I wish above all things that thou mayest prosper and be in health, even as thy soul prospereth.

"For I rejoiced greatly, when the brethren came and testified of the truth that is in thee, even as thou walkest in the truth.

"I have no greater joy than to hear that my children walk in truth." (3 John 2-4.)

We remember that as our Eternal Heavenly Father has introduced his Only Begotten Son he has said: "This is my beloved Son, in whom I am well pleased." May we so live that both our heavenly parents and our earthly parents will also say that of us.

To enable us to please God, one day out of every week was set apart as the Sabbath. This is the Lord's day. This is a kind of Heavenly Father's Day. This is a special time for pleasing God and honoring our parents. From the cross Jesus looked down upon John the beloved apostle and said: "Behold thy mother!" (John 19:27.) I suppose that that meant to pay attention to her and think about her and care for her. And on Mother's Day we might say to ourselves, "Behold thy mother!"

My own mother has long since departed this life, and yet I know what would make her most happy on the special Sabbath that has been set aside as Mother's Day, and that would be for her to know that her children were faithful to those noble ideals and high principles which she tried to instill into them. She wanted us to be happy, and she knew that that could only be brought about by righteousness. On this important subject the Prophet Joseph Smith has said: "Happiness is the object and design of our existence and will be the end thereof if we pursue the path that leads to it." And this path is virtue, uprightness, faithfulness, holiness, and keeping all of the commandments of God. But we cannot keep all of the commandments of God without knowing them, and we cannot expect to know all or more than we now know unless we comply with and keep those that we have already received.

So on Mother's Day we might honor our mothers best by making some Mother's Day resolutions to know the truth, to love God, and to obey that great command in which he said: "Honour thy father and thy mother: that thy days may be long upon the land which the Lord thy God giveth thee." To our mothers we might repeat the prayer in which some of the ancients extended their appreciation and conferred their blessings upon their loved ones. They said: "The Lord bless thee, and keep thee: The Lord make his face shine upon thee, and be gracious unto thee: The Lord lift up his countenance upon thee, and give thee peace." (Numbers 6:24-26.)

How Great Thou Art

WE HAVE a very interesting word called *great* that we frequently apply to persons or things whose real importance we may not fully understand. We sometimes speak of our great country, or a great business, or our great inventions. However, this word has one of its finest applications in describing people. It designates a human dimension of importance or quality or excellence or ability. We sometimes feel great, and frequently we are able to get a little greatness into our activities. Certainly if a person is not great in what he does, he is not great. Greatness is also one of our objectives for eternity, and if one plans to be a great soul in heaven, he ought to practice being a great soul here.

But whether our concern is for here or hereafter, we should be aware of those traits in human life that are great in magnitude, power, intensity, eminence, or elevation. The opposites of great are seen in those conditions where either things or people are described as little, brief, scant, slight, unworthy, undistinguished, and unimportant. Most of our personality traits, mental abilities, and character qualities fit some place in between the extremes of great and small.

The most exalted use of this great word *great* is when it is used to describe the function or the person of God himself. God represents the greatest good in the universe. He is all powerful. He is all wise. He is all knowing. He is all good. If we will follow him, his influence and rule can make us as he is. God is the Creator of the earth and all things that are therein. All of its laws were organized and ordained by him. He is the giver of all good things, and all of our hopes for future happiness depend upon him and how effectively we obey his laws. When we keep his greatness in our minds, we can bring important benefits upon ourselves. John Drinkwater has said,

> When the high heart we magnify,
> And the sure vision celebrate,
> And worship greatness passing by,
> Ourselves are great.

Sometime ago, Stuart K. Hine wrote an inspiring sacred song entitled "How Great Thou Art."* He said:

O Lord my God! When I in awesome wonder—
Consider all the worlds Thy hands have made,
I see the stars, I hear the rolling thunder,
Thy pow'r throughout the universe displayed.

Then sings my soul, my Savior God to thee—
How great Thou art, how great Thou art! . . .

And when I think that God, His Son not sparing,
Sent Him to die, I scarce can take it in,
That on the cross, my burden gladly bearing,
He bled and died to take away my sin:

Then sings my soul, my Savior God to Thee—
How great Thou art, how great Thou art!

When Christ shall come with shout of acclamation
And take me home, what joy shall fill my heart!
Then I shall bow in humble adoration
And there proclaim, my God, how Great Thou Art!

Then sings my soul, my Savior God to Thee—
How great Thou art, how great Thou art!
Then sings my soul, my Savior God to Thee—
How great Thou art, how great Thou art!

It is thought that probably the most important idea with which we ever occupy our minds is to try to comprehend the greatness, the power, the wisdom, and the goodness of God. This idea is even more important inasmuch as the human mind has some of the qualities of the tendrils of a climbing vine that attach themselves and draw themselves upward by what they are put in contact with. When we put our minds in contact with God, our lives are drawn upward. Jesus said, "And this is life eternal, that they might know thee the only true God, and Jesus Christ, whom thou hast sent." (John 17:3.)

Because we are gregarious by nature and have these climbing-vine tendencies, we are always attaching ourselves to or identifying with someone. We attach ourselves to the Democrats or the Republicans or the hippies, or hold on to the atheists or the Communists, and then we go up or down accordingly. We tend to absorb the essential parts of what we cling close enough

to and hold on to long enough. We take into our mental bloodstream the ideals, ideas, and mannerisms of those with whom
we identify. But the climbing vine has little chance to remain
standing after the wall to which it is attached has crumbled
away.

To satisfy our human need for someone to cling to and something to grow on, Jesus was sent into the world to be our example and give us our pattern. When he said, "Follow me," he was
providing us the safest wall to cling to and the finest ladder on
which to climb upward.

We are taking serious chances when we place our confidence
in any of the arms of flesh. Some have attached themselves to dictators or to wealth or to power or to evil, and they have always
eventually fallen. Many men have built their houses upon the
sand and placed their trust in human wisdom, and when the
storms have beat upon them, great has been the fall thereof. Certainly one of the most serious mistakes that has ever been made
in our world has been the tendency of men to downgrade God in
their own minds. We sometimes say that God has lost the power
to reveal himself, that we don't need him anymore, or that he is
old-fashioned and out of date. Sometimes we allow some mixed-
up, self-styled intellectual to get above the great God of Creation
in importance in our minds. Then we let go of God and cling to
the crumbling wall of man.

In preaching their false man-made doctrines, some so-called
religious leaders insist upon depriving God of his body, his personality, his faculties, and his senses and make him a mere nothing. Then we say that God is dead, and we discontinue our prayers
and cut off all of our other communications with him. Because of
our sins and disobedience, we alienate his spirit and lose his
blessings. In the foul sacrilege of our oaths, we profane the divine
supremacy of him whose names we desecrate. The scripture says
that "ere he is aware, he is left unto himself, to kick against
the pricks, to persecute the saints, and to fight against God."
(D&C 121:38.)

If we would sing with full appreciation, "How great thou
art," we would not disobey his commands and commit every possible crime against each other. Some whole nations have banished
God. Others have forbidden that prayers be said to him in the
public schools. One of the evidences of his greatness is that he

treats us as well as he does when we are such unprofitable servants.

In the antemortal estate Lucifer was the light-bearer, the brilliant son of the morning, but he rebelled against God and drew away after him one-third of all of the hosts of heaven. I suppose that it would be impossible to imagine a more gigantic waste. Even in mortality many of God's spirits are carrying on the evil activities of disobeying, disbelieving, seducing, deceiving, lying, and destroying. But at the glorious second coming of Christ the activities of Lucifer and all of those who follow him will largely be destroyed. Then that thousand years of a millennium of peace will be inaugurated upon the earth, and Satan's reign and his power to do evil will be greatly reduced.

We might wonder why God doesn't put an end to all of Satan's evil and force us to do right whether we want to or not, but in the council in heaven a two-thirds majority of God's children voted for the freedom of the human spirit, and God himself made a firm commitment to support man's free agency. God gave us a promise saying, ". . . thou mayest choose for thyself." (Moses 3:17.) This applies to the entire 6,000-year period that has been allotted as the time for man's mortality. This is the period when the earth will be in its telestial state. When this 6,000-year period has been completed, Christ will come to cleanse the earth of its sin and establish his own government upon the earth. Then after the thousand years are finished, the influence of Satan will be finally destroyed, and the earth will again be raised in status, this time to the rank of a celestial earth. It is very difficult to understand why Satan should continue to do evil in the face of many serious disadvantages. It is even more difficult to understand why so many mortals who followed God in the preexistence should jeopardize their eternal welfare by having such an estranged attitude toward him in this life.

From some points of view we got off to a bad start when Adam and Eve disobeyed God and brought the curse upon the earth with its telestial conditions. Cain started an extended crime wave when he murdered his brother, and since that time we have suffered through all kinds of wars, sins, floods, confusions, the crucifixion, and the dark ages because of our evil deeds. Even now in these last days of our world's telestial history, with the second coming just around the corner, we seem to be in a kind of suicidal race to see who can pile up the most serious evils, including the threat of blowing up our world, destroying our bodies, and condemning our souls.

It is interesting to inquire of ourselves why it is that we do as we do when we believe as we believe. Or why do we act as we act when we are who we are? We were created in the image of God, and we can be like him. He is the greatest being that our minds are capable of conceiving. He lives without committing any wrong. We cannot imagine him doing any evil thing. He is so opposed to the destructive nature of evil that no sin is permitted in his presence. God himself "cannot look upon sin with the least degree of allowance." (D&C 1:31.) While he gives us our free agency, however, he also grants us the full and unrestricted privilege of full repentance. Under some circumstances he grants us the promise of a full pardon. God is not only the greatest being in the universe; he is our eternal Heavenly Father and is by long odds our greatest benefactor. He has given us this beautiful, wonderful earth with all of its delightful interests, its abundant food supply, its great natural laws, and its wonderful opportunities. What is probably even more important, he has given us ourselves on a kind of lend-lease basis. We have these magnificent minds, these wonderful personalities, and these bodies capable of a glorious resurrection and an eternal life. God's objective for us is complete success and happiness. We are not our own while we are in this life. We were sent here to be tested and to prove ourselves worthy of those great blessings of eternal progression and everlasting happiness that he has held up before us.

After we have satisfactorily finished our second estate and passed our final examinations, then we may have glory added upon our heads forever and ever. Then we will be turned over to ourselves to live in our exalted state forever with God.

Under these circumstances, when we sing "How great thou art," we ought to respond in kind. We ought to show our Heavenly Father that we can be trusted to be faithful and devoted and righteous forever. Just think what our earth would be like if all of God's children conducted themselves as his children and as he desires us to conduct ourselves.

It is an interesting thought that we come next to God in the catalog of greatness for a very good reason. God hates our sins, but he loves us. We are his children, and that family relationship will last forever. We have inherited his great traits, and if we are faithful, the offspring of God may eventually be like their eternal parents and live with them in eternal glory. So we sing again,

> And when I think that God, His Son not sparing,
> Sent Him to die, I scarce can take it in,
> That on the cross, my burden gladly bearing,
> He bled and died to take away my sin.

> Then sings my soul, my Savior God to Thee,
> How great Thou art, how great Thou art!

How Much Should We Lose?

SOMETIME AGO an article was written by Myron Roberts with its interest centered in Las Vegas, Nevada. Mr. Roberts refers to what takes place there as an American phenomenon. He says that "nothing like it does or could exist any place else in the world." It is his opinion that Las Vegas expresses a trait of an affluent twentieth century America in about the same way that the Olympic games stood for ancient Greece, or the Circus Maximus expressed ancient Rome, or the pubs and coffee houses stood for eighteenth century London.

It seems to Mr. Roberts that to have lived in Rome during the days of the empire and not visited the Coliseum would have reflected a certain poverty of the imagination. By the same logic, he argues that someone who lives in America in the last third of the twentieth century and does not visit Las Vegas is not experiencing his own culture and doesn't know his own time. Of course, the primary business of Las Vegas is gambling. It is around this that all else revolves. Unfortunately gambling is evil, and it becomes the mother of many other human problems. It also calls our attention to the fascination that so many people have for it. This fascination might be compared to the story of the rabbit being hypnotized by the snake as a preliminary to its destruction. Will Durant once pointed out that there has never been a civilization in the history of the world without the two universal vices of drinking and gambling. Why this should be so, no one can adequately explain, but the fact seems to be that man is a betting animal, and he finds betting in its greatest abundance in Las Vegas. There is another interesting fact: the great majority of people don't go to Las Vegas with the idea of making any money by gambling. Rather, they usually start out with some kind of an idea in mind as to about how much they feel that they can afford to lose. The only real question involved during their stay is whether or not they can manage to keep within their self-imposed limit. They know that the slot machines and the gaming tables mean a sure loss to everyone who plays.

They know that all of the gambling devices operate with a mathematical precision that precludes any possibility of winning over a long period. This law of averages for the machines is so adjusted that the house eventually ends up with the money. As in most other things, those who play are usually those who cannot afford to lose. Inasmuch as the lure is not the anticipation of something for nothing, we must look for the attraction in some element of the gambling itself.

There may be some things about our human nature that are not quite clear even to us. Just as the members of our society usually do not go fishing because they want to eat the fish, so people do not gamble because they expect to win. There is something about the risk involved or the struggle engaged in that seems to supply its own inducement to play. It may be man's inexhaustible fascination with luck that causes his endless flirtation with this serious evil even if he loses money that he cannot afford. There are many people who would be more enthusiastic about *finding* a hundred dollars, or *winning* a hundred dollars, or even in *stealing* a hundred dollars, than in *earning* a hundred dollars.

Someone once asked Napoleon what sort of generals he chose for his armies. He replied, "Lucky generals." Many people feel that while it's nice to be smart or brave or reverent or true, yet it is even better to be lucky. Mr. Roberts feels that much of the lure of Las Vegas lies in the opportunity given for one to test his standing with Lady Luck.

An astonishing thing about Las Vegas is that based on this undesirable human weakness, men have created a city of a quarter of a million people in the midst of a barren and inhospitable desert and have almost exclusively given over the city's importance to gambling. There are other world famous resorts, spas, and places of amusement. There are also other places where one can gamble, but nothing remotely comparable in scope or scale to Las Vegas has ever been known in the world before. Alongside Las Vegas, Monte Carlo is merely a quaint little village. Only a couple of decades ago, Las Vegas itself was a curiosity. It was a rather disreputable remnant of an old frontier saloon town. But it has now become a major city financed by some of the world's richest and most celebrated capitalists.

The only part of Las Vegas that most visitors ever see or care about are the few miles of Las Vegas Boulevard called the Strip. The huge urban resort that has been created there is really a series of cities within a city, where the principal pleasures are to be found indoors. But even the outdoor sports, including golf, swimming, and other activities, are conducted with a certain high gloss not usually found elsewhere. Most of the great hotels of Las Vegas are new, and they are like completely self-contained luxury liners floating on the desert instead of on the sea; they offer to the visitor almost every imaginable form of recreation. There is a variety of restaurants from coffee shops to intimate cafes to elegant gourmet dining rooms. One gets the works in elegance as he visits the shops, golf courses, pools, and gymnasiums.

The hotel executives, the restaurant chefs, the entertainers, and the musicians who manage these vast enterprises have all been brought to Las Vegas from virtually every city in the world. Most of them were highly successful someplace else. As a result there is a certain professionalism that characterizes the typical Las Vegas resort hotel. Certainly there is nothing rustic or intimate about it. No one is likely to accuse Las Vegas of being a warm, friendly little town. As Mr. Roberts says, Las Vegas is fast and efficient.

A certain kind of success is one of the other commodities that Las Vegas also has a lot of. Mr. Roberts says that in Las Vegas everything works. The rooms in the hotels are uniformly attractive, the beds are large and comfortable, the TV sets turn on and off when you flick the buttons. At the International Hotel, Mr. Roberts was continually surprised at how smoothly the management manages things:

"The International is thirty stories high (the tallest in Nevada), it has 1519 guest rooms. It contains *three* theaters seating thousands of people and the casino is the largest in the world. In the convention hall, 5,000 people can sit down for dinner; there are six restaurants, a gigantic swimming pool, a golf course, a complete children's hotel within the hotel, 211 chefs and cooks in eleven kitchens with an annual payroll of 25 million dollars. And there are plans to expand it to twice its present size. The task inherent in keeping so gargantuan an enterprise running well boggles the mind. And either on the Strip or downtown, it is easier to hit a dollar jackpot than to find a bad room, or a service that is not swift, efficient and pleasantly given. . . .

"Of course, there is a shrewd, practical reason for the time, trouble and expense the management is willing to put forth in order to keep the guests amused and contented. The reason is to be found in that portion of the lobby given over to what the billboards describe as 'Nevada Fun':—namely, the casino. . . .

"Closely associated with the games are the other forms of entertainment. In about two decades, Las Vegas has become synonymous with a certain kind of flashy showmanship, the form of which has been polished and refined to a point of high excellence. In a way Las Vegas has resisted the recent downgrading that has taken place in so many other areas. For example, the trend in the moving picture industry, in night clubs and to some extent on TV is toward anti-art: We now have the plotless film, the bitter comic and the hero who slouches around dressed in ugly clothing in need of a haircut and an elementary course in Basic English. He refuses the bath and does the most sordid kind of things. Even in the movies and on TV commercials, the producers are now using many ugly girls as models to satisfy the current passion for a distorted realism."

Mr. Roberts says that Las Vegas has not lowered itself by any cheapening in its standards. It still clings to the American tradition of excellence. In Las Vegas, show girls still have to be beautiful and elaborately costumed. The men must be tall and handsome, their voices clear, powerful, and masculine.

The Las Vegas show girls look magnificent prancing around in their fantastic costumes, and Mr. Roberts says that he found them much more interesting to look at than the coeds one sees in many college towns with uncombed hair and faces to match. These college girls are frequently dressed in disorderly, unattractive, and unladylike clothing. At the International Hotel, the settings and costumes cost the management almost one million dollars. Certainly Las Vegas is good at "doing its thing." It is a place where the American art of packaging has been carried to new heights. Whether the subject is a pop song, a clean, attractive room, or the sight of beautiful girls resplendently clothed, Las Vegas delivers an experience that is uniquely its own.

The civilizations of ancient Greece and Rome have long since destroyed themselves. Their many points of excellence were outweighed by their sins, and Las Vegas might serve as an American symbol cautioning us of our own decay. This human weakness of gambling that manifests itself in Las Vegas also shows up with even bigger losses in the greater activities of real life. As we contemplate our own life's journey, we might ask ourselves the Las Vegas question: "How much can we afford to lose?"

How much can we afford to lose playing at the new morality? How much can we afford to lose to atheism? How much can we afford to lose to disloyalty, lawlessness, rebellion, and weakness? Anyone who plays those games involving nicotine and alcoholism knows that certainly there will be serious losses. All of the machines of evil are set so as to preclude any possibility of a gain. That gambler is very fortunate who never loses anything more important than his money, as there are many who also lose their faith, honor, ambition, and hope. Many people lose the very attitude of righteousness. Our great nations of the past lost all of their virtues to their vices. Our serious modern rebellions and our attitudes of permissiveness have also turned many people to an attitude of anti-art in real life. More and more people are going through life without an objective, without standards, without a design, and without an ability to appraise values. More and more we are getting ugliness and hate into our philosophies, and many are using criminals and other evil doers as their models. As we invest our effort in sordidness and sin, we greatly increase the loss ratios on those machines that we operate in the casinos of our own lives.

Actually, there are better ways to live than by the alcoholism and gambling mentioned by Mr. Durant. It is interesting that the men who have built up this giant gambling industry in Las Vegas do not themselves gamble. They always bet on a sure thing. Their machines and playing tables are so set that those who own them will get many million dollars of profit annually. All of the risk has been taken out of gambling so far as they are personally concerned. Every thousand times the handles are pulled on these one-armed bandits, their victims will be poorer and the owners will be richer by an amount known in advance. The owners themselves determine the ratios in their own interests. The same procedure is followed with dice, roulette, and cards. That is also about what happens in life. When anyone sets his hand to do any evil, a loss is always sustained.

When we pull the handles on our various indulgences, we lose our health, our wealth, our ability, our morality, and our hope for the future. Satan is the overall operator of a far greater gambling kingdom than the one seen in Las Vegas. Whenever we can be induced to take a chance with evil, we pay our tribute to him in our life's values. The ratios are set against any possible win by those who play. Whether evil is dressed in the glamour of a painted, scantily clad show girl or the squalor of the degenerate, yet its machines are set to collect an awful toll.

It is a sin to cheat. But it is also sinful to be cheated, and two of our most unprofitable sins are the sins of drinking and gambling mentioned by Mr. Durant. From time immemorial, these evil devices have broken up homes, distorted morality, and destroyed faith in God. These are two ways in which we most frequently lose our money, our success, our treasures in heaven, and often even our lives themselves. They represent the exact opposite of that way of life recommended by the Savior of the world. If we live those great principles called the principles of the gospel, then our every effort will bring us a profit. There is a fundamental law in the universe that says that all effort must be paid for. We can no more do a good thing without in some way receiving a reward than we can do an evil thing without suffering a loss. The basic law of the universe is that immutable, unchanging, inexorable, irrevocable law of the harvest which says:

"Be not deceived; God is not mocked: for whatsoever a man soweth, that shall he also reap. For he that soweth in his flesh shall of the flesh reap corruption; but he that soweth to the Spirit shall of the Spirit reap life everlasting." (Galatians 6:7-8.)

If we properly conduct our personal affairs, we will reap an abundant and profitable harvest.

In the Garden

O N SEVERAL occasions over the years I have had the inspiring experience of visiting in some of the world's famous botanical gardens. It is amazing what wonders an expert gardener can perform with a few seeds, some fertile soil, a good climate, and plenty of water. Of course many families in every part of the world maintain their own supply of beauty and utility in beautiful gardens of their own. Also many parks, hotels, business establishments, and others maintain gardens for many purposes.

The dictionary describes a garden as a lot of cultivated ground devoted to growing herbs, fruits, flowers, or vegetables. A garden might be a natural forest. It has been pointed out that groves were used as God's first temples. Frequently a garden is a place where people go for inspiration and uplift.

A lot of people have an uplifting hobby of working in their garden for relaxation and as a means for building up themselves. Many of the prophets and even Jesus himself have gone to the mountains and other places of peace, quiet, and beauty for rest, prayer, worship, and inspiration. It was to a high mountain apart from the world that Jesus, with Moses and Elias, was transfigured before Peter, James, and John. The record says: "And [he] was transfigured before them: and his face did shine as the sun, and his raiment was white as the light. And, behold, there appeared unto them Moses and Elias talking with him." (Matthew 17:2-3.)

Jesus spent a part of the period of his final preparation for death in the Garden of Gethsemane. Here he prayed to his Father in heaven. This was also the place of much of his suffering. Luke says:

"And being in an agony he prayed more earnestly: and his sweat was as it were great drops of blood falling down to the ground.

"Saying, Father, if thou be willing, remove this cup from me: nevertheless not my will, but thine, be done.

"And there appeared an angel unto him from heaven, strengthening him." (Luke 22:44, 42-43.)

Jesus was buried in the garden tomb of Joseph of Arimathea, and he was also resurrected in a garden. When Jesus first spoke to Mary after his resurrection she mistook him for the gardener. (John 20:15.) All of us have been inspired by being in beautiful gardens; we have also been inspired by the evident fact that God himself loves gardens. For our own starting point, our life upon this earth began in a garden. The record says:

"And the Lord God planted a garden eastward in Eden; and there he put the man whom he had formed.

"And out of the ground made the Lord God to grow every tree that is pleasant to the sight, and good for food; the tree of life also in the midst of the garden, and the tree of knowledge of good and evil.

"And a river went out of Eden to water the garden. . . ." (Genesis 2:8-10.)

It is interesting to try to imagine what this beautiful, beneficial place must have been like. At that time our earth itself was a paradise. The curse that was put upon it at the fall had not yet taken place. There were then no deserts, no weeds, no pollution, no evil, and the fertility of the earth was then new.

We think that this earth is a pretty nice place as it now is, but this earth is now in its telestial or fallen state. Then it was a terrestrial earth described as a paradise. The scripture says that the Lord had made to grow every tree that is pleasant to the sight and good for food. Even on our telestial earth we have some trees and flowers that are very pleasant to the sight, and we also have many whose fruit is very good for food.

The fruit of the tree of knowledge of good and evil made people wise. How helpful it might be to eat a little more from the fruit of this tree. What will it be like sometime when we are permitted to eat from the tree of life and the other wonderful trees that God had planted in the Garden of Eden for our benefit? Then, the record says, God made us gardeners: "And the Lord God took the man, and put him into the garden of Eden to dress it and to keep it." (Genesis 2:15.)

Adam was instructed that with two exceptions he might eat from all of the trees and enjoy their beauty. Even God himself must have greatly enjoyed this beautiful garden. The scripture says that God spoke to Adam and Eve as he walked in the garden in the cool of the day. (Genesis 3:8.) A place of natural beauty and peace is also a good place for us to go when we want to think and meditate and prepare ourselves for important things. It was with this kind of inspiration in mind that C. Austin Miles wrote his beautiful poem "In the Garden" in which he says:

> I come to the garden alone
> While the dew is still on the roses
> And the voice I hear falling on my ear
> The Son of God discloses.
> And he walks with me and he talks with me
> And tells me I am his own
> And the joy we share as we tarry there
> None other has ever known.
>
> He speaks and the sound of his voice
> Is so sweet the birds hush their singing.
> And the melody that he gave to me
> Within my heart is ringing.
> And he walks with me and he talks with me
> And tells me I am his own
> And the joy we share as we tarry there
> None other has ever known.

Of course there are other kinds of gardens. Many people have talked about their own heart as a garden—and so it is. Our minds can also be beautiful, fertile places where lovely flowers grow with wonderful fragrance, quiet order, and happy harmony. Or our minds can be places that produce noxious weeds that are harmful to human beings.

In God's garden he had every tree that was pleasant to the sight and good for food. The fruit of one tree brought mortality into the world. The fruit from the tree of knowledge of good and evil could make men wise in judging right from wrong. Luther Burbank spent his lifetime in cross-breeding trees and flowers. We can do something similar to that in our minds.

Jesus was not talking about plants; he was talking about people when he said that a tree should be judged by its fruits. We might imagine our lives as a great garden with its trees producing all kinds of good things. In the garden that I plant in my own mind I would like to have one tree, the fruit of which would make me dependable. Few things are more inspiring than those people who produce the fruit showing that they are trustworthy and predictable. I would like to have one tree the fruit of which would make me appreciative.

The old Roman statesman Cicero once pointed out that gratitude is the mother of virtues. Almost every good thing comes from a grateful heart. I would like to have a tree in my garden that would produce loyalty. So far as I know, the greatest sins that have ever been known in the world have been the sins of disloyalty. Lucifer was disloyal to God, and in his rebellion he induced one-third of all of the children of God to turn away from their Creator and lose their blessings. Judas sold Jesus for thirty pieces of silver. Benedict Arnold was disloyal. The reason for many divorces and spiritually bankrupt lives is disloyalty. How wonderful it would be if we could produce in ourselves the kind of devotion to God seen in the great old prophet Job. When his affairs were not going as they should, one of his advisers said to him, "Curse God and die." But Job's faith could not be shaken, and he said: "Though he slay me, yet will I trust in him." (Job 13:15.)

The sunflower has been called the symbol of loyalty, and because of its beauty and significance it has been chosen as the state flower of Kansas. As one of its distinguishing traits, the sunflower always follows the sun, not only in the early hours when the day is young, but also during the long afternoon when the heat is great. Even at the end of the day as the sun disappears into the ocean, it still looks directly into the face of the ever loyal sunflower.

Some years ago a movie showed a ship that had been torpedoed at sea. The captain, who had been blinded in the explosion, had made known his intention to be true to the tradition of the sea and go down with his ship. The mate had helped to launch the lifeboats and had seen to it that everyone had safely gotten away from the ship, and then he came back to the captain's cabin to go down with his chief. The captain was dressed in his smartest uniform and was ready to meet the end of his career in the best possible tradition. When the captain learned of the mate's intention to accompany him in death, he urged his faithful friend and aide to save his own life.

But the mate could not be dissuaded, and as the end approached, the mate was telling the captain the story of the sunflower with its symbolism of loyalty. As the water in the cabin of the sinking ship rose from the men's ankles to their knees, to their waists, and just before the great ship reared up on its end to plunge with its cargo to the bottom of the sea, the mate said, "The sunflower follows the sun; you go down with your ship; I go down with you." That's loyalty.

I usually keep around some sunflower seeds, and occasionally, when I need a little special tonic, I eat a few for the strength and motivation I may get from this loyalty symbolism.

As I work in my spiritual garden, I pay special attention to the fruit on my tree of faith. One of the greatest emotions is the ability to say, "I believe." It is difficult to believe in something that you do poorly, and it is a fine compliment to be able to say, "I believe in God. I believe in my country. I believe in my family. I believe in my life's work. I want to make that great Article of Faith grow stronger in me, which says: 'We believe in being honest, true, chaste, benevolent, virtuous, and in doing good to all men; indeed, we may say that we follow the admonition of Paul —We believe all things, we hope all things, we have endured many things, and hope to be able to endure all things. If there is anything virtuous, lovely, or of good report or praiseworthy, we seek after these things.' " (Article of Faith 13.)

We can make all of these virtues grow in the garden of our lives.

When I was young and lived out on the farm, we had a fruit orchard in which grew several varieties of apples, cherries, peaches, apricots, and plums. In addition, my father allowed me the use of some land of my own where I cultivated some smaller fruits and berries for my own pleasure. What a delight it was for me then to go into the orchard in the spring and see the beauty of the blossoms, smell their fragrance, and watch the bees go about their business of pollination. I could see the fruit of my youthful ambition as I went among the tomatoes, the cucumbers, the strawberries, the watermelons, the cantaloupes, and other fruits and vegetables.

In the long ago day I had something of the feeling of a creator because I had planted the seeds and helped to bring about so many wonderful things that were good for people. A half century later, I still like to go into a great supermarket and see the tremendous array of colors, flavors, vitamins, and tastes that have all come from this great miracle of creation that God has put into our human hands.

But we can also create a lot of other things, such as courage, industry, a knowledge of truth, morality, spirituality, and eternal life. Gardening was the occupation in which the Master himself was engaged. Jesus referred to himself as a gardener, a vinedresser, a horticulturist, the true vine, a good husbandman, a sower of seeds, and a pruner of trees. He always had a great concern about his plants.

As I think about him, it is easy for me to remember that each of us has been given some gardening responsibilities. When he said, "Follow me," one of his meanings may have been that he wanted us to plant and cultivate our own gardens—our gardens of virtues, our gardens of good deeds, our gardens of character values. He said, ". . . man shall not live by bread alone. . . ." (Luke 4:4.) I must decide the kind of trees and plants that will characterize my life, and all of these must be cared for, cultivated, fertilized, and vitalized.

Elbert Hubbard once said, "I am looking out through the library window into the apple orchard and I see millions of blossoms that will never materialize or become fruit for lack of vitalization." The destiny of an apple blossom is that it should someday become an apple. The destiny of a human soul is that it may eventually become as God is. Neither of those things happen without that vitalizing pollen that brings about accomplishment, so one of our greatest objectives in life should be that of being good husbandmen.

It Is Good to Give Thanks

ONE OF our greatest American holidays is Thanksgiving Day. This very special day is set apart each year by a proclamation of the president of the United States. Thanksgiving is a legal holiday. It is a day when we recount our blessings, and it is also a feast day. However, Thanksgiving was designed primarily as a day of religious devotion.

By presidential proclamation, Thanksgiving has been set apart as a day of prayer, and everyone is exhorted to go to church. We should certainly do all of those things that a good follower of the Master should do. Thanksgiving is also a day of national dedication. Two of the most important considerations of our lives are those of paying our allegiance to God and to our country.

Governments were divinely instituted for the benefit of men. The Church, officered by inspired men and instructed by the holy scriptures, was established to direct our lives toward the greatest success not only here but hereafter. Some other great institutions have been established for our benefit, such as the family and our occupational organizations, and certainly we should all unite in asking God's blessings upon all of those who have the responsibility for conducting the affairs of church, state, family, and providing our livelihood.

As we recount our blessings, we increase them; and as we ask God's blessings upon our leaders, we are motivated to help them.

In one of the very wise statements of the Old Testament, it is said: "It is a good thing to give thanks unto the Lord, and to sing praises unto thy name, O most High." (Psalm 92:1.) There are a great many reasons why that is a good idea. By being grateful we develop within ourselves those qualities of greatness. The best way to give life to such virtues as courage, love, happiness, prayer, faith, righteousness, health, and prosperity is to have a grateful heart out of which they may be born.

Those who are bitter toward God, disloyal to their country, unfaithful to their families, hateful toward life, and get satisfactions in ugliness are suffering from insufficient gratitude. It is easy to visualize the kind of man who said in his prayer:

> Oh God, I thank thee for each sight
> Of beauty that thy world doth give.
> For sunny skies and air and light,
> Oh God, I thank thee that I live.
>
> That life I consecrate to thee
> And ever as the day is born,
> On wings of joy my soul doth flee
> And thank thee for another morn.
>
> Another day in which to cast
> Some silent deed of love abroad
> That hastening as it journeys past,
> May do some earnest work for God.

At one Thanksgiving time a wise teacher asked her students to compose their Thanksgiving Day prayers and tell what they wanted to express appreciation for. Then the teacher wrote the following composite prayer. She said:

> We bow our heads and thank Thee, God—
>
> —for the sounds of laughter,
> —for the colored leaves that swirl and fall in the autumn,
> —for the smell of chocolate cake in the oven,
> —for big, red garden tomatoes,
> —for my playful kitten that gets tangled up in pink yarn,
> —for erasers that make mistakes disappear,
> —for the feel of wet grass on my bare feet,
> —for the good taste of hot cherry pie,
> —for my warm, soft bed,
> —for my sister's smile on Christmas morning,
> —for the boats and seagulls on the wallpaper that carry me across the sea when I look at them,
> —for the shade of the maple trees in our yard,
> —for the windows that let me watch the world go by, and
> —for God's care.

But this blessing of gratitude is taken away from us when we fail to use it. When one ties up his arm in a sling, the arm loses its strength. That is also the way we lose our virtues. When the mole didn't use his eyes, nature took away his eyesight. Some nineteen hundred years ago when the people didn't respond to

Christ's message, their ranks were soon devastated by apostasy. When one fails to be grateful, he soon loses his gratitude.

One of those unpleasant traits opposing gratitude is rebellion. This disease has broken out in epidemic proportions in our day. Under a recent newspaper title of "Runaways Find Tragedy," UPI women's editor Gay Pauley said that each year an estimated one million teenagers run away from their homes. Of this group more than one-half are girls and there are more thirteen-year-old female runaways than those in any other age group. Imagine this large group of little girls hating their parents and leaving their homes without supervision or any proper means of providing for themselves. Each year this delicate segment of our population is plunging into every conceivable kind of tragedy.

Real gratitude could prevent the disasters of rebellion. However, children are not the only ones afflicted with this plague. Thousands of adults are joining mobs to conduct rebellions against the government. Many are rebelling against decency, law, and order. Some young people have turned against cleanliness, beauty, and fairness. With a terrible vengeance some have dedicated their lives to fighting the establishment. They seem to feel that they have some kind of divine right to burn down property and destroy what has taken others a lifetime to build up.

But there are no vacuums in human personality. When people lose their gratitude there is always a supply of bitterness, sin, and rebellion that rushes in to fill up the vacated space. Some people have gone so far into evil that it soon becomes impossible for them to save themselves. Then they become victims of that truth stated by the scripture that says: "He that is unjust, let him be unjust still: and he which is filthy, let him be filthy still. . . ." (Revelation 22:11.)

In Paris there is a famous gallery of art called the Louvre where many treasures of uncalculated value are kept. In the centuries since it was converted from the royal palace of France into their national museum, the Louvre has acquired a great collection of masterpieces that unfailingly speak the poetry and drama of man's existence and inspire the full spectrum of emotion in some three million people every year from all over the world. They come away enthralled and uplifted by the majestic beauty of what they see. One of these paintings, which was exhibited for a short period in New York and Washington, has an insurance value of

$100,000,000. However, its real value may be much greater than that.

Once a group of tourists was being taken through this great gallery. There was considerable agitation among them in anticipation of seeing this famous painting. Further interest was added by the fact that it was protected twenty-four hours a day by an armed guard. As the tourists approached the picture, one of them said, "I don't see anything so hot about that." The guard said, "But don't you wish you could?"

What a tragedy it is when our hearts become incapable of appreciating beauty and righteousness. How fortunate they are who can fully serve God, love truth, and help to build up the establishment. Don't we wish that we could feel a genuine patriotism for our great country and be loyal to it under all circumstances?

How the quality of our lives would be improved if we had some of those traits possessed by Major Martin Treptow who, before the battle of Chateau-Thierry, wrote in his diary, "I will work, I will save, I will sacrifice, I will endure, I will fight cheerfully and do my utmost as though the entire conflict depended upon me alone." Don't we wish that we could feel that way? Don't we wish that we could get all of the bitterness, hate, and irreverence out of our hearts? What a tragedy it is for those poor unfortunates who betray their country, conduct senseless marches, foster race riots, hate law and order, and call law enforcement officers, who are only trying to do their duty, unsavory names.

It would help us to develop this profitable quality of gratitude if we knew more about God, truth, and our own possible destinies. It would also be helpful to know more about the religious origin of the United States and those who have built up our establishment. Our Pilgrim fathers were not rich or powerful; they were not highly educated, but they were real people. It took them 128 days to cross the Atlantic in their little ship of ninety tons. In that year they had one of the wildest winters that ever swept the North Atlantic.

The *Mayflower* landed in December, and it is cold in New England in December. Columbus landed in October, and his crew mutinied. Columbus had recruited a poorer grade of human beings and they were merely "summer sailors." But there was not a single

Pilgrim who even thought of mutiny. During the first terrible New England winter, ninety people were sick at one time, and only seven were well enough to care for them. One by one they died—wives, husbands, and children. Fifty-one out of 102 were laid in the frozen earth by the survivors. The Pilgrims had a lot of other problems that their faith and sturdy gratitude helped them handle. May God help us to build on their foundation that we also might have the strength and righteousness of real people.

How different our history might have been if our country's foundations had been laid by draft card burners, trouble makers, and idlers who spend their time in protest marches, causing trouble, and holding angry demonstrations. The lives of our Pilgrim forefathers were God-oriented. When they landed in America, the first public building erected was not a store, or a town hall, or a library, or a courthouse. It was a church. In their philosophy, the Pilgrims related everything to God.

It is interesting to take a close look at our own dollar bill. On one side of this paper money is a picture of George Washington, the father of his country. On the reverse side we see the front and back surfaces of the great seal of the United States. In the middle are the words "In God We Trust." There are certain super liberals who now want to have these words removed because they might offend the weak sensibilities of someone.

In one of the circles of the great seal is the picture of a pyramid that was left uncompleted at the top. Above the pyramid is the Latin phrase *Annuit Coeptis,* meaning "He has smiled on our undertaking," and below it says, *Novus Ordo Seclorum,* meaning "A new order of the ages," the idea being that with the blessings of God we can build the finest order of society, including a magnificent way of life. A successful way of life must always be a righteous way of life. It is God's way of life.

The pyramid is left incomplete to indicate that we are always building and always trying to improve. Above the pyramid is an eye that represents the eye of God. The fathers of our country resolved that under God they would build a greater order than had ever been known before. May we carry the torch they have lighted. It is a good thing to give thanks that we can make our good nation better.

There is only one thing that could go wrong either with our country or with the church or with our marriage or with our lives, and that is us. The only way for our country to fail, or for the church to fail, or for our marriage to fail is for us to fail. Our country is not made up primarily of buildings and real estate—it is made up of people. We have this nation because human beings were inspired by God to establish it on Christian principles. We cannot make a great nation out of criminals, atheists, hippies, or those possessed by an unholy mania for tearing down, burning up, and destroying. When we sing "God Bless America," we do not mean a drunken America, nor an ignorant America, nor a weak America, nor an atheistic America, nor an ungrateful America. And so at Thanksgiving time, we pray that we may help God to build up an industrious, successful, righteous America filled with happy, prosperous, God-fearing Americans.

Looking Backward

THE OTHER day I read an interesting article telling of the conversation of two men who were discussing the advantages and disadvantages of looking backward. One man said, "If I had my life to live over again, I would not change a thing." The other man thought this was a very unproductive and unprofitable attitude. He felt that anyone should be able to learn a great many things from a lifetime of experience and that every adult who couldn't see things in his own past that he could have done better must be very unperceptive and insensitive.

This man went on to say that when he was a young boy his mother had started him out taking piano lessons. But like many other young boys, he developed a serious dislike for piano lessons. Consequently he kicked up so much fuss about them over such a long period that his mother finally gave up in disgust and sold the piano. Now he thinks about what a thrilling experience it would be if he could occasionally sit down at the piano and effectively run through some great musical selections. With these he could not only please his many friends, but he could also inspire himself. He recounted a large number of other abilities and emotions that he could have had at a small sacrifice, and the effort required now seems to him very trivial.

This man had another interesting idea. He had been born and reared in Los Angeles when Southern California real estate was selling for a song, whereas it now brings a price of thousands of dollars per square inch. With a little ability to see ahead, every person living in North America then could now be wealthy. And it is probable that many people have neglected a great many other personal opportunities that they now wish they had taken advantage of. We fall down in our opportunities because, at the time, they are so easily available that we see them only in the dim misty view of our foresight. Because we don't have a trained hindsight to teach us how to look ahead, we frequently pass up all kinds of privileges that, if we could only turn the calendar back, we would most certainly do something about.

Therefore, just for the fun of it, this man sat down and made up a list of all of the things that he would do differently if he could live his life over again. Now just suppose that as a special favor to us, the clock of the universe could be turned back so that we could actually live our lives over again. What would we do differently? It may be that we would work a little harder in school and be a little more dependable in our social relationships. Or it may be that we would have left out of our life's mixture some of those bad attitudes and unfavorable experiences that have since caused us too many embarrassments. Of course, the cold facts are that we can't turn back the clock, and we can't postpone even the smallest crisis while we prepare for it. But we ought to learn to look back frequently as we go along.

Recently I talked with a man who had been fired from his job at the age of sixty-four who had never learned to do this. With a real fear for the future, which prompted a genuine regret for his past, he said, "I wish I could live my life over again." But trying to relive life is like trying to rehearse birth or death or success. One can't leave age sixty-four while he starts over again at age twenty-four. However, even regrets can be very profitable if we have them early enough.

Recently a friend was telling me about one of his greatest experiences. Because of financial problems, he had had to drop out of school for four years while he was young. Most of his friends went on to finish, and he was made to feel that the possibilities for success had already all passed him by. On one occasion after visiting with his former best friend, he sat down and cried about the uselessness and disappointment that in his opinion had already destined his life to permanent failure. But from his viewpoint at age twenty-five he couldn't see all of the picture. Actually he had received many benefits from these out-of-school years. Certainly they had taught him how to work hard, and they had given him a helpful humility. He learned something of that old proverb which says, "He who arises quickly and continues the journey is as though he has never fallen." Therefore he picked himself up and got started.

It is also helpful to understand the temporary failures of other men. One might review the letter that George Washington once wrote to his kinsman during the discouraging years of the Revolutionary War. He said:

"Such is my situation that if I were to put the bitterest curse on an enemy this side of the grave I would put him in my place. I see the impossibility of doing any essential service to the cause by continuing in command, and yet I am told that if I quit the command inevitable ruin will follow from the distractions that will ensue. In confidence I tell you that I never was in such a divided, unhappy state since I was born."

But because Washington kept going, he became the father of his country. Success is not in causes or in classes or in teachers or in locations or in situations, but in people.

A great corporation recently announced that all of its executive officers were college graduates except two, one of whom was president of the company and the other was chairman of the board. It is very interesting that neither Abraham Lincoln nor Brigham Young nor Jesus of Nazareth had very much formal education. Abraham Lincoln even lost more elections than he won, but he learned from his defeats how to become the President of the United States. Lincoln did a lot of looking backward, not only into his own life but also into the lives of others, and with the desperate ambition generated by his failure, he had soon passed up all of those about him.

Looking back is about the only way to develop hindsight, which is usually much clearer than foresight. If we develop the right combination of introspection, retrospection, and contemplation, our forward vision can be greatly strengthened by our rear views of life. From old Roman mythology we get the helpful story of Janus, the Roman god of January. One of the unusual things about Janus was that he had two faces. With one he was constantly looking back into the past, which made him continually aware of his previous mistakes and what had caused them, and with his other face he looked up into the future as he planned how he could avoid repeating his past errors. An effective hindsight is not limited to an examination of one's own errors. It is very helpful to learn from one's own mistakes, but it is much more profitable to learn from the mistakes of others. One may also be encouraged and enthused by his own as well as other people's successes. Both the successes and failures of every other person, past and present, can help him effectively plan his own future.

It has been said that planning is the place where man shows himself most like God. He is the one who borrows from the success of every other person to help him draw the blueprint for his own accomplishment. He is the one who builds the roadway on which his future success is to travel. He is the one who studies causes and consequences so that he understands why things happened as they did in the past and how he can use his knowledge to produce a more rosy picture for the future. We can build up our own success every day.

By looking backward into the past, we may be impressed with the idea that we have been stamping our minds with too many bad habits, too many sins, too much failure, and too many negative attitudes. Our futures will soon be our pasts. Because hindsight is very inexpensive and easy to profit from, the rest of our future may have all of the fumbles and mistakes removed from it. In a very substantial way we can read the future by looking backward.

A Detroit executive was once shopping for a new home and when he found the one that fit his liking, he was told by the realtor that it would cost him $70,000. The executive said, "I could have bought this house last year for $60,000." "That's right," said the realtor, "and next year it will cost you $80,000." Because the executive could see into the future by way of the past, he bought the house.

Values change and times change, but by looking back into the past we can discover the fact that music lessons and hard work now will always have a still greater value for the future. We may also discover that in the future we will still want to love more and to hate less. It will still be profitable to be more kind, more considerate, and more tolerant toward others. And no matter how important our past may have been, the next five years will undoubtedly be more important years than any up to this date.

In the financial markets, special importance is attached to what are called growth stocks. Whether our life's values are growing or diminishing will determine whether we are becoming wealthy or going out of business. If we can read the past and identify the causes of failure, we can change every recession into a boom. The records of the past show us clearly that crime does not pay and that disobedience to God is unprofitable. We can easily learn that industry and righteousness are vastly superior to sloth and sin as a way of life.

As we review the past records of Cain, Jezebel, Judas Iscariot, and Benedict Arnold, we can eliminate any of the seeds of their failures that may be getting a start in us. We can determine also the most profitable courses by comparing their failures with the successes of the great prophets, the great saints, the great patriots, and the faithful doers of good deeds. Righteousness is always profitable, and we can always sluff off failure by repentance.

In 1932 Walter Pitkin wrote an interesting book entitled *Life Begins at Forty,* but life begins every morning. Life begins when we begin. It is never too early to stamp personalities with righteousness, and some of the world's greatest successes have taken place after age sixty-five. Our real lives begin when we start enthusiastically doing those things that God's laws of righteousness say that we ought to be doing.

The great God of creation also looks in both directions. He has said: "I am Alpha and Omega, the beginning and the end, the first and the last." (Revelation 22:13.) God can see the end from the beginning and he can see the beginning from the end. He has offered us his objectives to go by and he has charted our course in such a way that if we follow we can't miss. What an unpleasant sensation it will be if, when we arrive at that great day of judgment, we can only say, "I wish I could live my life over again."

One of the greatest blessings is to live in this world of contrasts where we can learn by opposites. It is one of our greatest opportunities to look back that we may see what is ahead. We may look back into our antemortal existence. We can also look back to our mistakes of last month and last year. Then, with a look forward to the most magnificent successes, we can understand what someone has said: "Life can only be understood backwards, but it can only be lived forward." Our primary job is to live it well.

The Love of Truth

DURING THE ministry of Jesus he gave many great laws and profitable philosophies for people to live by. His two greatest commandments were centered in love. He said that we should love God with all of our hearts and our neighbors as ourselves. This great emotion of love is fundamental to any outstanding success. When one has a substantial love for something, he sets up a strong natural attraction that draws him toward it. This procedure might be compared to a piece of metal setting up a powerful magnet to draw it toward its goal.

An airplane can fly faster and much more easily when it is assisted by a strong tail wind. Every accomplishment can be multiplied when we fall in love with what we are doing. I knew a man many years ago who wanted to get married, and he needed to have a job that would allow him more freedom, help him to develop himself more rapidly, and pay him a larger income in order to do so. He was offered a job as a salesman that included all of these possibilities. The problem was that he was not a salesman and that he didn't like selling. But he had set up a worthy objective and he was willing to sweep the street in order to bring it about. Therefore, he changed his job from one that he liked to one that would give him what he wanted. With strong self-control, he forced himself to do what all good salesmen are required to do, and because he followed the laws of successful selling, he was an immediate success. The only problem was that he didn't like what he was doing.

But after a period of fighting the strong headwinds of dislike by forcing himself to do the things that he didn't like to do, he thought how ridiculous it was to hate something that offered the only way of getting him to his objective. Then he made a great decision to love his new job. He made a list of the good things about it and began building them up in his own mind. He believed in his product. His job had the advantage of forcing him to develop initiative, courage, and love for people. When he reasoned it out, every single thing about it was good. He also remembered what

Jesus had said about the advantages of loving one's enemies, and everyone should understand that when we love our enemies, we more or less automatically make them our friends.

When we do a good job well, we always learn to love and enjoy it. The reason that he hadn't liked selling was because he was not big enough to do it like a champion, and he would now either be forced to grow or to acknowledge himself a weakling. Therefore, because he forced himself to work harder than anyone else, he began to exceed everyone else in results. And it wasn't very long before he sincerely loved what he was doing.

Many years have passed since then, and this man has won many honors and received many recognitions in his field. But he still maintains his high standards of effort, because he knows that when one relaxes his excellence, his abilities soon dwindle and his love disappears.

Now, if we thoroughly understand how this principle of love works, we can get great pleasure from keeping the two greatest commandments. But we might ask ourselves, why should we love God? We should love God because our love will draw us toward him. We should love him because he is our eternal Heavenly Father. He is our best friend. He is the giver of all good things. He is the author of happiness, success, fairness, and the source of everything else that is worthwhile. When we love God, we find our lives in the very center of all good things. The Master said that we should love our neighbors and ourselves. These are both great ideas and both are fundamental to our success.

Someone once asked his friend which commandment came next to love in importance. His friend said that he didn't know there was one. Actually we fall in line with most of the other laws automatically when we obey these first two. Think what it would mean to us and to everyone else if we really loved fairness, righteousness, our country, our families, our work, our opportunities, and ourselves. It is important to remember that none of these loves come automatically; we must even earn the right to love ourselves.

The ancient Chinese had an interesting custom. If you became a visitor in one of their homes and were attracted to some particular object, you might find that your host would wrap the object up and send it to you as a present. That is, you loved it and that made it yours. Such a custom might seem a little strange to us, and yet life has a program that is just exactly like that, for it is a natural law of life that everything that you truly love and admire you get.

If you love courage, you get courage. If you love the great character traits, life wraps them up and sends them to you free of charge. Abraham Lincoln loved honesty and frankness, and because life gave them to him, they distinguished his life as long as he lived. One of the great privileges of our existence is that we may love the most important things to our heart's content. Someone once said, "I own the landscape." But you can also own the sunrise merely by loving it. Some people reap far more value from the beauty of a wonderful landscape than the one who actually possesses the legal title to it. You can own the most fabulous treasures of beauty, wisdom, righteousness, and happiness by loving them. When anyone really loves great wealth and power, he is already well on his way toward their actual possession. On the other hand, the failures in life are known by the numbers and degrees of their hates.

When you hate your job, you soon lose it. When you dislike people, you lose your friends. When we stop using those great character qualities that we already have, nature soon repossesses them. Everything that we have in life, whether it is good or bad, is only ours on a kind of a lend-lease basis. As long as we love it and use it, it is ours. When our love diminishes, our possession is lost. An interesting thing about this law of love is that it is unable to discriminate between good and bad. Therefore when we love liquor, we get liquor. When we love the new morality, life wraps the awful package up and writes our names on it. When we become disloyal, that trait is also registered in our name. How unfortunate are those people who hate the government, and hate the establishment, and hate their work, and hate their mothers-in-law, and hate their wives, and hate themselves. One of the most pathetic circumstances in our world is that people can learn to hate God, righteousness, beauty, and truth by contrary action.

When people sin against life, they become bitter and hateful. When we are lazy, we hate industry. When we are disloyal to the government, we soon dislike the government. When we lose the spirit of law and order, we may soon start calling law enforcement officers "pigs" and other unsavory names. It is interesting that every vice that we entertain is always extremely unprofitable, and sin is always very expensive to the one committing it. This is par-

ticularly true when one hates the church or hates the government or hates his wife. If one doesn't like where he lives, he ought
to repent because he is doing something wrong. If he can't correct
this situation, he ought to move immediately to a place where he
can fall deeply in love with some new homeland. Then his hates
will not have an opportunity to fester and destroy his soul.

One man recently told me that he had worked for a great
national company for twenty-two years, and he said, "I have hated
every minute of it." I said, "You can't be serious." He said, "I
am telling the absolute truth." I said, "Why didn't you quit this
hateful job twenty-two years ago and get one that you could fall
head over heels in love with?" He said, "Where could I find a job
like that?" He didn't even know that such a job existed. This
man didn't just dislike one job, he disliked all jobs. Hate is always
located in the hater instead of in the hated. This man would be
miserable in any job. Some people dislike the tenth job even more
than the ninth, and they dislike the fifth wife even more than the
fourth.

The scripture tells about a group of the ancients who loved
Satan more than God. This seems strange in view of the fact
that Satan stands for everything evil. He is everyone's worst
enemy. Satan is not even friendly to the hardest criminals or the
worst sinners. He is the father of lies. He delights in ugliness and
sin and poverty. He practices deceit. It pleases him to cause as
much misery and failure as possible. Those whom he injures most
are his own followers. He will destroy even them if he can, and
yet they continue in their evil, unprofitable, unpleasant course.

It is hard to understand why people in our enlightened age
continue to cater to unrighteousness and sin. We probably
wouldn't even believe that we were guilty if we didn't see it happening every day with our own eyes. Arsonists seem to delight in
setting fires and destroying the property of others, even though
they themselves have nothing to gain and everything to lose. That
is, if they are discovered, it may cost them their freedom, their
reputation, their job, their family, their friends, and their own self-
respect, and yet they just hunger to destroy something that
they have no right to. Kleptomaniacs steal merely for the sake
of stealing. Many adulterers carry on their own ruinous evil for
the mere glory of the conquest.

Some people, formed in the image of God, do everything
that they can to destroy God's likeness in themselves. They dress

themselves in dirty, ludicrous clothing, refuse to bathe, shave, or comb their hair. They destroy their minds with dope, their bodies with venereal disease, and their spirits with venereal attitudes. What a shocking sight to see God's glorious image distorted by human beings living at their worst. On the other hand, what a great joy when God's greatest creation effectively honors his Creator. What an accomplishment when one magnifies his office as a great human being and intensely loves to live life at its best.

Now of all of the things that we might like to love, which one thing would we put first? Jesus said that we should love God. God comes up at the top of the list, but God is also great for what he stands for. God stands for love, for righteousness, for beauty, and for truth. What could more effectively distinguish us as that greatest creation fashioned in God's own image than to develop a whole-souled love of truth? That would not merely mean to know the truth or even to be truthful—but to love the truth. That means to have a strong attraction for truth and to love it with a passion that would never allow us to deviate from it and would continuously draw us toward it.

One of God's highest and most noble titles is that he is "a God of truth. . . ." (Deuteronomy 32:4.) Jesus said, "I am the way, the truth, and the light. . . ." (John 14:6.) The dictionary says that truth is that quality or state of being true and faithful. It includes fidelity, constancy, and veracity. It is made up of a sincerity of character both in action and in speech. It implies a genuineness in expression, in feeling, and in belief. The scripture says: "And the Word was made flesh, and dwelt among us, (and we beheld his glory, the glory as of the only begotten of the Father,) full of grace and truth." (John 1:14.)

The thing that distinguished Abraham Lincoln and set him above others was his love of absolute honesty. This has also been the glory of many other people. We would not discount the importance of love, and yet someone has said that to be trusted is more important than to be loved. What trait would you rather have in a child or a parent or in a spouse or in an employer than that he could always be absolutely trusted under any circumstances? That is, one who is always true blue and always faithful.

On the other hand, what could be worse than to have to live with or work for or be associated with one who was a liar, a deceiver, a betrayer, and one who was undependable and irresponsible? If we were going to try to guess what trait God would like best in us, what could be more important than a strong love of truth? This would mean that we should understand the truth and that we should live the truth.

Jesus said: "And ye shall know the truth, and the truth shall make you free." (John 8:32.) But the truth will also make us prosperous, happy, and successful. Therefore, we ought to love it nobly and continually.

The Magic Beans

THERE IS a famous old nursery tale entitled "Jack and the Beanstalk." It is based on an ancient and widespread myth about some magic beans. Jack and his mother were very poor. In their desperation Jack's mother sent him to sell their primary asset, the family cow. Jack traded the cow to the butcher and in payment accepted a handful of magic beans. When he handed his mother the beans, she became very angry and threw them out the window, and I suppose that Jack went to bed without any supper. However, one of these magic beans immediately began to grow in the good soil of the garden, and by the time Jack and his mother awoke the next morning, the top of the beanstalk had already reached to heaven. Because it was a magic bean, it was also a magic beanstalk, and so Jack decided to climb it. When he reached its top, he was met by a fairy. The fairy directed him to the house of the giant from whom Jack obtained a bagful of gold without the giant's consent. With his new-found wealth, Jack hurriedly descended the beanstalk with the giant in hot pursuit. Then just in the nick of time, Jack chopped down the beanstalk, causing the giant to fall and be killed. With the giant's gold, Jack and his mother lived happily ever after.

This story itself has a little bit of magic in it as over the centuries it has reminded people to be on the lookout for ways of improving their own good fortunes. The writers of the fairy tales sometimes have the knack of transmitting their ability to think big. This in itself is a kind of magic, for it has always been true that as a man "thinketh in his heart, so is he. . . ." (Proverbs 23:7.) It has been said that science and magic are similar inasmuch as they both deal in cause and effect. However, the scientist rejects those things that lie beyond his science, whereas those are the things on which magic thrives. My own opinion is that we should not too quickly throw away those ambitions which appear larger than life. Nothing can be brought about without believing in it, but there is a very reasonable philosophy that says that anything that the mind can conceive can be realized by the ambition.

In our day there is much greater magic than that of climbing a beanstalk for a bag of gold that doesn't belong to us. Our world has always been filled with magic. We remember how Aladdin built a palace by rubbing a magic lantern, but magic has become much more powerful since then. We now have mechanical genies that can build far more impressive palaces than Aladdin's. We have also surpassed the wildest dreams of the ancients who traveled on magic carpets or used seven-league boots or wore magic wishing caps. Even the most ambitious imagination of those early days never even thought of putting a windshield or a steering wheel or a heater on a flying carpet. Sometime ago when out in my automobile in sub-zero weather, I thought how much more comfortable I was than if the trip had been made on a flying carpet.

A hundred years ago Horatio Alger wrote 235 books of the rags-to-riches kind of success stories. These tales had enough magic in them to uplift the accomplishment of many people. But probably the greatest magic is found in present-day industry, courage, ambition, and faith. Nowadays unheard-of things always seem to happen when someone goes to work or gets enthusiastic or becomes ambitious.

The dictionary says that magic is something exhibiting more than ordinary power. It is something that produces results beyond those that might have been expected. According to that definition, I know a lot of people who have magic in them. Many years ago, I knew a young boy who had a very serious inferiority complex that caused him great mental suffering. He played a role similar to the one described by Hans Christian Andersen in his story of the "Ugly Duckling" that became a beautiful swan. From this boy's point of view and from the point of view of many who knew him, he had a very bleak future to look forward to. But somewhere along the way he got hold of some magic beans, and now he brings home more gold every month than Jack got from his magic beans in a lifetime. Jack had to risk his life, kill a giant, and employ methods that would never have been approved by the Better Business Bureaus of our day, whereas the improved varieties of magic beans now available require none of these hazards or questionable practices.

Even those things that seem to us to be disadvantages almost have magic in them. There is an old proverb that says "Foxes are wise because they are not strong." Some used to think that only sickly boys unable to do hard work should be educated. Because of my young friend's early ugly duckling status, he didn't have the usual social demands made upon his time or attention. Therefore, he channeled his saved energy into the work on the farm. Naturally he was more effective than if he had been more popular socially. To cover up his hurts and loneliness, he lost himself in his work. He developed a great love for the soil and was delighted in making it produce all kinds of valuable crops. In this substitute interest he soon learned a better acceptance of himself. He stopped worrying about his ugly duckling image and became a very competent young farmer. His successes with the soil seemed to come about as easily to him as the social graces had been difficult. These abilities soon began attracting other responsibilities, and when people began taking a little more notice of him, he wasn't an ugly duckling at all. Following Mr. Andersen's example, he had transformed himself into a very acceptable person. Jack had given his mother's cow for a handful of magic beans—but my young friend gave himself to his work and in return received a whole pocketful of magic beans.

If some success expert were to put a scientific name on these magic beans, they might be called planning, initiative, industry, and a healthy outlook on life. Certainly my young friend's magic beans were more worthwhile than those that Jack's mother threw out the window. This young man saved the money that he earned and went on a mission for the Church. Soon he was acquiring such other magic beans as devotion, faith, conviction, and courage. It is the basic law of the universe that all effort must be paid for, that one can no more do a good thing without at some time, in some way, receiving a reward that he can do an evil thing without suffering a penalty. This is just not possible. The basic law of the universe is this immutable, inexorable, irrevocable law of the harvest that says, "Whatsoever a man soweth, that shall he also reap" (Galatians 6:7), and this young man was taking his pay in the magic beans of thoughtfulness and righteousness. The one of Jack's beans that fell in fertile soil provided the ladder on which he could climb to heaven, and our beans of virtue and ability will do the same for us. On them we may climb to heaven and make intermediate stops at every worthwhile accomplishment.

The dictionary says that a bean is an edible seed that grows in the long pods of the leguminous herb, scientifically called *ficia faba.* All beanstalks grow erect, and many of them are climbers. We call them by such names as kidney beans, lima beans, sieva beans, soy beans, and string beans. The dictionary points out that these edible seeds are very rich in protein and highly nutritious. They come in a great variety of colors. We have black beans, white beans, red beans, and spotted beans. An interesting phrase has been developed in American slang in which we refer to a man's skull or brain as his "bean." As a boy, I remember that in playing baseball when someone was hit on the head with the ball, they said he had been "beaned" or he had been hit on the "bean." In addition to stopping baseballs, our heads may serve us as our chief magic bean. If we put into our mental beans a few good ideas, some solid convictions, and a few determined ambitions, the resulting beanstalk may easily provide us with a ladder that will reach to heaven.

I know of a salesman who gives credit for his success to his set of ten beans. For a long time he suffered from the awful salesman's disease called "call reluctance." This occupational disorder has destroyed the effectiveness of thousands of salesmen since time began. It has much in common with the physical malady known as muscular dystrophy. Muscular dystrophy breaks down the physical muscles and prevents its victim from moving about very effectively. But call reluctance gets into the mind and paralyzes certain important attitudes so that the ambition refuses to respond. This is often a fatal disease and causes failure in sales work, certain kinds of church work, and many other important related activities.

But in the case of this particular salesman, he was saved by his magic beans. Every morning he put ten colored beans in his inner left-hand coat pocket. Six were white, three were black, and one was red. During the day whenever he merely made a call, he transferred a white bean over to the inner right-hand coat pocket. When he made a call that developed into a good selling interview, he transferred a black bean over to the right-side pocket, and when he made a sale, he transferred the red bean over to his accomplishment pocket. He had a strict irrevocable agreement with himself that he would never quit calling until he had all of his beans in the right pocket. It was quickly proven that these beans all had a great deal of magic in them, for his income, his job satisfaction, and his prestige began a growth almost as rapid as the beanstalk on which Jack was able to climb to heaven.

The Boy Scouts have an excellent program that calls for doing at least one good turn every day. This program is designed to make people happy by doing some helpful thing for them. If this irrevocable schedule of good deeds were religiously carried out by everyone, it would soon change our world into a paradise. However, the reason it doesn't work out as well as planned is that we so frequently forget to follow through. Just suppose that we had the tailor make all of our future suits with a right- and left-hand pocket for our good-turn magic beans. Then suppose we really lived under a rigid commitment to ourselves that we wouldn't go to bed until we had all of our good-turn beans in the right pocket. Some people have fallen down in this program because they have made the mistake of using jelly beans. There isn't any magic in jelly beans, and besides, the jelly frequently gets into the convictions, the backbone, and the muscles. When we get a little jelly in the will, we are done for. It is much better to go to the other extreme and use jumping beans. The jumping bean is the one with the highest content of magic in it. There can be no doubt about anyone's success if each morning he takes two jumping beans out of his bean bag. He should put one in his left-hand pocket and swallow the other. If a good man keeps on the jump all day, he will always be on schedule in having his beans in the right pocket.

The beanstalk on which we climb upward will also grow a little faster if we use jumping beans. There are no problems climbing either to financial, social, or spiritual success if each morning our minds swallow a few jumping beans. The most important thing we ever need to learn about success is how to get the right amount of magic into our beans. A few years ago Claude M. Bristol wrote an inspiring book called *The Magic of Believing.* Mr. Bristol points out that whether you want an increased income or a new home or a better job or a happier marriage or simply a better night's sleep, you may have any of them merely by getting a little more magic into your believing. Jesus said it more effectively when he said, ". . . all things are possible to him that believeth." (Mark 9:23.) He didn't say that just a few things were possible. He said that all things were possible.

When we really believe, then our faith is always supported by strong ambitions and good works, and any accomplishment is placed within our easy reach. Anyone who wants to change his ugly duckling status or legally get possession of the bag of gold that may now be in the possession of the giant called industry can easily do so by using a few of his magic beans. Then our beanstalks will grow to God's highest kingdom. This is the place that Paul refers to as the "third heaven" (2 Corinthians 12:2) and the psalmist calls the "heavens of heavens" (Psalm 148:4).

The magic of understanding and faith and works will enable us to perform the greatest miracles. Miracles are only happenings that presently are beyond our understanding. But we all know numerous people who are miracle workers and turn in great wonders of performance. We may also accomplish more than is expected of us, and we can develop that magic in our lives which will enable us to climb upward to our own greatest happiness.

Making the Most of Your Regrets

M ANY YEARS ago, I read an interesting article about success that impressed me very much. It pointed out the very small differences that frequently exist between success and failure. I remember that it gave one example from the meat packing industry. It pointed out that no one could succeed in that business if he prepared for sale only the finest cuts of meat. To succeed, he must also make the most out of those lesser items which at first thought might seem relatively unimportant. In fact, it has been said that to stay in business and show a profit, the meat packers not only must use the less desirable cuts of meat, but they must utilize such by-products as leather, glue, and fertilizers.

In the lumber industry, a firm may make enough money to run the business from selling fine hardwood lumber, but it will never realize a profit unless there is also a good market for the lesser grades of lumber, the telephone poles, the plywood, the paper pulp, and even the sawdust.

This situation has something in common with the way we succeed or fail in life. It is very helpful to utilize our great virtues, our untiring industry, our strong convictions, and our constructive abilities, but if we are to make the best and the most of ourselves, we must also make capital of our lesser talents. We must be able to use even our defeats and our faults to make a profit.

Reed Smoot once said that an ambition to excel is indispensable to success. Everyone has his own trade leaders that must be pushed to the limit. Each individual has some talent or some character quality or some personality trait that can be developed to the point where he may surpass everyone else in the world. But sometimes the margin by which we keep our lives in the profit column comes from the way we have handled some weakness. Jesus said: "I give unto men weakness that they may be humble; . . . if they humble themselves before me, and have faith in me, then will I make weak things become strong unto them." (Ether 12:27.) He also said: ". . . my strength is made perfect in weakness." (2 Corinthians 12:9.)

It has been said that Demosthenes did not become the great-est orator in the world *in spite* of his speech defect; he became the greatest orator in the world *because* of his speech defect. His inability to communicate so humiliated and embarrassed him that his extra effort to overcome it generated in his soul a giant power strong enough to turn all of his weaknesses into strengths. If properly used, handicaps, problems, and hardships can serve a useful end in our lives. For example, John Milton once said that no one can do his best until he has suffered much. Suffering puri-fies the soul. Even evil can serve a constructive purpose.

The villain serves our best interest quite as well as does the hero. One shows us the quicksands to be avoided, whereas the other shows us the best road to follow. Some of the greatest of all of life's lessons we learn from our own mistakes. In planning our lives, we should certainly spend a lot of effort in the development of our talents and abilities, but we should not neglect to turn all of our errors and even our weaknesses into a profit.

Among the unpleasant experiences of life are the mistakes we make and the regrets that we must live with. The word *regret* comes from some words meaning to weep and mourn. This is one of those experiences that most of us have in abundance, as many people spend much of their time in some kind of mourning. The dictionary says that to regret is to remember an experience with grief and sorrow. Regret is to feel distressed in one's mind and emotions because of some past failure or mistake. If we can find some way to make a profit from our regrets, we are in pretty good shape, since many of us have so many things about which to feel sorry. But these must be handled effectively, because even one unpleasant experience that is not taken care of may canker, fester, get infected, become inflamed, and turn malignant.

The human body is equipped with many organs to help it handle the various parts of its business. For example, the stomach receives all kinds of grains, herbs, fruits, vegetables, and meats. Then by a process of digestion, these raw materials are trans-formed into such usable products as tissues, sinew, blood, heat, vision, intelligence, personality, and power. However, if the diges-tive system gets out of order and stops functioning, in a very short time the food becomes rancid, sour, and poisonous.

We also have mental, spiritual, and emotional digestive sys-tems, and the dangers involved with these are even greater if we are unable to eliminate the harmful elements. Some people allow their souls to become sour, bitter, ugly, profane, and ungodly. However, it is one of the most fortunate circumstances of our lives that we are equipped with these miraculous personality digestive systems which can transform our disappointments, regrets, and bad habits into positive mental attitudes, great spiritual powers, and productive emotional traits. And, in turn, these can produce the finest qualities of beauty, industry, success, happiness, and godliness.

It is interesting to remember that the bee gets honey out of the same flowers from which the spider extracts its poison. This selection device is also a human ability. The apostle Paul gave an example of the functioning of this great human endowment when he said to the Romans: ". . . all things work together for good to them that love God." (Romans 8:28.) If we love God, if we think right, if we have the right attitude, and if we do the right things, then everything can be made to work in our interests.

It is to our advantage that we live in a world of opposites. We can always see light things best on a dark background. Lemonade tastes better if it has some sour lemon juice mixed with the sweet sugar. The world is planned for our benefit. Uphill is as good as downhill, night is as necessary as day, sickness and death serve our eternal purposes quite as well as health and life.

If we love God, even Satan serves our best interests. That is, God could destroy Satan and evil at any instant that he desired, and we might ask, "Then why doesn't he?" God himself has given us the answer. He has said: "And it must needs be that the devil should tempt the children of men, or they could not be agents unto themselves; for if they never should have bitter they could not know the sweet." (D&C 29:39.) If all of our prayers were answered, then no one would ever get sick, no one would ever die, and there would be no opposition. Everyone would always get his own way, but there would be no strength. God has made up our world of contrasts and opposites. He has made it possible for us to receive poverty, struggle, doubt, defeat, sickness, error, and weakness, and to transform them into prosperity, power, faith, health, happiness, and godliness.

Think what Lincoln made out of the lack of advantages that came with his backwoods origin. Much of John Bunyan's success was born in the prison where he wrote his masterpiece *The Pil-*

grim's Progress. About the many thorns in his flesh, the apostle Paul said: ". . . therefore will I rather glory in my infirmities, that the power of Christ may rest upon me." (2 Corinthians 12: 9.) There is one theory that says that in whatever aspect life expected us to excel, she gave us a weakness. Demosthenes was supposed to be a great orator, so life gave him a speech impediment to overcome. Beethoven's deafness led him to become a greater musical composer. His longing to hear the beauties of the finest music impelled him to create them. While Julius Caesar was conquering the world, he was an epileptic. Many people presently drawing total and permanent disability benefits are in better physical condition than Julius Caesar was while conquering the world. John Milton was blind for fifteen years before he wrote *Paradise Lost;* that is, he never saw paradise until he lost his eyes.

We ought to understand that those problems and difficulties which are a natural part of our lives can be used for our benefit. It was a part of the plan that our world should be filled with the opposites of good and evil, success and failure, uphill and downhill, struggle and ease. Even hell is a divine institution, and one of its functions is to serve as a place of purification for those who can't handle their own problems in this life.

How shall we get the most mileage out of our regrets and disappointments? One thing that we should not do is hide them from ourselves by our denials or our excuses or our alibis. If we say, "Everybody's doing it," we will probably so appease our minds that we will keep on making mistakes and our problems will get worse instead of better. Neither is it a good idea to let our regrets paralyze us so that we get so discouraged that we throw up our hands in despair and stop trying.

Our regrets can completely destroy us if we adopt the destructive attitude of unduly condemning and belittling ourselves. The best way to handle a regret is to let it arouse in us such a fighting spirit that we will overcome it. Then the more it hurts us, the more benefit we get from it, because we launch an attack against our offenses in a kind of a suit for damages.

The Bible gives an account of Jacob wrestling with an angel at Peniel. Jacob would not let the angel go until he gave Jacob a blessing. (Genesis 32:26.) We can get blessings out of our regrets, too, if we fight them hard enough. There is a law of regrets similar to the law of the pendulum. A swing in one direction gives a pendulum the power to swing an equal distance in the opposite direction. Life is also like that, except that the opposite swing can be made much longer and more powerful.

In his youth, one young man was arrested with some other young men for stealing a watermelon. He was very badly frightened, and he made a solid resolution that has lasted through the years that he would never again try to steal a watermelon or anything else under any circumstances. The recoil toward good caused by his regret was much stronger than the evil force that had set it in motion. Other people have used their regrets over little sins to build great virtues; their temporary weaknesses to build everlasting strength; their embarrassing blunders to cause satisfying thoughtfulness. Our regrets can be used to build over-compensations in other fields.

Vash Young once wrote a book on his regrets entitled *I Got Tired of Being a Fool.* He built a great fortune on a few miserable mistakes. His regrets built up some powerful extremes to carry him to success in the other direction. We can also powerize the swing of our own pendulums by harnessing the regrets of others. Mistakes in others can build virtues in us. There is also a natural compensation enabling us to get good out of weakness.

Many poor boys have become capitalists, and plowboys have become prophets. Napoleon rode his inferiority complex to become one of the most powerful of all our world military leaders. The apostle Paul fought the church in his early years and had a part in the stoning of Stephen. This caused him great regret, which lasted throughout his life and made his pendulum swing so far that he became one of the greatest of all Christian missionaries. Everyone should make a list of his weaknesses and then use his regrets to turn them into strengths. He should make a list of his mistakes and transform them into advantages.

The ancients spent much of their time in the ancient science of alchemy, trying to find ways to transmute the lesser metals, such as iron and tin, into silver and gold. Regardless of their success or lack of it, we can actually transmute habits of tardiness into punctuality. We can change ugliness into beauty. We can also change falsehoods into truthfulness, dishonor into honor, irresponsibility into dependability. One's insane angers can be changed into a quality of imperturbability; his doubts into faith; his disobedience into godliness; his sloth into industry, and his hate into a friendly consideration and love of others. One of our greatest possibilities is to learn to increase the motivating power of our regrets and then transmute them into pure gold.

Life is a most generous trader. She maintains a store stocked with every good gift in the most abundant supply, and she will give us peace for tension, happiness for misery, heaven for hell, and God for Satan. It is interesting that no one is ever sent to hell by somebody else. By the same token, no one is ever given a free ride to heaven, especially against his will or his industry. But if we build strong enough regrets around our bad habits, then our bad habits will disappear, and we will find virtues growing in their places. In trying to make the most and the best of his life, no one is compelled to remain as he is, even for one more minute, and no one ever remains down after he determines to rise. We can intensify our regrets, exchange them for virtues, and then let them take us to any desired destination.

Our Human Plurality

EDWIN SANFORD MARTIN once wrote some interesting lines about human personality under the title "My Name Is Legion." He said:

Within my earthly temple there's a crowd;
There's one of us that's humble, one that's proud,
There's one that's broken hearted for his sins,
There's one that unrepentant sits and grins;
There's one that loves his neighbor as himself,
And one that cares for naught but fame and pelf.
From much corroding cares I should be free
If I could once determine which is me.

Among the most important facts of our lives that all of us must learn to reckon with are the problems and responsibilities that go with our multiple personalities. To make the most of ourselves, our many virtues, abilities, and problems should all be effectively integrated under one central, righteous authority and not be allowed to go their own individual, contrary ways unrestrained. However, our personality sometimes gets so seriously divided and antagonistic that control, as well as accomplishment, is lost. Conflicts and rebellions within ourselves can easily be our undoing. Our society itself sometimes develops such serious conflicting factions that it becomes an unwieldy, uncoordinated, unmanageable combination of the positive and the negative, the good and the bad, the successful and the unsuccessful.

Sometimes we actually so much lose ourselves that we have difficulty with our own identity. Frequently someone makes an accurate description of his situation when he says, "I am all mixed up." "I've got to find myself." Then he is unable to distinguish between the good guys and the bad guys within himself. Sometimes one part of us wants to go forward while an antagonistic part is dragging us backward. Frequently our high gears, our low gears, and our reverse gears are all trying to operate at the same time.

We have many cases of mistaken identity where we can't even recognize ourselves. We believe that we are one kind of person when we are actually some other kind. We may be a different person when with our families than when we are at the office. This inconsistent plurality may also seriously confuse others because they are unable to tell which of our various personalities will represent us on any given occasion.

Recently I heard three men being discussed for employment. Of one it was said, "He is a wonderful person; he is very friendly; he knows his business, but he is undependable." Of another it was said, "He is absolutely honest, he has a good character, but he can't get along with other people." Of another it was said, "He likes people; he is nice looking; he is a very hard worker, but he is immoral." I decided that no matter what may be said about us during the first part of the discussion, we had better pay close attention when the discussion gets around to the *buts*.

Martin Luther once said that one small vice could overcome ten great virtues. One may be excellent in many ways and have his whole personality made useless by his *buts*. A movie actress with several divorces to her credit once said that getting married was like buying a house: the first time you buy a house you look at the paint job on the outside, but thereafter you always look for the termites in the basement. This lady had previously made the mistake of disregarding the *buts* in her situation.

Often we try to keep our worst faults hidden from general observation, but with the closer personality views that are offered in marriage, in employment, and in friendship, we may find that we or our friends often turn out to be someone else. How frequently we hear someone say, "I have never known John before." "He is a completely different person than I always thought he was." "This is not the man I married."

In addition to our confusing plurality, our many selves are continually changing. Someone once reminded his unhappy wife that she had married him for better or for worse. She replied, "Yes, but you are so much worse than I thought you were going to be." Frequently we fertilize some of the elements in our personality so that they grow very rapidly whereas other parts are afflicted with a disease called arrested development, and they grow not at all. Sometimes while improving in one place, we are losing ground in another place, and we become completely unpredictable even to ourselves.

We remember Robert Louis Stevenson's story of *Dr. Jekyll and Mr. Hyde.* Dr. Jekyll was a fine young physician who had within himself some of the usual conflicts of good and evil. However, instead of bringing all of his various inclinations into line by integration and self-discipline, he split off his bad traits and refused responsibility for them. Therefore, in a very real way, he became two people. When Dr. Jekyll's conscience was undisturbed by Mr. Hyde's misdeeds, Dr. Jekyll became better, and when Mr. Hyde's misdeeds were unrestrained by Dr. Jekyll's sense of right, Mr. Hyde became worse. Soon a kindly, helpful, completely good physician by day became a ruthless, immoral, unmanageable criminal by night. It was not long before this antagonistic duality destroyed itself.

This splitting-off or splitting-up of the personality is one of our most common and most serious problems. Goethe indicated the dangers of this possibility when he said, "I have in me the germ of every crime." One of the great abilities we need to develop is to keep the harmful germs from repeating in us the tragedy of the Dr. Jekyll and Mr. Hyde.

Sometimes a mother explains the delinquencies of her son by saying, "It's your father coming out in you." Some have also been accused of having the devil showing up in them. Our personality crowd may range all of the way from a group of angels of light to a company of evils resembling the devil himself. Everything in our lives depends upon how well we integrate and control and eliminate the factions of this plurality within ourselves. It has been said that everyone always carries a little child around inside of him. E. S. Jones, Jr., mentions this particular duality when he says:

Across the fields of yesterday
He sometimes comes to me,
A little lad just back from play,
The lad I used to be.

He looks at me so wistfully
Once he has crept within,
I wonder if he comes to see
The man I might have been.

I know a mature, intelligent, well-balanced woman who is so disturbed by the wind that she can't sleep at night when it blows. When she was five years old, there was an east wind in the community where she lived. She discovered that her mother was afraid of the wind, and this little girl developed such a severe childish fear that it stamped itself into her mind and personality so that she has been unable to get it out. Therefore, whenever the wind blows at night, the little girl in her returns, and this lady must not only carry her around with her but also be tormented by her childish fears.

Many people carry around with them even more serious kinds of childishness. I know of another woman who is allowing her childish selfishness to wreck many lives. When she was young, her parents were always engaged in quarreling and other forms of unpleasantness. In the parental contest for this little girl's affections, the child was rather seriously spoiled and became very selfish. Now the child in her has never ceased to believe that she should have everything to which she takes a fancy.

Her problem is increased because she thinks of herself as something of a glamour girl, and she has now taken a fancy to another woman's husband. She just knows that she can't live without him, and under her spell, he has agreed to give up his wife and five children, a very lucrative professional practice, as well as hundreds of friends, and to start over elsewhere with her where they are unknown.

To get what she wants and has no right to have, this selfish woman is willing to break up two homes, deprive two sets of children of their fathers, deprive the proper wife of the very things that she, "the other woman," is using her glamour to steal. Because of her unmanaged and unmanageable emotions, there will' be a serious loss for everyone in total honor, income, self-respect, stability, and love. This is all because an otherwise fine woman is still carrying around with her the terrible weight of her childish selfishness and a kind of Mr. Hyde's evil.

For good or for bad, many people also carry their parents around with them. From the top of Mount Sinai, God said that the sins of the fathers shall be visited upon the children (Exodus 20:5), and that is one of our greatest tragedies. However, it is also true that the virtues of the fathers may also be visited upon the children. As Nancy Hanks Lincoln lay on her death bed, she said to her nine-year-old son, "Abe, go out there and amount to something." Throughout the balance of Abraham Lincoln's life he always carried his mother around with him, and everything that he did was influenced by her love and desire for his success. Later on, Lincoln said, "All that I am or ever hope to be I owe to my angel mother."

It is even more important what kind of self we carry around with us. Each one of us has been endowed by creation with a set of magnificent equipment, including a brain, a heart, a conscience, and a will. These can be important influences for good if they are properly developed and used. If we are weak or sinful, we impose a heavy load upon ourselves and find ourselves stuck with our own evils. However, if we are the kind of people God intended, then every labor can be made a light and joyous experience. One of our greatest good fortunes is that we can carry the Spirit of the Lord around with us. We are all entitled to have the Holy Ghost as our constant companion. We can always have with us the Spirit of light, truth, righteousness, and intelligence. The apostle Paul said, "Know ye not that ye are the temple of God, and that the Spirit of God dwelleth in you?" (1 Corinthians 3:16.) If we heed the promptings of this Spirit, it will help us to purge ourselves of all selfishness, childishness, and evil.

The Bible says that if we draw nigh unto God, he will draw nigh unto us. (James 4:8.) However, when we follow Satan, in a very real way we must always carry his heavy satanic weight around with us.

Jesus went among people casting out devils. Before Mary Magdalene could solve her problems, the record says that seven devils had to be expelled. (Luke 8:2.) It is one of our primary responsibilities of life to learn to cast out devils in a very real way. The apostle James gave us one method when he said, "Resist the devil, and he will flee from you." (James 4:7.) However, if we do not resist him, we will soon have him on our backs. A little favorable entertainment, and Satan always tries to take us over.

On the other hand, Satan has no power over us except as we give in to him. His outside attractions are powerless unless they are connected with our own inside inclinations. We should never say, "How much the devil tempts," but only "How strongly I am inclined."

A little boy once said, "There ain't no Santa Claus. It's like the devil—it's your dad." But frequently other members of the family, including ourselves, insist on getting into the devil act. Certainly our generation needs to work a lot harder on this technique of casting out devils and getting rid of our own weaknesses. If everyone in the world would always keep all of the commandments of the Lord, Satan would be completely powerless, and this earth would be God's paradise. It might help us in this art if we got a little more practice in casting out those seven devils—selfishness, weakness, sloth, hate, alcohol, immorality, and atheism. Then if we would like to try casting out another seven devils, suppose we start with our indecision, our ignorance, and our indifference. We sometimes develop a devil of a temper that we allow to rule over us. We also develop a devilish habit of rebellion against right. We would be a lot better off if we would cast out the devil of falsehood and the devil of unfairness.

The greatest secret of success is to be able to coordinate all of our righteous powers into one cooperative effort involving a joint action of the heart, and the mind, and the might, and the physical strength. By this process of consolidation and joint action, one may concentrate all of the elements of personal power into one determined effort. He thereby achieves a centrality in his purpose. His effort becomes concentrated, highly focused, one directional, and all in one piece rather than being a bundle of many directioned impulses held loosely together by circumstance.

Our problem is that so many of us are neither one thing nor the other. We are made up of various fractions of good and bad going in all directions at once. Our weak convictions and minimum efforts tend to give us small accomplishments. Without a strong, central, righteous self-discipline governing all of ourselves, we degenerate into a mob of appetites. Then our lives become torn by evil, indecision, and conflicts. As we load ourselves down with guilt complexes and feelings of inferiority, we tend to reenact the age-old battle of good versus evil, which usually ends in some kind of stalemate.

It is interesting that when our food doesn't taste good, it is a sign that we are sick, and when we find ourselves unfriendly to the best things, then we can be certain that we need to repent and cast out a few devils. As James says, "Cleanse your hands, ye sinners; and purify your hearts, ye double minded." (James 4:8.)

The greatest opportunities of our existence are to fully integrate our lives under a righteous authority and then center all of our different abilities and powers into a divine focus.

The Paper Man

M ANY YEARS ago, Mao Tse-tung, the Chairman of Red China, referred to the United States as a paper tiger. He was trying to convey the idea that the military power of the United States looked good only on paper. His thought was that the United States may be a great power in theory, but in an actual demonstration of strength he felt that it would not stand up very well. While he believed that his own country might not have done as well in some places of actual accomplishments, yet it would be a veritable tiger in any test of actual performance. Mao used this particular figure because in his part of the world a tiger is thought of as the strongest of animals, and a tiger is frequently used as the symbol of the greatest strength.

There are many individual people who feel about this same way as they compare themselves with others. They feel that while they may not have many tangible favorable facts that they could put down on paper, yet when the need arises they will be able to perform like a tiger. But if one wants to be a tiger in any actual accomplishment, it is a pretty good idea to be a tiger on the paper first.

Recently I met with a group of church leaders where some of the statistics of their church activities were being discussed. Some of them seemed to show a considerable amount of resentment toward the records of their own work. One of them said, "We are not interested in the statistics; it's the people that count." They were saying to themselves, "Our statistics are terrible, but we are wonderful."

This human attitude of resenting our own statistics is all too common. Because our statistics are the best way of representing what we are, it might be a pretty good idea for us to pay a little more attention to how we look on the paper, especially in the bright light of day. How we feel in our hopes and ambitions or what our wishes and dreams are is very important, but we should also give some consideration to the facts.

We usually have more power for the actual contest when we have a strong reflection coming from the paper. It would be pretty difficult to develop an athletic program if we left out the paperwork. In football, every kick, every pass, every run, every down, and every penalty is measured and timed and counted and recorded. It is also interesting that we always add up the score. It is the score that makes the game. If the score is 6 to 7, and we are on the one-yard line with a minute and a half to play, everyone is excited. If the score is 50 to 0, most of the crowd will have gone home.

Everyone wants to know who won the game and what the score was. The statistics are a kind of itemized statement of the accomplishments. It is from the statistics that we get the final score. A football team's morale and a football team's prestige go up and down with their statistics. The team that looks the best on paper is the one that stays up at the top of the league.

In baseball we keep an accurate record of the hits, runs, and errors of each individual player. Life is also a great game, and in life the statistics are much more important than they are in football. One of our human weaknesses in life is that when we are losing the game, we don't always like to keep track of the score. Certainly we are not very enthusiastic about putting the errors down on the paper, and most people don't even know what their individual batting average is. This makes our success much more difficult both to figure out and to attain.

If you bat .350 in the big leagues, you may receive a salary of a hundred thousand dollars a year. If you bat .250, you may get ten thousand per year. This is quite a difference in pay when the difference in effectiveness is only one additional hit in ten times at bat. That is, the .350 batter gets on first base three and a half times out of ten tries, whereas the .250 batter gets on first base two and a half times out of ten.

The greater success is not always because of how frequently or how hard you hit the ball. The .250 man may be held back because he can't run. There are enough photo finishes at first base to indicate that if you had been half a step faster in 90 feet you would have been safe, but because you were half a step too slow, you were called out. It would not even have been necessary for the unsuccessful man to have been faster every time. He was fast enough two and a half times out of ten; all he needed was a little more speed in one out of ten tries.

However, it is far more important that we know our batting average in life than it is in athletics. We cannot separate our success from our statistics. That is, a banker may not be very favorably impressed if we say, "Our financial statistics are terrible but we are wonderful." The banker might want to know about such prosaic things as our assets and liabilities, our income and our outgo, our bank balances and our overdrafts. Planning and record keeping are so closely related in our success that they cannot be discussed separately.

Someone has said, "You cannot effectively increase accomplishment without some accurate measurement of the progress made." That is, you can learn to be a high-jumper much more quickly by laying a bamboo pole across on two measured uprights and then jumping over it than you can by merely going out onto the field and jumping up in the air without any knowledge of your effectiveness. It has been said that when accomplishment is measured, accomplishment improves, and when accomplishment is recorded and reported back, the improvement is accelerated. But when accomplishment is also publicized, our motivation is given gigantic power. If you want to help your son, don't give him an assignment and then fail to check up; and while your own planning, goal-setting, and motivation are good to watch, never fail to keep an accurate score on yourself.

It is an interesting fact that God is the creator of, and the greatest believer in, statistics. He not only keeps records, but he also advises us to do the same. He said to John the Revelator: "What thou seest, write in a book. . . ." (Revelation 1:11.) He also might have said, "What thou doest write in a book." And that is exactly what he does. John the Revelator records his preview of the final judgment as follows:

"And I saw the dead, small and great, stand before God; and the books were opened: and another book was opened, which is the book of life: and the dead were judged out of those things which were written in the books, according to their works.

"And the sea gave up the dead which were in it; and death and hell delivered up the dead which were in them: and they were judged every man according to their works." (Revelation 20:12-13.)

If each day we could see what God writes in his book about our works for that day, it would certainly motivate us to make better scores. We can most surely reach any goal by putting our results down on the paper every day. When our statistics are low, it is more important than ever that we keep them. How stimulating it would be to see our personal errors published every day on the front page of the newspaper. With this kind of situation, our errors would be much fewer. This would also help us prepare for that great day when all of our present secret acts shall be revealed. Of course, there are some things about ourselves that we can't get on the paper.

Many years ago Clarence E. McCartney compiled an important book entitled *The Great Sermons of the World.* After an exhaustive amount of research and selecting, Mr. McCartney collected in one book the greatest human utterances that had ever been made. He included two sermons by an old preacher named Whitefield who used to live in New England a couple of hundred years ago, and as kind of an apology, Mr. McCartney said, "No one can read the sermons of Whitefield and understand why thousands of people were always flocking out to hear him." Then by way of explanation, he added, "You can't get the man on the paper. You can get his words and his paragraphs and his questions, but you can't get the man." What he meant was that you can't get the light in his eye or the music of his voice or the love vibrations that come out of his heart. You can't get the fire of his personality or the warmth of his soul on the paper.

One famous minister was once approached by an admiring listener who had just heard what he thought was a magnificent sermon. The listener said, "I would like your permission to publish and distribute that sermon." The minister said, "You may print and distribute the sermon if you will also print and distribute the thunder and lightning that goes with it." It is pretty difficult to get human thunder and lightning on paper. It is very hard to get real love, personality, and faith on paper.

On the other hand, we can get on paper many of the things that cause love, personality, growth, and faith. And there are some things that must be put down on the paper. If a man's biography is not written down, the story of his life is soon lost, frequently even to himself. If one's plans are not put down on paper, they are soon forgotten. It has been properly said that "no plan is a plan until it is on paper." You wouldn't employ an architect who didn't know how to get the ideas out of his head onto the paper. If the bishop tries to keep the records of all of his ward members in his head, he is doomed to fail.

Suppose you take any group of even fifty people, no matter how well they may be known to you, and see how many of them you can remember without hesitation. You will be shocked at how ineffective are your powers of recall. But your brain was never intended to be a baggage room or a storehouse; it much more resembles a machine shop or a work bench. One of our greatest opportunities is that each of us may increase his total mental equipment by building a great paper memory. A good bookkeeper with an ordinary brain can have a fantastic paper memory. A lawyer sits in his library where he has on paper all of the legal experience of the greatest legal minds, and they are more readily available to him than if he had to depend on some kind of magic recall from his own mind.

We may make the greatest literature a part of our paper memories. You can't judge a man by watching him live or a baseball player by seeing him bat. I have personally watched Babe Ruth at bat three times, and he struck out every time. But at the very time that I was watching him strike out, the record said— and still says, even after he is dead—that he was the greatest home-run king who ever lived.

What a great thrill it would have been to have studied at the feet of the great thinkers and leaders of the past, and yet we have many of them down on the paper verbatim. Written expression can be much clearer as more care is taken in its preparation. We can hear the words and feel the ideas of Shakespeare, Washington, and Lincoln even better now than if we had lived in their own day. Abraham Lincoln once said, "What I want to know is in books." And the two most powerful books in Lincoln's life were the Holy Bible, which even in his youth he hungrily devoured before the open fire, and *The Life of Washington*, by W. R. Weems.

Weems put the life of George Washington on paper, and as a result Washington has favorably influenced Lincoln and millions of other people ever since. Through books we may know the greatest men and women with an intimacy and completeness that was never enjoyed by those who lived in their own time or even in their own household.

Recently a woman came to talk about some of her emotional and moral problems. She said that her boyfriend liked to go to X-rated, sex-oriented movies. She pointed out that when she went to any kind of a movie, she lived the events as they took place on the screen; and while she felt that she had high moral standards, when she came out of this particular kind of movie she felt like a different person than she had been when she went in. The people on the screen were actually getting over to her. The people in great books can, with real power, get over to us also because every contact that we ever make, either good or bad, modifies us. Some people make us feel like we are ten feet tall, and some can make us feel small, dirty, and sick.

Someone wrote a poem in which he said, "I love you for what you are but I love you even more for what you make me feel while I am with you." We have detailed editions of Shakespeare, Moses, and the apostle Paul all arranged on paper. We can be with them at our leisure and enjoy their inspiration to our heart's content, and, like the girl at the movies, we can absorb their spirits and breathe the atmosphere of those things that were in their minds and souls.

One of our greatest blessings is that even God has made himself available to us in a very real way on paper. We may spend a lifetime waiting for some sign or revelation from him, but on paper we may feel his inspiration immediately and listen to his words at will. At our pleasure we may witness the thunders and lightnings of Mount Sinai and be present in spirit while God gives again those fundamental laws. With Moses we may go and spend those memorable forty days and nights in God's presence. But that is not all. We may make ourselves a part of those other important conversations that God has had over the centuries with Adam, Enoch, Noah, and Abraham. We may read at our pleasure the revelations of his mind and will to all of the holy prophets and understand again his words that "whatever principle of intelligence we attain unto in this life, it will rise with us in the resurrection." (D&C 130:13.) One of the great opportunities of our lives is to learn to do the paper work on which a most happy and successful eternal life can be built.

A Piece of Paper

SOMETIME AGO I met with a group of Aaronic Priesthood bearers who had received certificates of achievement because of their religious excellence. A young man who had not thus achieved had tried to discredit to himself the importance of the award by saying that it was just a piece of paper. But actually it was much more than that. The merit identified on the paper was an outward representation of something much greater inside the lives of the boys themselves.

Very frequently a thing is not as important for itself alone as it is for what it stands for. Of course, a piece of paper may represent a great value in itself. A hundred dollar bill is just a piece of paper. A ten thousand dollar stock certificate or a deed to one's home or his baptismal certificate or his marriage license or his citizenship paper or his license to practice medicine is just a piece of paper.

The value of one particular piece of paper is indicated by a story of an explorer who many years ago was working in one of the world's primitive countries where writing was unknown. On one occasion it became necessary for this man to send a message to an associate working many miles away. It was arranged that a native who knew the country should be the messenger. The native watched as the explorer took pen and ink and made some written marks in a letter. Then the native was given an envelope enclosing the paper. After spending the necessary days traversing the jungle, he placed it in the hands of the one for whom it was intended. The native stood by as his host looked at the marks on the paper. Then, to the great astonishment of the native, without any word having been spoken, the man to whom this mysterious package had been delivered knew exactly where his friend was, what he was doing, how he felt, what his problems were, and what help he was asking for. The receiver knew all of these things merely by looking at signs on a piece of paper. Overcome by the powerful magic that was contained in the writing, the native fell down on his face and worshiped the paper.

Because we have a better understanding of this miracle of writing, it has lost much of its glamour and has become more or less commonplace to many people, and one who doesn't read is no better off so far as all practical purposes are concerned than one who can't read. In many cases, our apathy may be more of a deterrent to our progress than was the native's lack of learning.

In a little lighter vein, though not without some elements of truth, someone has said that out of our 200 million people, 30 million of them can neither read nor write. But then there is another 30 million who can read but don't, and another 30 million who can read and do read some but don't understand what they read. Then there is another 30 million who can read, and who do read and do understand, but they don't do anything about it.

Be that as it may, writing by any measurement is still one of the greatest wonders of our world. It is our most productive force. Its productive magic can still perform all kinds of miracles in our behalf. Writing is preserved speech. It is our greatest storehouse for helpful ideas, pleasant emotions, and profitable information. It has the ability to transfer to us the finest thoughts, the highest ideals, and the most powerful ambitions from the greatest men and make them negotiable in our own lives.

Writing is also our most effective way of communication as well as our most valuable avenue for receiving benefits. During the 1956 political campaign, a newspaper man pointed out that Dwight D. Eisenhower was ear-minded. That is, for most of his life he had served in the army where he had received his communications largely by means of the verbal commands that entered his mind through his ears. The same newspaper man said that Richard M. Nixon was eye-minded. He had been trained as a lawyer, and the main entrance to his brain was through his eyes. Mr. Nixon liked to get by himself among his books and look up the needed information as it had been written down by the best legal authorities.

Many of us are or ought to be productively eye-minded. Our eyes not only provide the chief entrance to our minds, but that is also the best way to our hearts as well. Most people can usually hear much faster through their eyes than they can through their ears. Sounds fade away, and even the ability for recollection is soon lost, but writing can make our ideas permanent. Its power defies time and continues on with undiminished effectiveness.

Writing gives value to our law books, our schoolbooks, our newspapers, our signboards, our great literature, and particularly our holy scriptures. Someone has said that without books God is silent, justice dormant, philosophy lame. Some of our most valuable possessions, our most powerful emotions, our most thrilling memories, our most motivating faith, and even our grandest experiences come from the written page. Even the word of the Lord himself spoken from the top of Mount Sinai thirty-four centuries ago can be re-run through our minds over and over again. God has specifically commanded that his greatest revelations should be put down on paper. In this way we can have the revelation renewed every day.

On one occasion, God said to John the Revelator, "Come up hither, and I will shew thee things which must be hereafter." (Revelation 4:1.) Then God uncovered to the gaze of the great apostle much of the future history of our world. He also showed him a clear vision of the resurrection of the dead and let him preview some scenes from the final judgment exactly as it would someday be. Important as this great communication from God was, it could not help us very much unless it could be preserved in some way, so the Lord said to John, "What thou seest, write in a book." (Revelation 1:11.) And God's command to write important things down has been repeated on many occasions.

As a consequence, a great volume of these important papers having a divine origin have been accumulated. Someone got the exciting idea of binding all of these life-giving documents together into books. Our great world literature is now headed by four great volumes of holy scripture that are God's own communications to us. For example, I hold in my hand a copy of the Holy Bible. On one of its pages have been written the Ten Commandments, and if we were to live by the writings of this one page alone, we could quickly transform our world for the better. On this one page, God has sent to us, across thirty-four centuries, many of the blessings of wisdom, law, righteousness, and religion. Also bound in the Holy Bible are the papers containing the beautiful poetry of the Psalms, the wisdom of the Proverbs, the hope of the Beatitudes, the wonder of the Golden Rule, and the great lifesaving doctrines of salvation providing for our own eternal exaltation. We not only have the important papers from God; we also have some wonderful communications from the greatest men who have ever lived in any land and in any age of time.

The greatest nonscriptural papers have also been made into books containing all of the wisdom, literature, beauty, enthusiasm, faith, experience, and even the enjoyment of some of our greatest men that they are able to transfer to us. All of this is as fresh and as exciting when it comes to us as it was when the events themselves originally took place. Someone put this idea into verse when he said:

> Every day in books
> Rip Van Winkle lies asleep,
> Moby Dick patrols the deep,
> Every day in books.

> Tall windmills turn in Spain
> Where across the empty plain
> Rides the rusty knight in vain,
> Every day in books.

> Falstaff laughs and Hamlet dreams,
> Camelot is all it seems,
> Kublai Khan in Sahna Du
> Hears the rivers running through.

> Marco Polo sails away,
> Mr. Pickwick has his say,
> Troy is falling every day,
> Every day in books.

However, we not only write our great messages on paper; we write them even more effectively on human minds and spirits as well as in their flesh and blood. Daniel Webster once said: "If we work upon marble, it will perish; if brass, time will efface it; if we rear temples, they will crumble into dust; but if we work upon immortal minds, imbue them with principles, with the just fear of God and love of our fellowmen, we engrave on those tablets something that will brighten through all eternity."

On many occasions our lives themselves have been compared to a piece of paper. One of the great educational processes is transferring the wonders from the paper into ourselves. We need to use our papers more effectively in this important process. Actually, our minds were never intended to serve by themselves as baggage rooms or warehouses. They are machines or spiritual work rooms, and many of the things that are written in our minds, if left by themselves, may sink below the level of consciousness or they may slip beyond our ability to recall them. But the things that are written on paper can be retained indefinitely. By the use of paper we may appropriate for our own pleasure and profit the finest ideas developed by all of the greatest men in the world.

Even the most vast paper memory has no forgetfulness, and we can transfer the substance of our greatest ideas from the paper into our own personalities. We can also appropriate the greatest ambitions of the greatest men from a written account and make them our own. We may also use the ideas from books written in other lands and in other ages to motivate our own souls and to bring about every desired success. We can preserve our physical food by freezing or canning, and we can preserve our most important mental and spiritual food by collecting the greatest ideas and getting them into their written form.

Through our four great volumes of the holy scriptures we may use for our own welfare the detailed directions from God himself. We can review the covenants and practice the training that he has given to other peoples in other lands. Through books we can rethink his thoughts and live in a way befitting his offspring and heirs.

James Russell Lowell puts this idea on paper and says to us:

> Life is a leaf of paper white,
> Whereon each one of us may write
> His word or two and then comes night.
>
> Greatly begin! Though thou hast time
> But for a line, be that sublime.
> Not failure, but low aim, is crime.

One of the greatest challenges of life is to try to understand what that paper of our lives will look like when we have finished with it.

Oliver Wendell Holmes once wrote an interesting poem entitled "To a Blank Piece of Paper." In his thoughts, Mr. Holmes speculated on the possibilities of this pale sheet of white paper before him. He wondered what his pen might write upon it that would be helpful for others to read. His brain might produce on this paper a poem of love or cast forward a projection of his own faith or picture an embodiment of his own courage, or he could give a forecast of the greatest accomplishment of which he was capable. Mr. Holmes said to his piece of blank paper:

> Thou hast no tongue yet thou canst speak,
> Till distant shores shall hear the sound;
> Thou hast no life, yet thou canst breathe
> Fresh life on all around.

No one except ourselves can read the unborn meaning of our lives, and yet many people will read as we write. And we can write such miraculous things as have never been known before. We can inscribe into our own hearts those great virtues which God himself possesses. We can transplant into our personalities the greatest enthusiasm that we can get from others, and they will radiate from our faces the love of beauty and the harmony of our lives as we develop the ambition to build up God's kingdom upon the earth. All of us are children of God, and each of us was sent from his presence with a message for general delivery.

As Joyce Kilmer has said:

> And since the way was hard and long
> And through a strange and weary land,
> God placed upon my lips a song
> And put a lantern in my hand.

We can shed that light and breathe that song of joy on all around us.

The Quitter

O N ONE occasion President Calvin Coolidge pointed out a great success idea that we might all do well to work at a little bit more effectively. He said: "Nothing in the world can take the place of persistence. Talent will not. Nothing is more common than unsuccessful men with talent. Genius will not. Unrewarded genius is almost a proverb. Education will not. The world is full of educated derelicts. Persistence and determination alone are omnipotent."

On the other hand we lose many of life's greatest blessings because we fail to make a continuous effort in the right direction. We form too many damaging bad habits that cause us to become quitters. All too frequently our success and righteousness lack persistence, and consequently the rewards are also lost.

The dictionary says that to quit is to abandon, to forsake, to terminate. It is common for otherwise fine people to just stop working, and because faith without works is dead, when we stop working we stop believing. A quitter gives up many things, including his employment, his faith, his family, his loyalty, his courage, his righteousness, and his rewards.

Our battalions of quitters include large numbers who are dropouts from education, dropouts from religion, and dropouts from the service of others. Many older people as well as younger people run away from home, and they also run away from duty and responsibility. They desert their families; their courage disintegrates; they betray their country; they allow their hope to wither, and they apostatize from God. The traits that characterize us as quitters are the exact opposites of those qualities that we need for all of our human success and happiness.

In one of his greatest statements, Jesus said, ". . . he that endureth to the end shall be saved." (Matthew 10:22.) Jim Sullivan, one-time heavyweight prizefight title holder, gave this idea a little different twist when he said, "The champion is the one who can stay on his feet and fight for one more round."

The other side of this proposition was demonstrated by Cato, the great Roman patriot who committed suicide on the very eve of his triumph. If he had only hung on to his courage and industry until morning, he would have been victorious. We have a natural human tendency to start a lot of good things that we never finish, and this unfortunate habit costs our world a lot of our success and happiness. An unknown author has commented on this trait under the title of "The Sticker." He says:

> Oh, it's easy to be a starter, Lad.
> But are you a sticker, too?
> 'Tis fun, sometimes, to begin a thing,
> But harder to see it through.
> If you failed sometimes when you did your best,
> Don't take it too much to heart;
> Just try it again in a different way,
> For it depends upon how you start.
> And sometimes a failure is best, my boy,
> To keep you from being too sure;
> Success that is built on defeat, you know,
> Will ofttimes longest endure.
> 'Tis the sticker who wins in the battle of life,
> When the quitter is laid on the shelf;
> You are never defeated, remember this,
> Until you lose faith in yourself.
> Oh, it's easy to be a starter, my boy,
> But are you a sticker too?
> You may think it is fun to begin a task;
> But are you game to see it through?

Under the title of "Perseverance" another unknown voice says to us:

> Genius, that power which dazzles mortal
>   eyes,
> Is oft but perseverance in disguise.
> Continuous effort, of itself, implies
> In spite of countless falls, the power to rise,
> 'Twixt failure and success the point's so fine
> Men sometimes know not when they touch
>   the line.
> Just when the pearl was waiting one more
>   plunge,
> How many a struggler has thrown up the
>   sponge?
> As the tide goes out, it comes clear in;
> In business 'tis at turns the wisest win.

And, oh! how true, when shades of doubt
dismay,
'Tis often the darkest just before the day.

There are many people who would have gone a long way in
the race of life if they had kept going for just one more round.
The most serious cause of quitting is almost always that destructive slowing-down process that precedes it.

These two faults of slowing down and quitting are like their
physical counterparts of disability and death. People usually get
sick before they die. The government attempts to measure the disability caused by disease as a percentage. The government might
say that one person is 10 percent disabled or that he is 50 percent
disabled or that he is 90 percent disabled. Actually disability is
merely a part of death. Death also comes as a fraction.

Sometimes one's faith dies or his industry dies or his morality dies or his loyalty dies or his enthusiasm dies. Then he may
be 10 percent dead or 50 percent dead or 90 percent dead. Jesus
said, "I am come that they might have life, and have it more
abundantly." (John 10:10.) But in most cases only some fraction
of us presently remain alive. There are many dead people who
have not yet been buried. On one man's tombstone were inscribed
these words: "Died at 30 buried at 65."

It is unfortunate that without knowing it we lose large fractions of our lives because we are quitters. And even quitting is
carried out a little bit at a time. We first slow down in our study,
we slow down in our enthusiasm, and we direct our attention to
some competing interest. We almost automatically slow down
when we allow antagonisms to destroy our effort, or doubt to
destroy our faith, or a guilty conscience to destroy our ability
to concentrate. If our excellence is allowed too many leaks, the
day finally comes when we are more dead than alive.

The actual dropout act is usually a mere formality that takes
place long after it has actually happened. We mold ourselves and
then we wait until some crisis shows us what we have become.
The Lord said: ". . . once more I shake not the earth only but also
heaven. . . . that those things which cannot be shaken may remain." (Hebrews 12:26-27.) The Lord provides the crisis that
shows us to ourselves.

Many years ago, out on the farm, I discovered a kind of
physical dropout process in operation. In our apple orchard I dis-

covered that the sound apples were not the ones most likely to
fall to the ground when the trees were shaken in the wind. It was
the wormy apples or the apples with other serious defects that
would fall at the least shaking of the tree. This is about what
happens to us in life. A few defects and we become quitters.

Of course there are many things that we should quit as
soon as possible, such as our bad habits, our negative attitudes,
our lethargy, our evil, and our sloth. But there is an important
difference in the reason for quitting these things. That is, we quit
bad things by design, whereas we usually quit the good things by
default.

Jesus gave us an idea about one way to prevent ourselves
from becoming quitters when he said that we should be careful
about what we begin and that we should make sure that we finish
what we start. He said:

"For which of you, intending to build a tower, sitteth not
down first and counteth the cost, whether he have sufficient to
finish it?

"Lest haply, after he hath laid the foundation, and is not
able to finish it, all that behold it begin to mock him,

"Saying, This man began to build, and was not able to finish.

"Or what king, going to make war against another king, sitteth not down first, and consulteth whether he be able with ten
thousand to meet him that cometh against him with twenty
thousand?" (Luke 14:28-31.)

Just think how many things there are in life that we quit
with serious consequences to ourselves. We frequently see disaster when we quit our marriage through a divorce, or we quit our
business through bankruptcy, or we quit our employment
through failure, or we give up our citizenship through treason,
or we quit our church membership through apostasy, or we break
off our relationship with God by our sins.

It is probable that no one ever does any of these things deliberately. We just let our personal situation deteriorate until it
almost falls to pieces of its own weight. Someone has said, "I
never had to put religion out of my mind; I was so open-minded
that it fell out." Some people say they have fallen out of love as

though they themselves had nothing to do with it. Or that they have lost interest in the church through no fault of their own. Or that their patriotism just happened to die for no reason at all. It is probable that none of these are ever true. Satan did not fall from heaven until after he had committed so many sins of rebellion and betrayal that his further residence in heaven was impossible.

Before Judas sold Jesus to the mob, he had sold himself to Satan. He first became Satan's serf, and then there was nothing left but to do his master's bidding. At one time Judas Iscariot was a member of the Quorum of the Twelve in good standing, but before he became a quitter, greed and selfishness had replaced those holy principles upon which a successful apostleship must be based. Benedict Arnold was a general of great ability in the American Colonial army, but when his greed and selfishness became stronger than his patriotism, he became a quitter and betrayed his country.

Recently a couple came in to talk about their projected divorce. Actually, the divorce began to develop even before the marriage took place. They had been drawn together by their natural instinctive urges, and for several years their forces of attraction fought with the evils that were tending to push them apart. Even before they were married, they had already started these forces of disintegration to work by committing some serious offenses against each other. By their immoralities and deceits, they had planted the seeds of failure and distrust in each other. After they were married, they made several arbitrary attempts to get their relationship on a better basis, but they never seemed to get around to obeying the fundamental laws of righteousness on which all real confidence and success rests.

If a student wants to avoid being a dropout, he should first quit doing those things that lead to it. If one wants to avoid causing a divorce, he should wipe out of his own life those personality and character defects that are the natural enemies of marriage. When the wife feels that her husband tries to dominate her unjustly, her resentments keep her in a state of continual rebellion. Some married couples are always bickering and quarreling and trying to outdo each other in imposing sanctions and penalties against each other.

In many cases both admit their share of the blame and because of the children both would like to see the marriage work. But each has an elephant's memory, and they can vividly recollect those sins which have now carried them beyond the point of no return. And like a school dropout, their future has been ruined by the wrong kind of a past that they are unwilling to let go of.

We should not try to rationalize that lover's quarrels are good, or that some little sins and offenses against God are all right. For like chickens, they will someday all come home to roost. The story is told of a man who jumped out of a window of a tall building. As he went by the third floor, he was heard to say, "Everything is all right so far." But the length of the fall will all be represented in the landing.

As our sins and personality problems are more securely established, they become more difficult to get rid of. Even a repentant mate can be almost unbearable to the other if the offense has gone far enough. Success in marriage is not so much in finding the right person as it is in being the right person, and we cannot have a happy marriage on our own terms unless those terms are also the terms of righteousness.

The trouble with most marriages is that we do not provide enough love, trust, congeniality, or pleasure for the marriage to run on. When too large a percentage of our energy is spent in generating unfairness, irresponsibility, and incompatibility, then our marriage is in real trouble.

We are told by the psychologists that everything that we hear, see, or think is registered in us. When our destructive emotions get set too deep, it is pretty difficult to get them out. When I make a mistake on the belt of my electronic dictating equipment, it is a very simple process to completely erase it and put on something that is more acceptable. Each belt can therefore be used over and over again whether the messages it carries are good or bad.

However, my previous dictating equipment had a plastic belt, and a recording needle cut the message into the belt itself so that after it had been used once it had to be thrown away. The Creator has given us some important procedures called repentance, reformation, restitution, forgiveness, and forgetfulness. Sometimes we are like an electronic belt and can completely erase those evils that cause our failures, but then again our sins sometimes cut themselves pretty deeply into our lives. And we also frequently cut our sins into the lives of other people. Then even the psychiatrists and the mental health people that we may hire have difficulty digging down deep enough into the dark regions of our lives to cut them out. We should avoid this great sin of quitting good things, and we should also avoid the deterioration in excellence that precedes it.

The Road Not Taken

O NE OF the greatest poets of our time was Robert Frost. He left us many helpful ideas dressed up in interesting language. He ornamented his thoughts and made them exciting and meaningful to us with constructive figures of speech. It has been said that the poets stand next to the prophets in their ability to influence and motivate our lives for good. We need the greatest truths presented in their most compelling form. Fortunately, we are the beneficiaries of a great array of literature that has been packed with the most helpful and significant meanings.

To make great thoughts usable to us, to light them up with greater meaning, and to make them more clearly understood, we have similes, poetic images, metaphors, symbols, and parables. They are used to uplift our feelings and improve our conduct. Symbols and figures of speech are not important for themselves alone. Frequently they are much more important for what they are a sign of, or for what they stand for, or for what they incite us to do and to feel.

The words that are used to form these pictures in our minds are the lifeblood of our language, and they vary in their constructive result according to the degree of identification that we make with them. Meanings are important not only for what their authors put into them; they are also important for what their readers can get out of them. More than anything else, every inspired author needs an inspired reader.

Many years ago Mr. Frost wrote a poem in which he pictures himself walking down a path through the woods. He came to a division in the pathway that required him to choose which way he would go. Both looked interesting and seemed filled with promise. Mr. Frost thought he would like to explore both roads, but obviously that was not possible, so he chose the lesser-traveled road.

One of the significant limitations placed on our experience is that we are required to make these choices every day. There may be a dozen roads, all of which have interesting sights to see and wonderful things to do along the way, but since we can't walk on many roads at the same time, we must reject all of the roads but one. Because this sometimes causes disappointment, Mr. Frost made a kind of compromise. He chose one road and then told himself that maybe he could come back later and explore the other. However, he knew that in all probability his hopes in this direction would never be realized.

Of course, Mr. Frost had something in mind that was far more important than merely choosing a path through the woods. There are also many interesting paths that run through life. Since time began, *road* or *journey* has always been used as the symbol for the course that we take in life. Our choices may make the difference between a life filled with serious regrets or one of eternal joys. No matter which road one takes, he will always remember his decision and will be compelled to live with whatever the results may be.

There are many decisions wherein the choices are not between good and evil. Frequently the alternatives may appear to be almost equally attractive, and yet, the road we take will determine what the volume and the quality of our experiences will be. Over the years, the particular road we travel can also make an important difference in the kind of people that we become. Actually, Mr. Frost's poem would have a different meaning for everyone to whom it was applied. In saying that he took the road that was less traveled, Mr. Frost may have been referring to his decision to become a poet instead of becoming a doctor, a lawyer, or a businessman, professions in which he would be on more heavily traveled roads.

To others who may read this poem, the fork referred to may have had reference to the need for deciding upon a hobby or an education or a wife. One might be selecting his own personality traits or selecting some of the minor trails that run through life. Actually, it is unimportant to us what choices the poet or some fellow traveler may have had in mind. However, it is very important that we clearly understand the truths that this poem holds up for our consideration.

The poem is a kind of expression of regret that the possibilities of our experiences in life are so limited that we can have but one native country or live with one wife or follow one profession.

Some people regret that they did not live in some other age or in some other country. Many people have wished that they had lived in the golden age of Greece or in the days of Jesus of Nazareth. Sometimes we express ourselves as wanting to get back to the good old days of the past, and with the poet, we may feel a bit sad that we are unable to explore all of the interesting roads instead of just one.

A person who has a wholesome craving for life may be completely satisfied with the choices he has made, and yet, he may long for some of those additional realms of experience that he had to pass by. However, if he had lived in the good old days, he would have been required to forfeit the privilege of living amid the miracles and wonders of our own days. If he had been Abraham Lincoln, he could not have been who he is.

Solomon was born to great wealth and power, and he ascended one of the most desirable thrones in the world while he was yet a teenager. As a consequence, he was denied the thrill of working his way up to success. Many men who have been born in poverty and have known a life dedicated to struggle have said that this was one of the greatest benefits of their lives. The football spectator who sits safely in the bleachers, wrapped in warm clothing and enjoying his ease and comfort, may not get as many thrills as the quarterback playing to the very limit of his strength, fully exposed to accidents and exhaustion. In every place that we find ourselves, there are choices that must be made.

The symbolism of Frost's poem is very rich and may be given many meanings. It teaches us something about the important doctrine of choices, as well as the equally important doctrine of responsibilities. We should understand, of course, that our choices not only govern the present; they also limit the range of all possible future choices. Since our lives are made up as we go along, once we have traveled the road of being a poet, we cannot easily go back to the crossroads to travel the path of being a great physician. One must either decide to give up the wonder and delight of curing men's bodies or he must miss the music, fascination, and excitement of his poetry. And even though one chooses between paths that are as equal as possible, the choices still will have far-reaching consequences. In his poem, Mr. Frost centers his attention on "The Road Not Taken." He says:

Two roads diverged in a yellow wood,
And sorry I could not travel both
And be one traveler, long I stood
And looked down one as far as I could
To where it bent in the undergrowth;

Then took the other, as just as fair,
And having perhaps the better claim,
Because it was grassy and wanted wear;
Though as for that the passing there
Had worn them really about the same,

And both that morning equally lay
In leaves no step had trodden black.
Oh, I kept the first for another day!
Yet knowing how way leads on to way,
I doubted if I should ever come back.

I shall be telling this with a sigh
Somewhere ages and ages hence:
Two roads diverged in a wood, and I—
I took the one less traveled by,
And that has made all the difference.

Mr. Frost's poem tells of selecting one path that seemed just as desirable as its alternative. Whatever his specific decision was, it was made between two good choices. We can understand that even this kind of a choice is often very difficult to make. Frequently we have another kind of decision wherein the choice lies not between good and good but between good and evil. This latter decision should not be so difficult, and yet, mounting crime waves and increases in atheism and delinquency indicate that a lot of wrong choices are being made in preference to good ones that are available. This involves a different kind of thinking and a greater contrast in the rewards that await at the end of the trail.

Someone has written a poem about making a selection between a good path and a bad one. Although each of us must be personally responsible for which road is taken, some of the differences may lie in the kinds of counsel that we pick up along the way. This poem is entitled "The Crossroads."

He stood at the crossroads all alone,
    The sunrise was in his face;
He had no thought for the world unknown,
    He was set for a manly race.
But the road stretched east and the road stretched west,

And the boy knew not which road was best.
So he strolled on the road that led him down
And he lost the race and victor's crown.
He was caught at last in an angry snare,
Because no one stood at the crossroad there
To show him the better road.

Another day at the self-same place,
A boy with high hopes stood;
He, too, was set for a manly race,
He, too, was seeking the things that were good,
But one was there who the roads did know
And that one showed him which way to go
So he turned from the road that would lead him down,
And he won the race and the victor's crown.
He walks today the highway fair,
Because one stood at the crossroads there,
To show him the better road.

One of the significant characteristics of our lives is that we live in a world of contrasts. Always before us there are choices of good and evil, sickness and health, light and darkness, pleasure and pain, God and Satan, heaven and hell, and labor and ease. The road that seems the fairest and the easiest may not always be the best. Frequently our blessings come disguised in their work clothes. Struggle and adversity sometimes look upon us with an unpleasant countenance, and yet they often prove to be our best friends sent to challenge us and make us strong. We might try to understand what it would be like to find failure at the end of our lives because the road not taken was the road of industry and struggle.

One of the most prominent teachings of Jesus has to do with this two-road concept of life. One road was that straight and narrow way which leads to eternal life, and the other was the broad road which leads to death. In Mr. Frost's poem, he took the road that was the least traveled. That is also the one contended for by Jesus. The most heavily traveled road is that broad road which leads to the place that no one wants to go. The broad road is wide enough to accommodate atheism, dope, alcoholism, and lung cancer, but on the straight and narrow road, dishonesty, profanity, Sabbath day violations, and many other evil pleasures must be excluded. When we get to the end, how will we feel if the straight and narrow way is the road that was not taken?

The road we choose continues to be one of the most important parts of life, and the straight and narrow road that leads to life in God's eternal city is the one that will prove more profitable in the end.

A Salute to America

SOMETIME AGO I listened to an interesting radio program entitled *A Salute to America*. It was a provocative discussion about some of the unusual opportunities that are granted and the duties that are required of those who live in this great free nation. It was pointed out that America is made up of many things, including real estate, buildings, climates, minerals, rivers, and other resources. But primarily America is made up of Americans. Among its many assets is a Constitution that has a divine origin and background. America is based on noble ideals with some great traditions for freedom, fairness, and democracy. It is governed by laws and founded upon basic Christian principles.

Not the least of America's assets is the fact that our founding fathers were raised up by the God of heaven to stand in the forefront of our civilization and give our nation its start toward its destiny. As I listened to this tribute, I was very proud to be an American, and I was motivated by a wholehearted desire to make my own salute more meaningful by a greater personal contribution to my country's strength and greatness.

The dictionary says that to salute is to address with expressions of kind wishes, courtesy, and honor. Then it gives some interesting examples, such as the lark saluting the dawn by bursting into song with its wholehearted welcome of the new day. The crocus salutes the spring with its new life and color. In some of our military salutes we fire cannon, dip the colors, uncover our heads, and stand at attention. We also have several kinds of hand salutes to show our approval and express our goodwill. There is an old Anglo-Gallic gold coin that bears a representation of Mary of Nazareth receiving the salutation of the angel Gabriel, indicating her new position as the prospective mother of the Savior of the world.

We might ask what would be an appropriate salute for good citizens to make to America, particularly at this time when she has such an urgent need. We might begin our personal salute to America by trying to understand America and by believing in

America. Governments have been instituted by God for the benefit of men, and he holds us responsible for our own acts in relation thereto. We have the word of the Lord himself that the American Constitution was established by wise men whom God himself had raised up for that very purpose. God caused that this land should be redeemed by the shedding of blood, and the government of this land was founded in honor and based upon Christian principles. Good government means order and righteousness. We are certain that many centuries ago God became sick and tired of dictators. What would a just God think of the kind of men who use Stalin blood purges, Hitler gas ovens, and Castro indignities as instruments of government?

God not only had a hand in the establishment of our government and in fostering the ideas of life, liberty, and the pursuit of happiness, but he also established his divine church here in these latter days. America, with its freedom and democracy, was about the only logical place where the restoration could have been effectively made. Certainly the two greatest present responsibilities of our lives have to do with our allegiance to God and our loyalty to our country.

An ancient prophet said: "Except the Lord build the house, they labour in vain that build it." (Psalm 127:1.) Under his favor, the United States of America has become the greatest and most powerful nation ever known in the world, but it will continue to prosper only as we obey the God of this land, who is Jesus Christ. From the time of the great council in heaven, God has continually made the strongest kind of commitments to freedom and democracy. In our time America has been ordained by him to serve as the citadel of freedom, and America has been given the divine mission to keep freedom, righteousness, and human dignity alive in the world.

In the days of ancient Israel, God also tried to establish a great nation based on freedom and democracy, but the people turned away from God in favor of a king, and as a consequence, their hoped-for success fell into the evils of dictatorship, and the whole undertaking failed. But now again in the last days God has established upon the earth a great free nation with special powers. This is his final attempt, before the glorious second coming of Jesus Christ, to promote his primary objectives of producing righteousness upon his earth and establishing peace and goodwill among men.

What a great benefit was conferred upon the entire world when God inspired our Constitution and raised up God-fearing, freedom-loving, righteous men to give it implementation. And every individual in the world should continually pray for a strong, enduring United States of America, for if any Communist combination of nations should ever gain control in the world, then none of our other problems would ever again seem of much consequence. As Emerson, an earlier spokesman for America, has said: "Of what avail is plow or sail, Or land or life if freedom fail?"

If they thought they could, the Communists would enslave every person in the world without a moment's hesitation. Enslavement is not the spirit of the great God of the universe. The spirit of God is the spirit of liberty. The spirit of God is also the spirit of righteousness, and it must also be the spirit of America.

Goodness is the basic law of nations, and freedom and righteousness are the two primary safeguards of America. If we hold these traits sacred, we will not fail. The people failed in the days of Noah, Babel, ancient Israel, ancient America, and in the days of Jesus himself because they ignored these primary laws of righteousness and freedom.

We need to understand the God-given American purpose. We need to believe in its destiny and to serve the true interests of its people. Someone has said that he likes to think of an American citizen as a person who helps to put out the fires of disagreement between people, who picks up a bottle in the street so that someone else's tire won't be ruined. A good citizen is also one who loves God and serves his fellowmen. The greatest discovery that has ever been made is not fire nor the wheel nor the internal combustion engine nor atomic energy nor any other material thing. Man's greatest discovery is teamwork by agreement, which brings about the righteous objectives of God-fearing, patriotic men.

Patriotism is a love of country, and it is also a determination to safeguard those important benefits that God would not want to see lost in the world. Patriotism indicates a real faith in our country's future and a sincere, unselfish dedication to her best interests. Patriotism is a challenge based on the religious concept of the dignity of man. It rests on the thesis that righteousness and freedom are the greatest objectives that any age can foster.

One of the outstanding characteristics of an intelligent citizen is that he learns from the past. The past is the source of many of our greatest benefits, which were bought for us at an incredible cost. There are very few privileges or opportunities that we enjoy that are not the product of other men's labors. Every day we eat from vines that we haven't planted and drink from wells that we didn't dig. We warm ourselves by fires that we did not kindle; we are the beneficiaries of a government that we did not devise; and we are benefited by those great religious, social, and business institutions that we had no part in forming.

As we are made aware of the fact that no man lives unto himself alone, we might well resolve to pass on undiminished to our children those great blessings which we have received from our fathers. All of the past has been an investment in us, and because of it we are under obligation to accept our share of the responsibilities for the world's future. We have inherited duties as well as benefits and opportunities. It has been said that the Lord fits the back to the burden, and only as we assume a greater load do we get a stronger back.

A young soldier who had just returned from a faithful service overseas was asked where he hailed from. He said: "I was born in Philadelphia but I grew up in Viet Nam." And what a wonderful way to grow up—by carrying the responsibilities of that great nation under God that he has established to provide liberty and justice for all.

Jesus gave an important success formula when he said: ". . . by their fruits ye shall know them." (Matthew 7:20.) God has prospered our land until it has become without question the greatest nation that has ever existed upon this planet in any age. But we are not without problems. There are some very serious changes that have been taking place in the last few years. Some enemies have come among us and have sown tares among our wheat. As a consequence, some of our attitudes toward law and order have been corrupted. Many have deserted the high ideals of our fathers upon which our nation was originally established. Upon our shoulders now falls the responsibility of taking up the load, and unless we can root out the evils, we cannot avoid suffering the consequences that will fall upon many people.

We are presently mounting some devastating crime waves. We are allowing ourselves to be overrun by the influences of atheism and sin. Our enemies from without are infiltrating our ranks, and with subversion and evil they are destroying our morale and our righteousness. Satanic slogans, with the purpose of demoralizing our attitudes, are being sponsored by Communist troublemakers who are attempting to tear down the greatest establishment ever known in the world. They shout their traitorous battle cry of "Tell it as it is," meaning, tell it as their lies say it is and as their evil ambition would like it to be. They mean tell everything at its worst; tell it as the enemies of America would like to make it.

We know that God could not possibly condone Communism with its dictatorship, its anti-God, its slavery of other people, its blood purges, its deceit, its trickery, and all of the other evils that from the beginning have been so offensive to him. However, this is not fatal to us except as we are seduced by it. There is only one way that any ungodly dictators can cause our fall, and that is by our making ourselves unworthy of our promised blessings by our own ungodliness.

Our civilization is now balanced on the razor's edge of a possible destruction, just waiting to see which way we will go. But as grave as the dangers are that threaten us from without, they are minor compared to those that threaten us from within. It is not underestimating the dangers from without to say that our foreign enemies can never hurt us if all Americans remain solid in our convictions about our own righteous Americanism, as it is still true that no one can hurt us except ourselves.

We may well fear the Communists. They stand for evil and subversion. They have already demonstrated that they will not hesitate to enslave everyone over whom their evil power can be extended. If we allow ourselves to become the victims of apathy, indifference, and complacency, what hope can we have? Our greatest fear should be for those misguided Americans who have lost their patriotism and their devotion to God. Some have already put on the uniform of ugliness, rebellion, and evil. They have become strangely behaved, ludicrously dressed, irresponsible agitators, spending their time in every kind of subversion and protest demonstrations against everything that is good.

We should be afraid of those Americans who have become so hardened to all types of crime that the chief offense is no longer the criminal act itself but being found out. We should be afraid of those traitorous, so-called Americans who operate in and under the protection of our courts in helping to destroy law and order. Before it is too late we should do what we can to help all Americans to recognize and love those ancient landmarks of our heritage that in the past have been so tremendously important. We should make permanent in our lives such real American strengths as reverence for God, dignity in our work, honor among our fellowmen, and always promote and safeguard that priceless heritage of freedom. We have good reason to be afraid, for the time is growing very short. May we lose no time in making effective our own enthusiastic, whole-souled salute to America.

Self-Management

ONE OF the most important skills that everyone should strive to develop is the ability to successfully manage himself. The dictionary says that to manage is to control and direct. It is to guide, administer, conduct, and handle successfully. The dictionary gives an example of management as that of a trainer of horses putting his charges through their paces. And what a delightful sight it is to see beautiful, graceful, powerful, well-trained horses perform. However, there is something much more exciting than a well-trained horse, and that is a well-trained human being.

The most valuable of all commodities is human life, and the greatest of all development is human development. Development comes from training. A well-trained man is always more effective than an untrained man. We think of a highly trained manager or teacher as among our greatest benefactors. And our greatest possible accomplishment is to become a great human being who is well-trained in the arts of manliness, effectiveness, nobleness, and godliness.

I have great authority over my finger. If I tell it to bend, it bends; if I tell it to unbend, it unbends. When I tell my eyes to close, they close; and when I give my feet an order, they obey. Now when I can get that kind of control over my brain and my objectives and my tongue and my emotions and my ambitions, then I am well on the way toward any accomplishment.

We have great possibilities in several fields of training. There is a physical training, a mental training, a social training, an emotional training, a moral training, and a training for our spirits. We sing a song in which we say: "School thy feelings, O my brother." And good social training is a high objective. Solomon points out the value of mental training when he says, "For as [a man] thinketh in his heart, so is he. . . ." (Proverbs 23:7.) A great human brain is undoubtedly the most wonderful creation ever known in the universe. Everyone born into the world is given free of charge a brain with the most fantastic possibilities for training.

A prominent British neurophysicist recently pointed out that no one could construct an electronic computer for three billion dollars that would be the equivalent of a human brain. Even so, who could endow an electronic computer with insight, foresight, kindness, understanding, and goodwill? But so many of us waste our potential because we either let our minds go undeveloped or we develop rebellious minds, negative minds, or closed minds.

Woodrow Wilson once gave an indication of this waste when he said, "The greatest ability of the American people is their ability to resist instruction." And many of us have our full share of that unfortunate talent. Thomas A. Edison gave his own appraisal of our human neglect when he said, "There is no limit to which a man will not go to avoid thinking." The most disagreeable, unpleasant thing that many of us ever do is to try to think constructively. Mostly we say "Everybody is doing it," and so we play follow the leader with such people as alcoholics, nicotine addicts, rebels and the followers of the new morality.

The human mind can either give us the greatest pleasure, produce the most outstanding success, and develop the greatest godliness, or it can be perverted, criminalized, and Satanized according to the evil of our own self-management. The mind, heart, spirit, and personality are all like rich, fertile, well-watered fields, and our husbandmanship can make them the most productive and profitable, or they can all be made to produce a poison fruit. Unless these human fields are planted with good seeds and the plants cultivated and cared for, the ground of our lives will always bring forth noxious weeds. Our minds are like horses, and unless they are well-managed, well-disciplined, and well-trained, they will run wild. What may at first be a small mental imperfection can soon become strong enough to take over the territory. John Richard Moreland once said in his poem "Growth":

> It was such a little, little sin
> And such a great big day,
> And I thought the hours would swallow it,
> Or the wind blow it away.

> But the moments passed so swiftly,
> And the wind died out somehow,
> And the sin that was a weakling once
> Is a hungry giant now.

But how tremendous is our potential ability to manage ourselves and make ourselves productive. It is probable that the greatest gift that God has ever given to man is the ability to think and dream and imagine. In one's mind he may go backward or forward across time or space with greater facility than he could get across the street. The mind can plan and meditate and construct and enjoy.

> Mind is the master power
> That builds and molds,
> And mind is man,
> And ever more he takes the tools of thought
> And fashions what he wills,
> Bringing forth a thousand joys, a thousand ills,
> We think in secret, and it comes to pass
> Environment is but our looking glass.

The mind can put together any kind of success. It can work out all of the necessary details and supply the discipline for bringing any accomplishment about. But unless we hold a tight rein on our thinking and our activities, our minds can get us into all kinds of trouble. Many minds are guilty of alibiing, rationalizing, crooked thinking, and mental agitation based on error and false reasoning. Sometime ago J. P. McEvoy wrote an article entitled "Want to Borrow a Jack?" He said:

"One day I went to a lawyer friend for advice. 'I'm in real trouble,' I said. 'My neighbors across the road are going on vacation for a month and instead of boarding out their two dogs they are going to keep them locked up and a woman is coming to feed them—if she doesn't forget—and meanwhile they'll be lonely and bark all day and howl all night and I won't be able to sleep and I'll either have to call the SPCA to haul them away or I'll go berserk and go over there and shoot them and then when my neighbors return they'll go berserk and come over and shoot me. . . .'

"My lawyer patted back a delicate yawn. 'Let me tell you a story,' he said. 'And don't stop me if you've heard it—because it will do you good to hear it again.

" 'A fellow was speeding down a country road late at night and BANG! went a tire, he got out and looked and—drat it!—he had no jack. Then he said to himself, "Well, I'll just walk to the nearest farmhouse and borrow a jack!" He saw a light in the distance and said, "I'm in luck; the farmer's up. I'll just knock on the door and say, 'I'm in trouble, would you please lend me a jack?' And he'll say, 'Why sure, neighbor, help yourself—only bring it back.'

" 'He walked on a little farther and the light went out so he said to himself, "Now he's going to bed and he'll be annoyed because I'm bothering him—so he'll probably want some money for his jack. And I'll say, all right, it isn't very neighborly—but I'll give you a quarter. And he'll say, do you think you can get me out of bed in the middle of the night and then offer me a quarter? Give me a dollar or get yourself a jack somewhere else.'

" 'By this time the fellow had worked himself up into a lather. He turned into the gate and muttered, "A dollar! All right, I'll give you a dollar. But not a cent more! A poor devil has an accident and all he needs is a jack. But you probably won't let me have one no matter what I give you. That's the kind of guy you are."

" 'Which brought him up to the door and he knocked—angrily, and loudly. The farmer stuck his head out the window above the door and hollered down, "Who's there? What do you want?" The fellow stopped pounding on the door and yelled up, "You and your damn old jack! I don't want to have anything to do with either of you." '

"When I stopped laughing, I started thinking, and I said, 'Is that what I've been doing?' 'Right,' he said, 'and you'd be surprised how many people come to a lawyer for advice, and instead of calmly stating the facts, they start building up a big imaginary fight—what he'll say to his partner, what she'll say to her husband, or how they'll tell the Old Man off about his will. So I tell them the story about the jack and they cool off.'

"I thought, How true! Most of us go through life bumping into obstacles we could easily bypass; spoiling for a fight and lashing out in blind rages at fancied wrongs and imaginary foes. And frequently we don't even realize what we are doing."

This wonderful creation of our minds can be so used that it will work against our own best interests in many ways. If it is not properly managed, it often turns against the right, it builds up our hates, it nurtures our glooms, enlarges our discouragements, alibis, and sins. It fights against the government, tears down the establishment, and rebels against God. The mind can easily bypass success and happiness because of our indecisions, our procrastinations, our indifferences, and our ignorance. Many people are perpetual hesitators with a slothful follow-through. Some are able to convince themselves that wrong is better than right, that idleness is superior to industry, and that ugliness is more desirable than beauty, health, and cleanliness.

Our earth is made up of contrasts and opposites. When we are without the proper training and discipline, our minds themselves may become addled, mixed up, and confused. Some people become tyrants and saddle their families with all kinds of unpleasantness and shame. Some people develop weaknesses and tell themselves that it is too difficult for them to live the religion of Christ. They can easily make themselves believe that crimes, sins, weaknesses, and negative thinking are in their own interests.

But minds can also be charged with righteousness. They can be trained to understand that there are no successful criminals. There are no happy sinners. And everyone may choose for himself what he will become. William James once said, "The greatest discovery of my generation is that we can change our circumstances by changing our attitudes of mind." No one need remain as he is for even one more day. Jesus said that we should be born again. Each of us may be reborn as many times as we like, and each time we can be reborn better.

This process may be what the apostle Paul had in mind when he said: ". . . be ye transformed by the renewing of your mind." (Romans 12:2.) In addition to the renewing of our minds, we can also renew our faith and our industry and our attitudes and our success and our happiness.

In 1926, Emile Cue announced his famous system of psychotherapy based upon auto-suggestion. He taught that we could have better health, increase our general well-being, and make improvement in every way by saying and thinking and living the ideas embodied in the phrase, "Every day in every way I am getting better and better." By our own effective self-management our foreheads can get broader, and our hearts can get bigger, and our emotions can become more intense, and our success can be increased, and our love of God and good can be given more power. And to develop one of the greatest advantages for our lives, we need to learn how to effectively manage ourselves.

Social Services

ONE OF the important activities of our world is its social services. This is something in which all of us have a personal as well as a general interest. The dictionary describes social services as any activity designed to promote social welfare. It refers to specifically organized philanthropic programs for giving assistance to the sick, the destitute, the unfortunate, or any group of people who are below, or who are likely to get below, the community standards of well being.

These groups include the poor, the neglected, the maladjusted, and the abnormal. The field of social services covers the entire area of physical, financial, mental, spiritual, moral, and social problems. We think of prostitution as a social problem. We refer to the venereal diseases as social diseases. When we speak of social hygiene, we have in mind the prevention of those sicknesses that are socially communicated.

Our social problems are those human problems that affect the community. Many business problems, family problems, and personal problems may become social problems. There are a great many organizations and groups engaged in social service, including governments, churches, clubs, hospitals, penal institutions, and such groups as Alcoholics Anonymous, and all are social service organizations to some extent.

Every morning I walk by three large, home-type buildings filled with groups of men who are trying to get away from the afflictions of that traditional demon called alcohol. In an attempt to help, there are also large groups of people who are presently spending vast amounts of money and a great deal of their time trying to rehabilitate dope addicts, those who have nervous troubles and criminal inclinations, as well as those with mental, spiritual, and moral weaknesses.

We have a continuing problem with unwed mothers, irresponsible fathers, child neglect, and many other kinds of sins that leave people scarred for life with feelings of emotional imbalance and guilt. Like alcoholism, dope addiction, immorality, and feelings of deep-seated inferiority are diseases that we largely bring upon ourselves. However, in spite of the great number of people engaged in social services, we are still losing ground at a tremendous rate. There are many people who actually spend their lives dragging other people down, and they are helping to produce those problems that afflict our entire community. We have many new sources of problems, and some of them center in that vast modern breed of hippie-type individuals who foster sexual promiscuity and other kinds of moral and intellectual irresponsibility that are probably far more damaging to human lives than all of the moral problems of the past put together.

Individual sins, like individual apples that are spoiling by themselves, are bad enough, but a rotten apple in a barrel, or an immoral person in a group, has a much more destructive power. The new development of communal nests where human beings foster social disease, moral decay, and physical filth in bunches gives an effectiveness in spreading problems that probably surpass in trouble-making ability anything that our world has ever previously known.

It might be difficult for anyone to imagine what our world may soon be like if we continue to go downhill at our present rate. Certainly the most serious problems of our world are not its food supply or its populations explosions or any shortages in scientific progress or military power. Our biggest problem is our inability to solve our social, spiritual, and moral difficulties.

Sometime ago a great businessman gave his accomplishment formula, which applies particularly to social success. He said that when contemplating any achievement, one of the first steps to be taken was to definitely decide on those things that just must not be done under any circumstances. That is, if one is going into a business, there are certain dishonest policies and improper practices that must never be engaged in if the business is to succeed.

If one is planning a happy marriage, there are certain things that must be ruled out of bounds. The best example of this technique was demonstrated by the Lord himself when he began his project to make the ancient country of Israel into the greatest nation in the world. The Lord sent Moses into Egypt to liberate the people from their bondage and to bring them up to meet God at Mount Sinai to there decide on arrangements for their national greatness and to make the necessary mutual covenants.

Three months after their liberation they were encamped before the Mount and God came down onto the top of the Mount and gave them their law. In giving them the Ten Commandments, he enumerated some of those things that they just must not do under any circumstances, for even God couldn't make a great nation out of a group of atheists, murderers, thieves, liars, profanity users, and violaters of the Sabbath day. In getting into their minds the things that they must not do, the Lord said:

1. Thou shalt have no other gods before me.
2. Thou shalt not make unto thee any graven image.
3. Thou shalt not take the name of the Lord thy God in vain.
4. Remember the sabbath day to keep it holy.
5. Honour thy father and thy mother.
6. Thou shalt not kill.
7. Thou shalt not commit adultery.
8. Thou shalt not steal.
9. Thou shalt not bear false witness.
10. Thou shalt not covet. (See Exodus 20:3-17.)

These sixty-seven words probably make up the greatest statement of social services ever made in the world. If all members of our society would definitely make up their minds not to do these things, then we would have all of our time and enthusiasm to devote to those things that we should do.

Joseph Malius once wrote some lines indicating two different kinds of social services. The one centered in prevention and the other in cure. He entitled this poem "A Fence—An Ambulance":

'Twas a dangerous cliff, as they freely confessed,
Though to walk near its crest was so pleasant.
But over its terrible edge there had slipped,
A duke and full many a peasant.

So the people said something would have to be done
But their projects did not all tally.
Some said, "Put a fence round the edge of the cliff,"
Some, "An ambulance down in the valley."

But the cry for the ambulance carried the day,
For it spread through the neighboring city.
A fence may be useful or not, it is true,
But each heart became brimful of pity,

For those who slipped over that dangerous cliff
And the dwellers in highway and alley
Gave pounds or gave pence, not to put up a fence
But an ambulance down in the valley.

"For the cliff is all right if you're careful," they said,
"And if folks even slip or are dropping,
It isn't the slipping that hurts them so much,
As the shock down below when they're stopping."

So day after day, as these mishaps occurred,
Quick forth would their rescuers sally,
To pick up the victims who fell off the cliff
With their ambulance down in the valley.

Then an old sage remarked, "It's a marvel to me
That people give far more attention
To repairing results than to stopping the cause
When they'd much better aim at prevention.

"Let us stop at its source all the mischief," he cried.
"Come neighbors and friends let us rally.
If the cliff we will fence, we might almost dispense
With the ambulance down in the valley."

"Oh, he's a fanatic," the others rejoined,
"Dispense with the ambulance? Never.
He'd dispense with all charities too, if he could,
No, no we'll support them forever."

"Aren't we picking up folks just as fast as they fall
And shall this man dictate to us? Shall he?
Why should people of sense stop to put up a fence
While the ambulance works down in the valley?"

But a sensible few who are practical too,
Will not bear with such nonsense much longer.
They believe that prevention is better than cure,
And their party will still be the stronger.

Encourage them then with your purse, voice and pen,
And while other philanthropists dally
They will scorn all pretense and put up a fence
On the cliff that hangs over the valley.

Better guide well the young than reclaim them when old,
For the voice of true wisdom is calling.
To rescue the fallen is good but 'tis best
To prevent other people from falling.

Better close up the source of temptation and crime,
Than deliver from dungeon and galley.
Better put a strong fence round the top of the cliff
Than an ambulance down in the valley.

Even since this poem was written our situation has so drastically worsened that we are seriously overworking many ambulances. It has always been a fairly simple matter to put some criminal in jail in the public interest or to feed a few hoboes or close up an offending house of prostitution. But what do you do when a large crowd of hippies almost takes over a whole community? Or what can you do with those thousands of marchers whose loyalty and reason are seriously distorted?

It is interesting that the Lord looked forward to our day and made a rather uncomplimentary comparison for us when he said, ". . . as the days of Noe were, so shall also the coming of the Son of man be." (Matthew 24:37.) The social problems of Noah's day were so severe that they could only be solved by sending a universal flood. If our age gets much worse, some comparable methods may have to be used on us. Certainly prevention is far superior to any known cure either in handling our social or our individual problems.

There is an interesting old proverb that says that God always sends the remedy before the plague. The Savior of the world provided a cure even before the problems arose. In fact, the religion of Jesus constitutes a great social gospel. The teachings of the holy scriptures have the best possible answers to all of the problems of sin, crime, weakness, and delinquency. The scriptures are very clear on declaring the infinite worth of the human personality. Jesus said: ". . . what shall it profit a man if he shall gain the whole world, and lose his own soul? Or what shall a man give in exchange for his soul?" (Luke 8:36-37.) We might ask what indeed. This great social gospel teaches the Fatherhood of God and the brotherhood of man. It holds love up before us as the greatest redemptive force in the world. Love is also the finest method of procedure.

When the Son of God established his church upon the earth, he intended that every single person should belong to it and should live by its principles. Even as Jesus stood above the Mount of Olives as he was about to ascend into heaven, he represented a great way of life when he said to members of the

Twelve at his feet: "Go ye therefore, and teach all nations, baptizing them in the name of the Father, and of the Son, and of the Holy Ghost: Teaching them to observe all things whatsoever I have commanded you: and, lo, I am with you alway, even unto the end of the world." (Matthew 28:19-20.)

Again he said: "He that believeth and is baptized shall be saved; but he that believeth not shall be damned." (Mark 16:16.)

The church and its doctrines were not just for a few. They were for everyone and should be lived with an intensity that would permit no vacillation or exception.

As Charles Kingsley once said, "What I want is not to possess religion but to have a religion that shall possess me." The greatest need in the world is still and always for every individual to make a full and complete return to the religion of Christ. That would solve all of our social problems for the here and also for the hereafter.

So Little Time—So Much to Do

THE MOST important power that anyone ever acquires in this world is a righteous control over his own life. Solomon said: "He that is slow to anger is better than the mighty; and he that ruleth his spirit than he that taketh a city." (Proverbs 16:32.) And Socrates added: "He who would move the world must first move himself." How one uses his power over himself determines his every success, his every happiness, his physical comfort, his peace of mind, the future welfare of his family, and the riches that his own eternal life will include.

It has been pointed out that in order to make the best and the most of one's own life one needs to be: well bred, well fed, well read, well led, well wed.

It is also helpful if his ideas are well said. The final evidence of his success comes only when the final curtain has come down, and he is well dead. But in the meantime everyone needs a good supply of physical health, mental health, spiritual health, moral health, and social health.

We need to be able to visualize our opportunities, analyze our problems, supervise our efforts, energize our industry, and spiritualize our objectives. But more than almost any other thing, we need a greater sense of urgency about life. We need to be able to wind up our enthusiasm and raise the level of our righteous activity. It is important that we have some inspiring experiences reminding us of the shortness of life so that we will be impelled to make the most of it while it lasts.

I happen to be a member of that part of our national population who are politely called senior citizens. We are those members of the human race who are over age sixty-five, which is the generally accepted age for occupational retirement. Age sixty-five is an imaginary line that is drawn across the path of every individual, making the subtle suggestion that his working life may be about over. At least it is time for him to begin that tapering off period leading to complete inactivity. It also suggests that he should now surrender his occupational place so that his share of the world's load of work and responsibility may be carried on younger and safer shoulders.

This important transition presents many problems for many people on both sides of the retirement line. Sometimes senior citizens themselves find that they are not prepared for retirement. They may be unprepared financially, socially, and spiritually. They may also be lacking in that sense of fulfillment and satisfaction that should come at the end of every fully lived life. To indicate the shortness of these sixty-five years, someone has pointed out that six of them are spent in childhood; another twenty are spent in getting an education; then of the thirty-nine remaining, one-third are spent in bed.

Because we only work five days per week, eleven more full years are subtracted from our working lifetime for Saturdays and Sundays. A lot of additional life is lost because of sickness, vacations, and holidays. We use up more of our time in eating and going to and from work. Then if we add the time that is wasted and eaten up by our sins, we don't have very much left. Just as we begin finding out how to live, we find that it is time to die. If anyone will work out the arithmetic to find the shortness of his own life, he will probably be shocked into a sense of urgency, as this short allotment is all he has in which to learn to support himself, educate his family, and build a foundation capable of bearing the burden of eternity.

Liquor and tobacco may cut down the length of life; ignorance may reduce its breadth and interest; sin may diminish the depth and intensity of life; and lethargy and sloth may thwart its purpose. But even at best we haven't much time. Reading has always been very pleasant to me, and because I have spent a good deal of time in the last few years on airplanes, I have looked forward to my flying time as a period when I could settle back and lose myself for a few hours in the comfortable enjoyment of some good book that I had been longing to read without any interruption from telephones or personal callers.

But because of some of the incidents of my advancing years, my reading ability has recently been greatly restricted, and I have had a few problems trying to find other ways to profitably occupy myself while flying. Sleeping, or looking out the window, or talking to my neighbors, or even thinking, have not always proven to be very good substitutes. I have thought how wasteful we sometimes are of this precious, available combination of great literature, vision, and time. I have never discovered anyone who had eyes to rent so that I might still discover some of the many interesting, helpful things that are hidden within the covers of books.

Without eyes, some people get very lonesome for the great scriptures and other great pieces of literature or even the printed news of the world. Many people never think in advance of the other doors that will be closed in our faces as we get older or the other of life's privileges that will be withdrawn as time advances. Finally, all of us must eventually come up against that stop sign that is marked with the words *The End.*

One of our greatest regrets may sometime be the benefits of life that we have missed because our time has been cut off by advancing years. Recently I talked with a comparatively young woman who has been made almost totally incapacitated by muscular dystrophy. She has four children who are also completely helpless because they have inherited her disease. Her husband deserted her on the grounds that he did not want to be married to a cripple. She has been told that she cannot live more than one more year. At one time she had visions of being with her children as long as they needed her to lead them from a helpless babyhood to a strong, self-reliant adulthood. But now her own strength has vanished, and time itself will soon run out for her.

She has no money, no influence, no friends, and no hope. Her overwhelming desire to build the proper character qualities into her children and to see that they know how to earn a living will both be denied her. And although her children are hopeless cripples, they are rebelling against her, against life, and against God. Their bitterness against life provides for a further reduction in the possibilities for any feelings of fulfillment in them.

Every day some additional people are cut off from life and from accomplishment by such things as muscular dystrophy, cancer, accidents, and heart disease. But an even greater number are being cut off by negative attitudes, bad habits, and sins. It seems very unfortunate that many young people think that they can solve their problems by tearing down the establishment, destroying the government, and ignoring the finest conventions that our society has been capable of building up. But in the process, they

also waste their own precious time. It does not seem to help anyone very much when they dress themselves in unconventional
clothing and congregate for a joint venture in such wrong things
as dope addiction, draft card burning, placard carrying, and
senseless marches. It doesn't seem to help to solve our problems
when people put on the ugly uniform of hippieism, and rebel
against wholesome, necessary, self-supporting, useful work.

As I go about a little bit, I wish that I could do something
for these thousands of misguided young folks by suggesting that
whether or not they are successful in breaking down the establishment, and no matter how dirty they are or how immoral they
become, they cannot stop their own calendars, which are always
recording a daily advance of their own years. Sometime their
eyes will begin to fail, and their hearts will get weak, and some
of the lessons that life has been trying to teach them will have
been missed because of their preoccupation with less important
things. Life at best passes rapidly, but our vices bring us to our
end much more quickly.

The other day a young mother was seeking a divorce from a
husband who spent much of his time in such things as Sunday
motorcycle races and doing other questionable and improper
things on the other days. I thought how bitter may be the regret
of those who, because of their sins, have broken up their homes
and helped to wreck the lives of their own children. This particular father and husband has the physical body of a man, yet in
some ways it seems that he has not matured beyond the spoiled
child stage. He has a wonderful wife and three fine children,
but he claims that he doesn't like his eleven-year-old son because
he thinks that this son is not as alert mentally as the other children. Instead of giving this son the extra amount of love and help
that is necessary, the father is actually doing more to agitate this
condition than to cure it, as he is continually criticizing him and
calling him unpleasant names.

When this fine little boy was seven years old his teacher
found him quietly sobbing in school. She inquired as to the cause
of his tears, and between his sobs and through his tears, he halt-
ingly said, "My daddy doesn't love me." Under these circumstances there isn't much chance that this little child is going to
do very well. Even if this man were living at his possible best, he
would scarcely have time to develop sufficient love in his heart to
solve the problems of his children and properly expand the soul

of his wife by his love, devotion, and care. How pitiful that he uses the few brief years that are granted him to break down the life of this little boy by his cowardly inhuman treatment of his own flesh and blood. What punishment could be severe enough for a mature adult who would deliberately destroy the soul of his own child?

So many of us spend too much of our lives in unproductive things and not nearly enough in the serious business of living and helping our children to live and mature. Many of us are working at cross purposes to good and are staging some rebellions against our wives, children, and our own eternal futures. We are also rebelling against reason, religion, education, and useful work.

Sometimes by these processes we inflict upon ourselves the terrible consequences of some distorting personality diseases. How awful are the mental and moral afflictions that some poor, misguided young people may pass around among themselves by an actual contamination of each other. It is helpful to remember that sins are contagious, and the results of our sins manifest themselves in us. Recently I talked with a young man whose long idleness was showing itself in his emaciated, sunken-chested body. His immorality, caffeine addiction, alcoholism, and nicotine-ism had all left their awful marks upon him.

When one rebels against study, it is not long before it will show itself in his form and features. When Lucifer rebelled against God, he began looking and acting like the devil. But even for the rebellious, their time will also finally run out, and the end of all rebellion is hell. The end of all evil is also hell. Satan is the most expert in rebellion. He is also the most effective evil-doer, and hell is the place where Satan must forever be confined. Rebels are presently having a heyday, but what will they do when they run out of people to rebel against and when there is no more time left for them to vent their antagonism? People in America are allowed to rebel against their country, but those under Communist rule don't rebel against the Communists because the Communists would not permit it. It might not be as pleasant for a rebel to try to start a rebellion while locked up in hell with Satan. How would one go about rebelling against the father of lies and the father of force and the father of slavery?

The time may come when even under the program of the God of freedom, there will be no time left for rebellion and sin. A great prophet once said:

"But wo unto him that has the law given, yea, that has all the commandments of God, like unto us, and that transgresseth them, and that wasteth the days of his probation, for awful is his state!

"And, in fine, wo unto all those who die in their sins; for they shall return to God, and behold his face, and remain in their sins." (2 Nephi 9:27, 38.)

Then the great scripture will be fulfilled which says: "He that is unjust, let him be unjust still: and he which is filthy, let him be filthy still: and he that is righteous, let him be righteous still: and he that is holy, let him be holy still." (Revelation 22:11.)

To develop a greater sense of urgency about life so that we may make the most of our opportunities is probably our finest challenge.

Soul Power

THE MOST interesting as well as the most important thing in the world is a great human being, and the thing that we actually know less about than about any other thing is ourselves. If someone asks us questions about science, inventions, history, or politics, we may be able to answer them. But if they should ask us to sit down and .write out an analysis of ourselves and describe our mind and soul qualities, we might not give them very good answers, or if someone asks us about where we came from or what the purpose of our life is, or if they ask us to describe our eternal destiny, we may stand silent and uncomprehending before them. Yet the two most necessary things to know about ourselves is where we are going and how we are going to get there.

We learn something about ourselves from the two scriptural accounts given of our own creation. The first chapter in Genesis tells of our spiritual creation, which took place in heaven and about which it is said, "So God created man in his own image, in the image of God created he him; male and female created he them." (Genesis 1:27.) But no one had yet been placed upon the earth to carry on its work. Then in the second chapter of Genesis we are told about our important bodily creation, in which it is said, "And the Lord God formed man of the dust of the ground, and breathed into his nostrils the breath of life; and man became a living soul." (Genesis 2:7.)

We are all aware of that interesting quality that exists in ourselves. Certainly it is evident when we look upon the dead as we stand at the bier of a loved one that the one we loved is not in the casket and that we are merely looking upon the tenement in which the spirit lodged. The body and the spirit were temporarily joined together at birth, and they are temporarily separated at death. The process of death has been described by the writer of Ecclesiastes, who says: "Then shall the dust return to the earth as it was: and the spirit shall return unto God who gave it." (Ecclesiastes 12:7.)

Following death there is a period of varying length during

which time the body and the spirit are separated so that they can most effectively be prepared for that great event of their own resurrection. At the resurrection their bodies and spirits are inseparably joined together. A great modern scripture calls our attention to this important event when the Lord says, "And the spirit and the body are the soul of man. And the resurrection from the dead is the redemption of the soul." (D&C 88:15-16.) The prophet Alma also comments on this important fact when he says, "The soul shall be restored to the body, and the body to the soul; yea, and every limb and joint shall be restored to its body; yea, even a hair of the head shall not be lost; but all things shall be restored to their proper and perfect frame." (Alma 40:23.)

The scriptures frequently use these terms *spirit* and *soul* interchangeably, and yet in the interests of our own understanding we might make some distinctions between them. Before we were born, we existed as spirits. We had antemortal bodies made of a substance much finer than that making up our mortal bodies. The spirit has many abilities that our flesh does not have. It has much greater power than do our bodies alone. At birth we are added upon with these beautiful, wonderful bodies of flesh and bones without which we could never have a fulness of joy either here or hereafter. Then our cleansed spirits and refined bodies are inseparably joined together, and we begin that happy period of eternal progression and increase. If in this life we qualify for a celestial designation, we will then be able to resurrect a celestial body, and our immortal souls will belong to that exalted order of which God himself is a member. But whether we speak of spirit or the soul, we are speaking of that entity or substance or essence that is the animating, activating part of our lives. This is where our greatest powers are developed. The spirit is the vehicle of our individual existence which, until the time of the resurrection, may exist either in connection with or separate from the body, and it determines our welfare. The soul is that magnificent finished product of life which is life as God knows it. And it is by the power of our spirits that we are perfected.

The spirit is that rational thinking, reasoning, deciding, willing part of us. It is the source of our strength and success and the power by which our flesh is trained and perfected. In its resurrected, immortalized state, our soul will have far greater influence and power than our spirits did or than our spirit and body did during our mortality. Even that great creation called our brain cannot function in the absence of spirit. The soul also controls our moral and emotional natures. Soul is more than intellect; it is the seat of all real life, vitality, and action. The spirit can live and act without the body, but the body cannot live or act without the spirit. The fruits of the spirit are courage, fervor, and the power to accomplish.

On several occasions, the Lord has discussed the development and use of soul power. This is an ability to coordinate all of our strengths of mind, body, and spirit into one cooperative, unified effort. In the fourth section of the Doctrine and Covenants, the Lord said, "Therefore, O ye that embark in the service of God, see that ye serve him with all your heart, might, mind and strength, that ye may stand blameless before God at the last day." (D&C 4:2.) To carry out this command involves a joint action of the heart, the mind, the might, and the physical strength.

To serve God with all our hearts means that our love and our devotion should be genuine and whole-hearted. To serve him with all of our might is to employ to the utmost our determination and our will power. It does not mean to walk the irregular pathway of vacillation and procrastination. To serve God with all of our mind requires a clear understanding, a strong positive mental attitude. It means study, meditation, and the ability to make firm positive decisions on each of the questions of life. To serve him with all of our strength requires vigorous persistence and continuous physical activity.

By this process of consolidation and joint action, one may concentrate all of the elements of personal effectiveness into one united powerful effort. We thereby achieve a centrality in our purpose. Our effort becomes not only highly concentrated but accurately directed. Psychologically speaking, a person whose life is characterized by this united effort is all in one piece rather than resembling a bundle of many directioned and conflicting impulses held loosely together by circumstance. Such a consolidated personality is capable of the maximum of efficiency and accomplishment.

Someone has said that the soul is a synonym for God, but it is more than that. As the children of God we are all actually gods in the making, and we sometimes refer to the vital energy of this inner man by saying that he is the soul of honor, or the soul of righteousness. It is interesting that during this life, no one ever sees this magnificent creation which is his own spirit. In some ways our spirits are like the proverbial iceberg that for the most part keeps itself hidden and out of sight. Yet like the iceberg, the unseen part of us is the most important part. It is also the most valuable of all other things in the universe. The whole purpose of our preexistence as well as our mortality is to develop and save our souls.

Sometimes we lessen our chances for success by allowing ourselves to be afflicted with certain soul sicknesses. The worst enemies of the soul come upon us in the form of those moral poisons of atheism and weakness. All sin tends to kill the spirit of success and happiness and thereby to destroy our eternal prospects. To keep ourselves at our best, we need to occasionally work ourselves over with the scrubbing brush of repentance. Only in righteousness are we able to develop enough power to bring about those great eternal blessings which make up our natural destiny.

When Columbus arrived in America, the Indians told him about an herb that was supposed to be growing here that could take away fatigue, but this herb is one that grows in the soul. There are also other herbs that can be made to grow in us that can produce faith and energy and love and power. These are the herbs of our own enthusiasm for life and the effort we are willing to make in our own interests. That is, when we are ahead of our job, we love it. When our job gets ahead of us, we hate it. No one ever gets tired while he is winning. No one ever quits while he is ahead, and everyone likes to do that which he does superbly well. The spirit of success can make the body strong, and almost all strength is the strength of the spirit.

The poet was speaking of soul power when he wrote "The Champion." He said:

> The average runner sprints
> Until the breath in him is gone,
> But the champion has the iron will
> That makes him carry on.
>
> For rest the average runner begs
> When limp his muscles grow,
> But the champion runs on leaden legs—
> His spirit makes them go.

The average man's complacent
When he's done his best to score,
But the champion does his best
And then he does a little more.

In 1923, there sat in a prison cell in Germany a young man by the name of Adolf Hitler. He was writing in his book *Mein Kampf* his plan to make Germany the greatest nation on earth. The fact that starting out single-handed he almost upset the world indicates that he had something. How did he do it? The answer is in his book. He said: "The question of Germany regaining her power is not how to manufacture or distribute arms but how to produce in people that will to win, that spirit of determination which produces a thousand different methods, each of which ends with arms." That is, we don't win wars with tanks or guns or airplanes or oil; we win wars with that spirit of determination inside of people, and that is how we save our souls. That is also how we do every other worthwhile thing in the world. By the development of our soul power we can turn every evil into a good. We can build up our weaknesses until they become our strengths. We can build courage and righteousness into our lives in the greatest dimensions. We can build up the kingdom and please God. We can worship with Mary as we say: "My soul doth magnify the Lord. And my spirit has rejoiced in God my Saviour." (Luke 1:46-47.)

We may not only become living souls; we may also become faithful souls and happy souls and productive souls. The soul of the righteous produces godliness and righteousness and success. We need to feed our souls on some new success every day. We should have something to do that we can get excited about. The greatest objective of life is to develop the kind of soul power that will give it eternal life. Isaiah said: ". . . hear, and your soul shall live." (Isaiah 55:3.) God said: "For my soul delighteth in the song of the heart; yea, the song of the righteous is a prayer unto me, and it shall be answered with a blessing upon their heads." (D&C 25:12.)

For many years Grantland Rice was the dean of American sports writers. Most of his life he followed the great champions of sport. He tried to identify those important traits that made athletic champions. Then during his life he wrote some seven hundred poems about those qualities that gave power to such great sports figures as Red Grange, George Gipp, Jim Thorpe,

Babe Ruth, and Jack Dempsey. One of these poems is entitled "Courage," in which Mr. Rice says:

> I'd like to think that I can look at death and smile and say
> All I have left now is my final breath; take that away,
> And you must either leave me dust or dreams or in far flight,
> The soul that wanders where the stardust streams through
>   endless night.

> I'd rather think that I can look at life with this to say:
> Send what you will of struggle or of strife, blue skies or gray,
> I'll stand against the final charge of hate by peak and pit
> And nothing in the steelclad fist of fate can make me quit.

It is our minds and spirits that make our bodies rich. We are moral beings, and the great driving forces of the world are not only intellectual but spiritual and emotional. When our minds are aroused and our souls are set on fire, we develop the kind of soul power that may bring about the greatest accomplishments of our eternal lives.

Stored-up Gladness

O NE OF the great stories of the world is the Bible story of Joseph, the son of Jacob. When Joseph was seventeen years of age he was sold by his jealous brothers for twenty pieces of silver to a wandering band of Ishmaelites going down into Egypt. In Egypt, Joseph arose to great fame and power. One of the main events of his life was Pharaoh's dream in which Joseph learned that the next seven years would be years of plenty when the land of Egypt would yield abundant harvests. This seven years of plenty would be immediately followed by seven years of famine. In order to favorably meet this situation, Joseph built great granaries in which he stored away 20 percent of all of the corn grown in Egypt during the seven years of plenty.

When the famine began, Joseph opened the granaries. Thus, with one good idea, two nations were saved from starvation. However, this idea of storing up food for the future always has been and probably always will be one of our greatest ideas. To begin with, in one way or another these alternating periods of feast and famine continue to come with some regularity as an important part of life.

In the year 1800 the French Government offered a prize to anyone who could discover a way to preserve food so that it could be carried over beyond the season in which it was produced. Without sufficient variety, many sailors died from scurvy and other diseases caused by deficiencies in their diet. Malnutrition also took a heavy toll both in the military forces and among the civilians.

The prize was won by a Frenchman by the name of Nicholas Appert. Stimulated by the government's offered prize, he went to work on the problem. Finally he discovered a way to preserve fruits, vegetables, and other foods by putting them in glass bottles, heating them to the boiling point, and then hermetically sealing the containers.

The French press, in praising the winner, said: "M. Appert has discovered the art of fixing the seasons. With him spring, summer, and autumn exist in bottles like delicate plants that are protected by the gardener under a dome of glass against the intemperate seasons." From this small beginning has grown the great modern canning industry. American can manufacturers alone turn out in excess of twelve billion cans each year, to say nothing of the bottles and freezing used to preserve foods. For many years The Church of Jesus Christ of Latter-day Saints has advised its members to always have on hand a year's supply of food to enable us to tide ourselves over those emergencies that may arise unexpectedly.

This interesting and productive possibility of storing up food for the future is an idea of God himself. That is, it was the Creator who put a hoarding instinct into the squirrel so that each fall he is stimulated to hide away enough acorns to provide for his food needs for the winter. God also put some other kinds of storing abilities into some of his creatures. For example, the bear lays up an extra supply of his own fat in the summer to provide him with the necessary heat, energy, and life during the period of his long winter's hibernation. However, the most important example of this ability to store things for the future is found in man himself. Man is by far God's greatest creation, and this ability in man has been given many different facets.

We can store up energy in our bodies so that when our stomachs are empty, our physical and mental operations can continue to run for a long period out of our reserves or on a very limited supply. Provision was also made for a mental, emotional, and financial storage. One reason that human beings go to college is to store up enough learning in four years to enable them to provide for a lifetime of occupational needs.

We also have another ability in our society, which is, to store up wealth. Many centuries ago the Phoenicians invented money, which we use to represent wealth. Money serves us as a medium of exchange. This makes it unnecessary for us to live too close to our food supply. Money is preserved industry. It is labor made negotiable. It is our most effective barter system. Money is materialized ambition, and because we can carry our labor over from one period to another, we can benefit from our labor even when it is not available.

The great business organizations have made several uses out of this storing idea. On a very large scale they store up money for the future to serve many needs. They not only carry large business reserves, but they also put away a part of one's individual wages to help him bypass the non-income periods of vacations, unemployment, and disability. Inasmuch as a famine frequently comes every day in the year beyond age sixty-five, some employers store up wages during the earning years to enable employees to enjoy an adequate income when the famine of retirement sets in.

This is a kind of supplement to that natural instinct for self-preservation that God put in each of his children. That is, each of us has a natural fear of the proverbial rainy day, and therefore we have built up a strong hoarding instinct in order to provide for it. This vigorous inclination to save has built up the great insurance companies and other saving institutions that teach us to save while the good financial weather lasts.

Some of the most common commodities that we save are food, clothing, shelter, and fuel. But money also has a great value because it is the recognized medium of exchange. It is also very convenient, and it does not deteriorate. Frequently it actually increases because of its ability to earn interest while we are waiting for the famine to arrive. This common medium of exchange makes it possible for our labor, our planning, and our foresight to be given a kind of economic immortality. Therefore, we may enjoy the benefits from our labor even after the energy itself has been exhausted.

But we also have been endowed with other abilities for storing up things for the future. For example, God has provided us with some large mental, emotional, and spiritual storage reservoirs in which we may impound spiritual strength, faith, enthusiasm, success, and happiness for future use.

Sometime ago I read of a man and his wife who spent a wonderful vacation in Hawaii. They had a delightful time admiring the beautiful scenery, listening to the music, eating the food, enjoying the climate, and visiting with the friendly people. They went bathing in the ocean and spent many hours lying on the beach absorbing the warm, healing sunshine, and listening to the delightful sound of waves washing upon the shores. But when this couple came home, they brought the islands, the ocean, and the beauty back with them in their memories. Then whenever they wanted to rerun their vacation and refeel their pleasure, they could just lean back in their easy chairs, close their eyes, hold each other by the hand, and relive their memories.

James Russell Lowell describes this same technique as he tells the story of Sir Launfal's life-long search for the Holy Grail. This great knight was a very wealthy man, and one beautiful June day he left his castle and money to spend his life searching for the Holy Grail. This was the cup out of which the Savior was supposed to have drunk at the Last Supper. Years later, after a fruitless search and when he was old and poor with threadbare clothing, he returned in the middle of a hard, cold winter to the area of the palace that had once been his home. As he huddled alone trying to keep himself warm, he thought about his past. Mr. Lowell says:

> Sir Launfal's raiment thin and spare
> Was idle mail 'gainst the barbed air,
> For it was just at the Christmas time,
> So he mused, as he sat, of a summer clime,
> And sought for some shelter from cold and snow
> In the light and warmth of long ago. . . .

Sir Launfal had stored up in his heart many pleasant memories of long-ago comforts that had stayed with him all of these years and now could be utilized to help to keep him warm.

In some ways we have the same ability as a tree that grows in the forest. It stores up the warmth of the sun for a hundred summers before being cut down to provide a happy family with a yule log. Then, as it is burned in the Christmas fire, it releases to the yuletide worshipers the warmth and sunshine which required a hundred years to accumulate.

James M. Barrie once said God gave us memories that we might have roses in December. But we may also enjoy many other things that we have stored up in advance. Isn't it interesting that all habits, all happiness, and all character qualities are accumulative? Rome was not built in a day, and neither are we. But each day we may stamp our minds with the finest ideals, the greatest enthusiasms for life, the most patriotic loyalty to the government, and the most fervent devotion to God. Then when any problems arise, or when our spirits need extra power, or when icy winter winds tend to chill our faith, we may call upon our reserves of strength to carry us through the storm. The prophet Job had stored up so much faith in God that when he had the shock of losing everything he said of his Creator, "Though he slay me, yet will I trust in him." (Job 13:15.) Nathan Hale had laid away a large reserve of patriotism, and while he was waiting to be hanged as a spy by his country's enemies, he said, "I only regret that I have but one life to lose for my country."

Many powerful decisions and stimulating emotions can be stored up to be used when needed at some later date. We have also learned how to bottle and preserve gladness. Someone wrote a poem in which he said:

> There was a dachshund, one so long
> He hadn't any notion
> How long it took to notify
> His tail of his emotion.
> And so it happened while his eyes
> Were filled with woe and sadness,
> His little tail went wagging on
> Because of previous gladness.

This idea of storing up gladness is a great one. We can acquire an unlimited amount of previous gladness to be rerun, revitalized, and relived and to last us through a lifetime of problems and needs. Great righteousness can also be stored up and hermetically sealed in. Every day that we love God and do our duty, we put a little extra fat on our spiritual bones to increase that reserve of strength and power which gladdens our immortal souls. We sing a song about some accumulations in which we say:

> There's sunshine in my soul today,
> More glorious and bright
> Than glows in any earthly sky,
> For Jesus is my light.

> There's music in my soul today,
> A carol to my King,
> And Jesus listening can hear
> The songs I cannot sing.

> There's springtime in my soul today,
> For when the Lord is near,
> The dove of peace sings in my heart,
> The flowers of grace appear.

> There's gladness in my soul today,
> And hope and praise and love,
> For blessings which he gives me now,
> For joys "laid up" above.

> Oh, there's sunshine, blessed sunshine
> When the peaceful, happy moments roll,
> When Jesus shows his smiling face,
> There is sunshine in the soul.

It is very important for us to understand that love and all other good things are accumulative. Companions in marriage who have been faithful and true to each other usually have very few misunderstandings. But if a problem should arise, it is quickly absorbed by that great reserve of love that has been accumulated in earlier years. Those marriage companions who have had many happy experiences together have built up a substantial balance of love that goes on increasing. This kind of situation might be compared to a large bank account yielding an interest income large enough to pay all of the bills so that the principal goes on increasing every year.

However, if one neglects this principle of building up a reserve and begins to withdraw from his capital account, he may seriously reduce his capital balance. It is those who skate on thin ice who most frequently break through to bring about disaster. Those who run their lives on deficit financing keep their love, happiness, and goodwill in a continual state of bankruptcy. The superior way to live is to store up gladness and all other good things in advance.

The Success Scrolls

THE OTHER day as I was riding down the highway, I passed an old abandoned fruit orchard where most of the trees were totally dead. Their bare, ugly, dry limbs looked like skeletons standing up against the sky. But over on the fence-line where there was water, the trees were still alive and green. About 10 percent of the trees there were neither one thing nor the other. They were live trees that were largely dead. Out of a possible five main trunk branches, it might be that just one had a few green leaves. All of the others had long since passed away. And I imagined that that might be about the way that we sometimes appear to God as he rides down the highway of our lives.

Someone once wrote a provocative book for us on this subject entitled *How to Stay Alive the Rest of Your Life.* That is one of the greatest do-it-yourself projects in the world, and all of the programs of Deity are designed to help us in this accomplishment. Jesus announced the purpose of his own mission by saying, "I am come that they might have life, and that they might have it more abundantly." (John 10:10.)

To help us attain this abundance for both here and hereafter is the purpose of the Church. It is the purpose of our lives. That is also one of the primary purposes of our occupations. In our own day, the Lord has said: "Wherefore, verily I say unto you that all things unto me are spiritual, and not at any time have I given unto you a law which was temporal; neither any man, nor the children of men; neither Adam, your father, whom I created." (D&C 29:34.) To build effectiveness into our lives through our work becomes one of our greatest opportunities and our most demanding responsibility, as well as one of our most important blessing possibilities.

Recently I read a helpful little book on this subject written by Og Mandino. It recounts an interesting legend of some two thousand years ago about a young camel boy by the name of Hafid who served in one of the important trade caravans of the wealthy Pathros. Pathros was a very prosperous merchant, a dealer in fine linens, rugs, robes, parchments, honey, carpets, glass, nuts, and figs. He had oil from Asia; balsam from his own country; textiles and drugs from Palmyra; ginger, cinnamon, and precious stones from Arabia; corn, paper, granite, and alabaster from Egypt; tapestries from Babylon; paints from Rome; and statues from Greece.

Hafid had been very happy while serving as a camel boy for such a successful man, but when he had fallen in love with Lisha, the daughter of wealthy Calneh, he had suddenly been impressed with the idea that he wanted to become a man with more difficult and important things to do than watering camels. He also wanted to do some part of the work of the world that carried a greater reward than watering camels. Hafid was a fine young man and he desired to grow. He wanted to be a good family man, to be helpful to other people, and to have some importance in his own right. He had often heard his master say that no other trade or profession offered more opportunity for one to rise from poverty to success and great wealth than that of a salesman.

It was the men who sold his goods that had made the great warehouses, caravans, and trade empire of Pathros possible, and because Pathros was getting on in years, he needed someone to whom he could pass the custody of the great secrets responsible for his own outstanding success. All of his life, Pathros had treasured this understanding of success above all of his other wealth. It was not only the source of all of his other wealth, but it was also the source of much of his happiness as well. This knowledge had come to him as a special gift. The principles were written down on ten scrolls that Pathros kept securely locked in a wooden chest. Pathros felt that Hafid might be the one who should follow him as the possessor of these important success secrets.

After questioning him and giving him special instructions, Pathros gave Hafid the scrolls. He pointed out to Hafid that there are certain fundamental laws of success, just as there are laws of gravity, laws of electricity, and laws of health. If the laws are followed, the results are absolutely certain.

Hafid started out with a great advantage because he firmly believed this. He had a solid faith that if he could master the laws written on these scrolls, he would become what Pathros had been —the greatest salesman in the world. In trying to teach right principles, Pathros said: "If this room were filled to its beams with diamonds, their total worth would not surpass the value of the ideas written on these ten scrolls."

One of the requirements for receiving the scrolls was that Hafid should give one-half of all the money that he earned to those in need. What we give to help others is a kind of seed corn for our own success. As a good farmer always puts withdrawn fertility back into the soil, so a good worker puts back into the community a large part of that which he takes out. He always does more than he gets paid for. He always produces more than he consumes. He always goes the second mile.

Hafid agreed to follow instructions and to fully memorize each scroll in turn. He would understand, believe, and master every word. He was committed to repeat each law to himself three times each day for thirty days—once when he arose in the morning, a second time just after he had had his noonday meal, and again just before he went to sleep at night. Then he would specifically practice the law each day for thirty days. After thirty days of drill on one law, he practiced for a similar period on the next law, and the next, until all had been perfectly mastered.

Hafid believed without any question that if he properly followed these instructions, the law could not fail. But following these laws of success would also make one a great husband, a great banker, a great teacher, a great church worker, or a great human being, and it would be worth a room filled to its beams with diamonds. These are the ideas written on the scrolls:

Scroll No. 1: "I will form good habits and become their slave." The greatest power in the world is the power of habit. Good, well-established habits absolutely control our success. Our habits determine what we are. Most of us err in this important success requirement because we don't know how to build a habit. Most people do things only when they feel like it. When we do things irregularly, we are doing as much toward tearing the habit down as we are in building it up. We should all make a list of our necessary habits and then become their slaves.

Scroll No. 2: "I will greet this day with love in my heart." I will love the sun, for it warms my bones. I will love the earth, for it furnishes me with food. I will love life, for it is my most precious possession. I will love my job and with a whole heart carry on that particular portion of the world's work that life has given me to do. I will love great ambitions, for they can inspire me. I will even love failures, for they can teach me. I will love people, for they are a part of me. I will love myself with such honor and respect that I will never allow myself to do one wrong thing. I will remember that the most important part of my wealth is not in my purse but in me.

Scroll No. 3: "I will persist until I succeed." I know that failure will never overtake me if my determination to succeed is strong enough. I will remove from my vocabulary such false words as fail, quit, and discouragement. I will avoid despair, but if this disease of the mind should infect me, then I will work on in despair. I know that the easiest thing in the world to do is to quit, and it doesn't matter much what the thing to be discontinued is.

Scroll No. 4: "I am nature's greatest miracle and I will believe in myself." I have unlimited potential, only a small part of which I have ever used. I will increase the accomplishments of yesterday by a hundredfold. I will practice my skills, and I will improve and polish the words and expressions that I utter in selling my goods. Many have attained great wealth and success with only one good sales talk. I am nature's greatest miracle, and my nature shall never permit any defeat.

Scroll No. 5: "I will live this day as if it were my last." Because the sand cannot flow upward in the hourglass, I will waste not a moment of this precious day. I will make this day the best day of my life. I will push my muscles until they cry for relief, and I, not they, will determine when I rest. I know that no one ever found himself on the top of the mountain because he fell there. I will work harder, sell more goods, and have more joy than I or anyone else has ever had before.

Scroll No. 6: "Today I will be the master of my emotions." The great driving forces of the world are not intellectual but emotional. Therefore, I will control, purify, and powerize my feelings. I will develop the finest attitudes. I will motivate my greatest ambitions. I will bring about my own highest destiny. I will think no little thoughts, no groveling thoughts, no cowardly thoughts, no ugly thoughts, and no dirty thoughts. I will have no traffic with hatred or folly. I will make no little plans and do no little deeds.

Scroll No. 7: "I will laugh at the world." I will always have great joy in my heart. No living creature except man can laugh or even smile, and yet a man who can't smile is not much worse off than one who doesn't smile. The emotion behind a smile is a fine medicine for the soul. It has an untold value. Joy is the wine that sharpens the taste of life.

Scroll No. 8: "Today I will multiply my value a hundred-fold." I shall set great goals and achieve them. I shall have high aims and reach them. I shall live by a schedule. Others may build a cave out of the clay of their lives if they wish, but I will build a castle with mine.

Scroll No. 9: "I will act now." I will be a doer. I will not vacillate nor procrastinate. I will remember that the firefly gives off light only when it is on the wing. When the lion is hungry he eats. When the eagle is thirsty he drinks; unless they do, they must both perish. I hunger after success. I thirst for happiness and peace of mind, and if I do not act, I will perish also. I will not waste my success in failure, misery, or sleepless nights. I will effectively command myself, and I will strictly obey my own commands. I will not expect success to wait for me. I will be there on time. This is the hour! This is the place! I am the man, and I will act now!

Scroll No. 10: "I will trust in God." He is my Father who has given me breath and an opportunity for all of life's good things. I will honor him. I will follow him. His commandments are the greatest of all success laws. I will always work for the best interests of all right principles. I will always work for the best interests of those whom I serve. I will allow no shoddiness in my work or in my goods or in my life. I will never compromise with sloth or mediocrity or evil. I will always trust God so that he can always trust me.

And I promise God and myself that I will always think and live and worship and work at the very top of my condition.

Titles

W E HAVE an interesting custom among us of putting titles on things and on people for various purposes. The dictionary says that a title is an inscription or a label. It is a notice put over, under, or upon something to distinguish or explain it. On June 30, 1906, the Federal Congress passed the national Pure Food and Drug Act, which prohibits the manufacture of adulterated foods or drugs. It also requires that the ingredients with which foods and drugs are made up be clearly specified on the labels.

We do something similar to this when we put titles on our books and give them chapter headings describing their contents. The deeds for our properties usually show their metes, bounds, and descriptions. There is also a kind of pure food and drug act for people, where we attempt to specify the ingredients in the title. The scripture speaks about Elijah the prophet, John the Baptist, Simon the sorcerer, Judas the betrayer, and doubting Thomas. We call one group of people doctors and another group lawyers. We have bankers, teachers, students, and citizens. Some titles show rank, some are a mark of virtue, some indicate an office held. Some show an achievement made or a privilege given or respect granted. Titles may be classified as those having to do with sovereignty, heredity, ability, money, rank, or membership. Frequently we honor men by bestowing their titles upon them as they are earned.

We crown kings, elect presidents, and appoint a great variety of people to rank and office. We develop titles for warriors, rulers, businessmen, and educators, and we put such labels on them as presidents, managers, salesmen, bookkeepers, or professors. We sometimes raise or lower our own titles. A student may finish his school work with the designation of magna cum laude, and another may have the title of dropout placed on him long before he reaches graduation. It is about the same with life.

This Pure Food and Drug Act idea provides for our stimulation as well as for our protection. If we are dealing with one who has the title of Communist or dope addict, we may better judge how we should proceed with him. It may also help us if we know which man is the general and which is the private. We should also be aware of a man's label before we go too far in identifying with what he has in the package, as we usually adopt the traits and use the motivation of those with whom we associate and identify.

Sometime ago an enterprising life insurance sales agency organized among themselves what they called a Barons Club. Formerly the title of baron was widely used in some European countries. This title was placed upon certain people whose lives contained very special ingredients. An order of barons was founded in England in 1611 by James the First, and later Napoleon the great established an order of barons in France. Napoleon bestowed this title of baron on those who rendered a high grade of effective service to their country and to their emperor. In some cases a baron was also entitled to have the title of sir prefixed in his Christian name. These barons were not only honored and held in high esteem, but they were also men having great possessions. This idea has seemed to carry over in our minds as we still speak of land barons, steel barons, and oil barons. With a related idea in mind, this enterprising group of life insurance men organized themselves into an association of sales barons.

Of course, with every honor there must always be a corresponding responsibility, and to qualify as a member of this Barons Club, the applicant must prove his continuing ability each month by having a specified volume and a satisfactory quality in his sales. Just as there would be no point in Napoleon bestowing the title of baron upon someone who was disloyal to France or incapable of rendering effective service to Napoleon, so these salesmen must demonstrate their increased knowledge, growing industry, more dependable character, and greater ability to serve the needs of those with whom they do business. To add something to the spirit of their enterprise, they have some smart-looking dinner jackets tailored with a baron's crown and shield embroidered thereon as well as a few points of extra significance which they themselves have added.

The bottom of the crown is lined with ermine, signifying royalty. The crest is ornamented with the six-crown points, which was the number permitted the French barons by Napoleon. These standards on the crown's crest symbolize such traits as high spirits, self-confidence, courage, loyalty, character, and their pride of accomplishment. Of course, no sales baron would ever be guilty of allowing himself to be crestfallen or violate any of the other emblems shown on his crown. The shield is also embroidered on their dinner coats to serve as a kind of protection against any unwanted weakness. Three battle axes are shown on the shield, signifying the salesman's fight against the economic miseries of death, disability, and old age.

In this idea these salesmen identify themselves with James, who said, "Pure religion and undefiled before God and the Father is this, To visit the fatherless and widows in their affliction, and to keep himself unspotted from the world." (James 1:27.) When these insurance men visit the widows and the fatherless, they want to be able to notify them that the proper financial benefits have already been provided and this before the ravages of death, disability, or old age have done their damage. It is their responsibility to put into force in the lives of all breadwinners the philosophy of the apostle Paul, who said, "But if any provide not for his own, and specially for those of his own house, he hath denied the faith, and is worse than an infidel." (1 Timothy 5:8.)

Once each month the members of this group put on their baron jackets and have dinner together. In the pleasant company of each other, they relate their experiences, exchange ideas, and motivate themselves to greater accomplishment and better work. They do not tolerate improper conduct in themselves or in each other, and they try to avoid such occupational vices as ignorance, idleness, and call reluctance. As they work and eat together, and as they are interested in each other, they make and increase their own strength and ambition sufficient to cover their own needs.

There are some other organizations and titles that we should be familiar with. In the meridian of time, the Son of God came into the world and organized his church. He placed his own name on its label. He ordained twelve men to preside over it whom he called apostles. Others were called to be high priests, seventies, elders, bishops, priests, and deacons. He gave each of these office holders a set of job specifications to go with their labels. The purpose of this organization was to build character, educate people, and save souls. The title placed on the church members themselves was saints. Christ also placed in his church the doctrines of eternal truth, and he included his program of redemption, resurrection, and eternal happiness. He also established the rules of conduct necessary to bring about the eternal exaltation of all those who lived his laws. He sent out his messengers to perform the prescribĕd initiatory ordinances, saying to them, "Go ye into all the world, and preach the gospel to every creature. He that believeth and is baptized shall be saved; but he that believeth not shall be damned." (Mark 16:15-16.)

In projecting the future of the faithful he said, "Ye are gods; and all of you are children of the most High." (Psalm 82:6.) Jesus made no little plans for members of his church, nor did he set low goals. He said, "Be ye therefore perfect, even as your Father which is in heaven is perfect." (Matthew 5:48.) Later in vision John the Revelator saw a great group of the redeemed with the name of God "written in their foreheads." (Revelation 7:3, 14:1.)

The Master directed that church members should meet together often to teach and inspire each other. He prescribed that each Sabbath day they should partake of the emblems of his atoning sacrifice. The words of a sacred prayer were also prescribed by him with which those authorized should bless the emblems, and all should renew their covenants of faithfulness. This prayer is, "O God, the Eternal Father, we ask thee in the name of thy Son, Jesus Christ, to bless and sanctify this bread to the souls of all those who partake of it, that they may eat in remembrance of the body of thy Son, and witness unto thee, O God, the Eternal Father, that they are willing to take upon them the name of thy Son, and always remember him and keep his commandments which he has given them; that they may always have his Spirit to be with them. Amen." (D&C 20:77.)

He has indicated that we should be informed on all of his doctrines and his directions for salvation. He said, ". . . seek ye out of the best books words of wisdom; seek learning, even by study and also by faith." (D&C 88:118.) It is important that we think noble thoughts and do great deeds, for as has been said, "As a man thinketh in his heart, so is he."

What a great idea it would be if in our work, our worship, and our study we actually lived his precepts and identified ourselves effectively with him. We are the children of God, and we should cling to our inheritance and be constantly reaffirming it in our lives. We should never corrupt ourselves by profaning that glorious being in whose image we were created nor think of ourselves as something less than we are.

When Jesus tried to get the people to think of themselves

as children of God, they refused his concept of their future and straightway accused him of blasphemy and sought to crucify him. Generally most people are too prone to load themselves down with all kinds of guilt and inferiority complexes. We are too accustomed to identifying ourselves with sinners, weaklings, and ne'er-do-wells, and then that is what we become. The Hungarians and the Czechoslovakians once began a friendly association with the Russians, and they were soon made into Russian slaves. That is also something like what happens to those who put themselves in Satan's sphere of influence.

On the other hand, what a great privilege it ought to be for us to take upon ourselves the name of Christ and join his church. We can identify with the Lord's program and follow him in our lives. Every Sabbath day we can put on our best clothes, dress ourselves in our most happy attitudes, and go to the house of worship and offer up our hearts to God. It is in our interest to frequently sing the great hymns of praise to worship God and to motivate ourselves with the great scriptures. It helps us to get the spirit of devotion when we have the fellowship of the saints and heartily shake hands with our brothers and sisters in greeting.

Through our own repentance we need to get all of the evil out of our hearts and then learn to love God and each other with more sincerity and vigor. This would not only make us more happy, but it would solve almost all of our other problems more or less automatically.

A man who is now a patient in a mental hospital began one of the most unhappy portions of his life by hating his little brother. The hating habit grew on him until it spread to a dislike for many other people. When anyone crossed him or disagreed with him, he would get a little more antagonism settled in his own soul. Then he denied forgiveness and refused to identify with any of those who had offended him. His problems started a number of internal conflicts. He taught a Sunday School class and drank a little liquor on the side. He was unfaithful to his wife and unfaithful to God. Because he was not very successful financially, he began downgrading those who were.

He found employment with a racial minority group because their members would give him more attention than he deserved. He built up this outside relationship to the exclusion of his own family and people. He asks for God's blessings while violating

God's laws. He tries to get people's sympathy by throwing tantrums and feeling sorry for himself. He has lost his power to reason clearly or to see justice in any fact that is unfavorable to himself. He makes a very high percentage of bad decisions because he lives on the low level of his emotions, and he does only what pleases his distorted, undependable tastes. Even when people try to help him, he rejects them if they disagree with him.

He says that he feels like Satan and wants to go to hell where he belongs, and he seems to be deliberately trying to make himself as depressed, lonely, and unhappy as possible. He has no peace in his heart and seems to want none. He has joined the wrong club and has the wrong rules of behavior and is labeling himself with the wrong kind of titles. Unless he can make an almost impossible change, he may have a long, unhappy, unbalanced eternal life ahead of him. Under a kind of divine pure food and drug act, he may be accused of manufacturing adulterated products. Even the inscription of his eternal label may not give him much hope.

This again brings us back to the thought that the greatest idea there is in the world is to take upon ourselves the name of Jesus Christ and to live in the way that he has directed. He would not have organized his church unless he wanted us to join it and to live its doctrines.

To Be Complete

EMERSON ONCE said that he had never seen a whole man but only parts of men. What he meant was that he had never seen any man as perfect as the man that he could imagine. There are millions of perfect birds, flowers, trees, and animals. But there are no perfect men. A one-year-old mother bird is a model of faithful performance. She never deserts her young; she never gets drunk; she never loses her way. Similarly, there are millions of others of God's plants and animals that fill the measure of their creation in a way that leaves nothing to be desired. Certainly all people have some good in them, but it is also people who launch the crime waves, break the laws, and fill the earth with sin.

Someone has given his opinion that this would be a great world if it were not for people. It is the primary job of every individual during his lifetime to make himself whole, wholesome, holy, and complete. The Master said: "Be ye therefore perfect, even as your Father which is in heaven is perfect." (Matthew 5: 48.) In one of the most important pronouncements of our literature, Jesus pointed out the fact that "man shall not live by bread alone, but by every word that proceedeth out of the mouth of God." (Matthew 4:4; Deuteronomy 8:3.) To maintain our physical health, we must have a well-rounded and well-balanced diet of bread. But by itself that is not sufficient. We also need to live by those all-important doctrines that are necessary for our eternal exaltation. We need a strong vitalizing faith that needs to be nourished by a lot of good ideas. We can live much more fully if we have strong convictions and high ideals supported by righteous activities. It is necessary that we have a wholesome diet of bread, but there are also necessary diets made up of hope, ambition, enthusiasm, and joy that we cannot very well get along without. Someone has pointed out that we can live on less if we have more to live for.

Mark Twain once said that he could live for two weeks on a compliment. But we can live for a much longer period on the right quality of love, righteousness, success, and that comfortable feeling that our own lives are worthwhile. We need a feeling of acceptance by God and a pleasant fellowship with our fellowmen. The purpose of our lives is to develop in ourselves the greatest possible abundance of good.

One of the most important sources of this life's abundance comes from heeding the Master's two-word success formula in which he said: "Follow me." Our greatest life's abundance depends upon a strong obedience to the word of the Lord as found in the holy scriptures. One of the magnificent treasures of our literature is the apostle Paul's famous thirteenth chapter of First Corinthians. This is the finest discussion of the great law of love that we have in our language. In his twelfth chapter to the Corinthians Paul made another famous statement on completeness. As an example for every success, the great apostle sets up God's incomparable invention of the human body. He says:

"For the body is not one member, but many.

"If the foot shall say, Because I am not the hand, I am not of the body; is it therefore not of the body?

"And if the ear shall say, Because I am not the eye, I am not of the body; is it therefore not of the body?

"If the whole body were an eye, where were the hearing? If the whole were hearing, where were the smelling?

"But now hath God set the members every one of them in the body, as it hath pleased him.

"And if they were all one member, where were the body?

"But now are they many members, yet but one body.

"And the eye cannot say unto the hand, I have no need of thee: nor again the head to the feet, I have no need of you.

"Nay, much more those members of the body, which seem to be more feeble, are necessary:

"And those members of the body, which we think to be less honourable, upon these we bestow more abundant honour; and our uncomely parts have more abundant comeliness.

"For our comely parts have no need: but God hath tempered the body together, having given more abundant honour to that part which lacked:

"That there should be no schism in the body; but that the members should have the same care one for another.

"And whether one member suffer, all the members suffer with it; or one member be honoured, all the members rejoice with it." (1 Corinthians 12:14-26.)

It is interesting to try to imagine a more magnificent creation than the human body, where even the smallest members have great importance. It would be difficult to conceive a more important lesson on completeness, unity, and cooperation than this one that the great apostle is trying to teach. We could greatly increase our own productivity and the constructive joy we might get from our own self-image if we fully appreciated those mighty individual body members which distinguish us as God's greatest masterpiece. Think of the boost that we might give to our self-prestige if we understood and fully employed the majestic wonders of the human brain. God created man out of the dust of the ground, to which a great deal of water has been added. It has been said that the brain itself is 70 percent liquid. The brain is made up of fourteen billion cells and may contain more information than can be put in ten truckloads of books. A well-trained brain is the greatest problem solver. It is the most magnificent creator.

Out of the brain of Thomas A. Edison came a whole string of electric lights, radios, refrigerators, phonographs, washing machines, and all sorts of things that no one had ever heard of before. But just think of the many uses to which each individual may put his own brain. He may endow it with occupational know-how, financial skill, reason, discernment, good judgment, love, and compassion that is worth everything in life. Just suppose that we were minus this great mental organ. If our brains do not meet their full potential, then God is not getting a good return on his money and neither are we. We ourselves may upgrade our minds and make them as alert and capable as we desire.

Or who can conceive of anything more miraculous than that eyesight which reaches out across space and brings back to us all of the beauty and harmony of the universe. Or think of that great manufacturing plant called the digestive system, which takes into itself all kinds of grains, meats, fruits, vegetables, and liquids and out of them manufactures intelligence, reason, energy, love, and compassion. Or think of the mighty wonders of the human personality, the reproduction system, and a pair of willing hands. Then add to these the miracle of the circulation system, the nervous system, the body's locomotion facilities, and its self-healing ability. Man is the only part of God's creation that can smile or pray or aspire, and we have literally hundreds of the most worthwhile members and abilities, every one of which is absolutely necessary. If we took a dime's worth of iodine out of the thyroid gland or robbed the body of its functioning pituitary, our great human masterpiece might lie in ruins. A couple of pin pricks and one may be blind. Even the greatest member cannot say to the least, "I have no need of thee."

However, in his famous twelfth chapter, Paul did not exhaust all the possibilities of this idea of cooperation and unity. The scriptures also compare the parts of the body to the members of the church, and the Lord has said, "Also the body hath need of every member, that all may be edified together, that the system may be kept perfect." (D&C 84:110.) In his great human creation God made no duplicates, and everyone is given a mission that no one can do except him. No one is ever born into the world whose work is not born with him. Each can do some part of the work of the world better than anyone else. The world is not complete if anyone is missing. The world cannot say to any of its members, "I have no need of thee."

For a very important purpose the Lord has organized his church upon the earth and has placed in it certain necessary officers. And he has said to us:

"Now therefore ye are no more strangers and foreigners, but fellowcitizens with the saints, and of the household of God;

"And are built upon the foundation of the apostles and prophets, Jesus Christ himself being the chief corner stone;

"In whom all the building fitly framed together groweth unto an holy temple in the Lord." (Ephesians 2:19-21.)

All of these offices and officers are necessary, and all of them were to always remain in the true church organization.

Paul said:

"And he gave some, apostles; and some, prophets, and some, evangelists; and some, pastors and teachers;

"For the perfecting of the saints, for the work of the ministry, for the edifying of the body of Christ:

"Till we all come in the unity of the faith, and of the knowledge of the Son of God, unto a perfect man, unto the measure of the stature of the fulness of Christ." (Ephesians 4:11-13.)

Some churches have said to these offices, including the very foundation of apostles and prophets, "we have no need of thee." Some churches have also done this with great life-saving doctrines of salvation. A great furor is going on in so-called Christendom about which parts of Christ's theology they are to believe. But we must live by every word that proceedeth forth from the mouth of God. Following are some of the doctrines that Jesus put in the church that have been deleted and yet are as necessary now as they ever were. First, we cannot say of faith, repentance, baptism, and the gift of the Holy Ghost, "I have no need of thee." We need the Ten Commandments, the Sermon on the Mount, the doctrines of the eternity of the family unit, marriage for time and eternity, the payment of tithing, the Word of Wisdom, the literal bodily resurrection, the three degrees of glory, and salvation for the dead. There is the Lord's command that church ministers must not choose themselves or minister in his name without his authorization.

Jesus taught the necessity for continual revelation upon which his church itself was built. He taught the literal second coming of Jesus Christ, the millennium of a thousand years of peace, and the reality of the final judgment. These were given specifically "for the perfecting of the saints, for the work of the ministry, for the edifying of the body of Christ: Till we all come in the unity of the faith, and of the knowledge of the Son of God, unto a perfect man, unto the measure of the stature of the fulness of Christ." (Ephesians 4:12-13.) But sometimes in our lethargy or disbelief we say of these great doctrines, "We have no need of thee."

The Lord has also placed certain necessary gifts in the church. The Bible says:

"For to one is given by the Spirit the word of wisdom; to another the word of knowledge by the same Spirit;

"To another faith by the same Spirit; to another the gifts of healing by the same Spirit;

"To another the working of miracles; to another prophecy; to another discerning of spirits; to another divers kinds of tongues; to another the interpretation of tongues:

"But all these worketh that one and the selfsame Spirit, dividing to every man severally as he will." (1 Corinthians 12:8-11.)

The Lord also put some signs that were to always identify the true church of Christ. He said:

"And these signs shall follow them that believe; In my name shall they cast out devils; they shall speak with new tongues;

"They shall take up serpents; and if they drink any deadly thing, it shall not hurt them; they shall lay hands on the sick, and they shall recover." (Mark 16:17-18.)

Nature also effectively operates on this idea of cooperation. The scientists have discovered 104 elements in nature. There are nitrogen, hydrogen, oxygen, carbon, iron, etc. These are nature's building blocks. When nature puts these elements together in the right combinations and proportions, she is able to fashion any of the material things of the world. But this same idea also works in our individual success. Someone has pointed out that in human personality we have fifty-one elements. We have kindness, faith, intelligence, integrity, courage, industry, judgment, righteousness, friendliness, and ambition. When these are put together in the right combinations and proportions, we have what someone has called a magnificent human being. We sometimes fall far below what God intended us to be because we say to our industry or our morality or our faith, "I have no need of thee." Then we become mere parts of men.

When someone mentions the word *automobile* we may think of just one thing. But recently I saw a sign posted on an automobile sales window that said that an automobile is actually 3,375 things. There is a steering wheel, a speedometer, a gas tank, a rear seat, a bumper, and some 3,370 other things. And if even the slightest gadget is not functioning in the carburetor, the most beautiful, valuable automobile may be made comparatively useless. There are some people who want to become followers of Christ while believing just a few of his doctrines and keeping just some of his commandments. Even some churches specialize in a limited area of doctrines. Their belief centers in healing, or they focus their faith in a particular day on which they should worship, while they let other things that may be even more important pass them by unnoticed.

Jesus mentioned this kind of situation when he said to the Pharisees, "But woe unto you, Pharisees! for ye tithe mint and rue and all manner of herbs, and pass over judgment and the love of God: these ought ye to have done, and not to leave the other undone." (Luke 11:42.)

When God created the world, he looked out upon it and pronounced it very good. I suppose that the thing that would now please him more than any other thing would be to look out upon it and to see it inhabited by his children, all of whom were complete. That would be where they understood all of his doctrines, honored all of his commandments, and lived by every word that proceeds forth from him so that they would make the greatest possible development of themselves.

The Tree of Knowledge

I NEVER CEASE to feel lifted up as I read that thrilling story of creation found in the book of Genesis. Moses records part of the great revelation given to him by saying:

"In the beginning God created the heaven and the earth.

"And the earth was without form, and void; and darkness was upon the face of the deep. And the Spirit of God moved upon the face of the waters.

"And God said, Let there be light: and there was light.

"And God saw the light, that it was good. . . ." (Genesis 1:1-4.)

Then God went on to create for our benefit our topsoil, our seasons, our atmosphere, our rainfall, and all of our plant and animal life. Moses recorded the most important event that ever took place when he said:

"So God created man in his own image, in the image of God created he him; male and female created he them.

"And God blessed them, and God said unto them, Be fruitful, and multiply, and replenish the earth, and subdue it: and have dominion over the fish of the sea, and over the fowl of the air, and over every living thing that moveth upon the earth." (Genesis 1:27-28.)

This was a heavenly creation. The record says: "Thus the heavens and the earth were finished. . . . And every plant of the field before it was in the earth, and every herb of the field before it grew: for the Lord God had not caused it to rain upon the earth, and there was not a man to till the ground." (Genesis 2:1, 5.)

Then the record says:

"And the Lord God formed man of the dust of the ground, and breathed into his nostrils the breath of life; and man became a living soul.

"And the Lord God planted a garden eastward in Eden; and there he put the man whom he had formed." (Genesis 2:7-8.)

Then the first question that Adam and Eve had to decide was whether or not they would eat the fruit from the tree of knowledge of good and evil. And after they had eaten God said, "Behold, the man is become as one of us, to know good and evil. . . ." (Genesis 3:22.) I would just like to point out in passing that the right kind of knowledge still tends to have that effect on people. To know good and evil still tends to make men and women become as God.

A flaming sword was placed in the Garden of Eden to guard the tree of life, but fortunately for us there is no flaming sword guarding the tree of knowledge, and everyone may eat to his heart's content. One of the distinguishing characteristics of our world is that it is full of opposites that must be decided, and one reason for having opposites is that we can always see light things best on a dark background. We have the contrasts of knowledge and ignorance, good and bad, success and failure, right and wrong, struggle and ease.

The great prophet Lehi said: "For it must needs be, that there is an opposition in all things. If not so . . . righteousness could not be brought to pass, neither wickedness, neither holiness nor misery, neither good nor bad. . . ." (2 Nephi 2:11.)

He explains what would have happened if Adam and Eve had not partaken of the tree of knowledge of good and evil. He said:

"And they would have had no children; wherefore they would have remained in a state of innocence, having no joy, for they knew no misery; doing no good, for they knew no sin.

"But behold, all things have been done in the wisdom of him who knoweth all things.

"Adam fell that men might be; and men are, that they might have joy." (2 Nephi 2:23-25.)

Above almost every other thing it is important that we be able to distinguish between good and evil. To help us to do this, God has given us a mind and a conscience as well as his own written direction on almost every important question in life. Yet one of our most serious mistakes is that we do not always distinguish between right and wrong.

A young woman was recently asked by a reporter for a national magazine whether or not she believed in the Ten Commandments. She said, "Who am I to say what is right and wrong?" This young woman is making a very serious mistake. If she claims not to know whether or not the Ten Commandments are true, what *does* she know? If she believes the word of God, she can easily know whether or not the Ten Commandments are true. And if she lives these laws of righteousness, she will have a second avenue for knowing that they are true.

Jesus said, "If any man will do his will, he shall know of the doctrine, whether it be of God, or whether I speak of myself." (John 7:17.) And if one uses his own righteous reasoning, he would also know that the Ten Commandments are right. However, it is pretty difficult to teach a group of sinners what is right, for when someone is doing what is wrong, they are usually persuading themselves that it is right.

In one of the greatest success formulas ever given, Jesus said: "Follow me." If we follow him we will believe him, and we will know that his word is truth. Where else could we turn? God is the only sure and dependable judge. He is the God of truth and cannot lie. He does not rationalize nor alibi nor weaken nor fail. It is human nature to be very interested in what other people think. We conduct polls to find out what the Republicans think and what the Democrats think and what other groups think. But a poll has already been conducted to tell us what God thinks. If everyone in the world would do exactly as he is directed in the written word of the Lord, this world would be God's paradise.

Unfortunately, even many ministers do not believe in or follow Christ. On many occasions the Lord has made a serious accusation against so-called ministers—that they teach for commandments the doctrines of men, having a form of godliness, but they deny the power thereof.

The Prophet Joseph Smith describes a part of his first vision as follows. He said:

". . . I saw a pillar of light exactly over my head, above the brightness of the sun, which descended gradually until it fell upon me. . . . When the light rested upon me I saw two Personages, whose brightness and glory defy all description, standing above me in the air. One of them spake unto me, calling me by name and said, pointing to the other—*This is My Beloved Son. Hear Him.*

"My object in going to inquire of the Lord was to know which of all the sects was right, that I might know which to join. No sooner, therefore, did I get possession of myself, so as to be able to speak, than I asked the Personages who stood above me in the light, which of all the sects was right—and which I should join.

"I was answered that I must join none of them, for they were all wrong; and the Personage who addressed me said that all their creeds were an abomination in his sight; that those professors were all corrupt; that: they draw near to me with their lips, but their hearts are far from me, they teach for doctrines the commandments of men, having a form of godliness, but they deny the power thereof." (Joseph Smith 2:16-19.)

This judgment might seem a little harsh, as everyone knows religious ministers who are kind, thoughtful men who want to be helpful. But how many virtues would it take to make up for teaching any false doctrine or perverting in any measure the word of the Lord?

Sometime ago I listened to one of the most famous ministers in the world. The people he influences are numbered by the millions. Yet he has never been baptized, and he freely and eloquently teaches everyone else that baptism is not necessary. To teach false doctrine is a very serious sin, and the Lord has said: "Whosoever therefore shall break one of these least commandments, and shall teach men so, he shall be called the least in the kingdom of heaven. . . ." (Matthew 5:19.) Actually, no one should be very interested in what I think or what this minister thinks. The thing that is important is what the Lord thinks. And on this point the facts are perfectly clear. As Jesus was about to ascend unto his Father in heaven, he stood above the Mount of Olives and said to the apostles who stood at his feet: "Go ye therefore, and teach all nations, baptizing them in the name of the Father, and of the Son, and of the Holy Ghost." (Matthew 28:19.) He said: "He that believeth and is baptized shall be saved; but he that believeth not shall be damned." (Mark 16:16.)

His meaning here is also perfectly clear. More than about any other thing, the Lord has said over and over again that no man should tamper with his doctrines or change them in any way. But this minister stands up and directly contradicts the word of the Lord by saying that baptism is not necessary. Jesus himself thought it necessary for him to be baptized, but this minister disputes the issue. The young woman previously referred to might say, "Who am I that I can judge between the Son of God and this minister who so freely airs his own mistaken opinions as the truth?"

The apostle Paul was speaking for Christ when he said: "But though we, or an angel from heaven, preach any other gospel unto you than that which we have preached unto you, let him be accursed." (Galatians 1:8.)

It is small wonder that the Lord has been so disturbed at ministers who presume to take his name upon themselves to teach what they believe. Unauthorized ministers, teaching their own doctrines, have caused some of our world's most serious problems. As Isaiah has said: "The earth also is defiled under the inhabitants thereof; because they have transgressed the laws, changed the ordinance, broken the everlasting covenant. Therefore hath the curse devoured the earth, and they that dwell therein are desolate. . . ." (Isaiah 24:5-6.)

In the very last and one of the most important ideas in the New Testament the Lord said:

"For I testify unto every man that heareth the words of the prophecy of this book, If any man shall add unto these things, God shall add unto him the plagues that are written in this book:

"And if any man shall take away from the words of the book of this prophecy, God shall take away his part out of the book of life, and out of the holy city, and from the things which are written in this book." (Revelation 22:18-19.)

The sin of changing his doctrines has also been reemphasized by God in our own day. And yet this changing continues to go on. Some people have taken it upon themselves to change every one of the Ten Commandments. One minister said that he never taught the Ten Commandments in his church anymore because they were so much out of date, and besides, their strong language was too harsh for our weak sensibilities. Therefore the new morality has been substituted for the seventh commandment. Many ministers openly teach that hunting, fishing, picnicking, athletics, immoral movies, and other so-called recreational activities are as acceptable to them on Sunday as on any other day of the week. One minister said, "We have no special Sabbath day." He said,

"We leave our people free to be guided by their own consciences before God. We look on Sunday as being like any other day. The man who works might well spend his Sabbath on Saturday or Monday or any other day, it makes no difference." But it does make a difference, as this is the one day a week set apart for worship and study. If we destroy this day, we largely destroy our worship and study.

Those people who remember the Sabbath day to keep it holy will be a different kind of people from those who don't. As we get to the place where we are using the Lord's day for everything but worship, we are on dangerous ground. Very frequently, we ought to reread all of the Ten Commandments and all of the others and then follow them to the letter.

In the fourth commandment the Lord said:

"Remember the sabbath day, to keep it holy.

"Six days shalt thou labour, and do all thy work:

"But the seventh day is the sabbath of the Lord thy God: in it thou shalt not do any work, thou, nor thy son, nor thy daughter, thy manservant, nor thy maidservant, nor thy cattle, nor thy stranger that is within thy gates." (Exodus 20:8-11.)

I can understand that some people might disobey God and desecrate the Sabbath day, but we must know what we are doing. Certainly I must know the right answer when someone asks us about one of the Ten Commandments. If I don't know that which God has said is true, then I should eat a little more fruit from the tree of knowledge of good and evil.

In addition to my faith, my reason also tells me that it is right to obey God, to avoid profanity, to honor my parents, and to keep every other one of the commandments. Our final success will depend upon how well we can distinguish between good and evil.

The Uniform

IT HAS been said that one of the greatest inventions of all time took place at Platea when an obscure Greek perfected the process of marching men in step. When it was discovered that the attention of a great group of men could be coordinated and focused on a single objective, that day civilization began. Another great invention took place when someone invented the uniform with which all soldiers could be given an added significance.

A recent moving picture showing the life story of General George W. Patton goes into great detail about his insistence that all of his soldiers should take proper care of their uniforms. They always had to have their shoes shined, their trousers pressed, their hair cut and combed, and their bodies clean. Their spirits also should be dressed in the proper attitudes. General Patton would not tolerate cowardice or any of the other forms of improper spiritual dress in those soldiers who fought under his command.

It has been said that things are sometimes more important for what they stand for or are a sign of, or what they get us to think about, than they are for themselves alone. And, of course, this is an idea that reaches far beyond the army. Knute Rockne was one of the most famous football coaches who ever lived. Rockne borrowed a lot of ideas from the theater. He always went to the sell-out performances to find out why some plays attracted more people than others. He discovered that the spectators were pleased with the beauty, rhythm, harmony, color, and timing of the girls singing and dancing in the chorus. He noticed that when their costumes were new and pretty, they made a better impression than after their outfits had become frayed from many performances.

Audiences also liked to see rhythm and color. So Rockne organized his football plays on this basis. He arranged for his players to have the smartest-looking uniforms that could be seen on any football field. He said to the members of his team, "We want to look like football players, even if we aren't." Each player stood for the team and the team stood for Notre Dame. Rockne had their uniforms specially designed, not only to promote comfort and speed in the players, but also to give pleasing sensations of style and color to those in the stadium. Rockne not only had color in the uniform; he also had colorful plays. Because Notre Dame had color and excellence in its traditions, there must be color and excellence in all of Notre Dame's players.

A player once came out onto the field with a hole in his stocking. Rockne said, "What team do you think you are playing on—Coxey's Wildcats?" Then he said to the player, "Go back into the dressing room and change your stocking and don't come back onto the field until you get a proper sense of pride about your dress."

Every Notre Dame player understood that Rockne would not stand for carelessness or slovenly habits or negative attitudes. These are lessons that should also be learned by every salesman and every doctor and every wife and every husband and every other person desiring to make the most of his own life. Someone has said that clothing doesn't make the man, but it does make 95 percent of what you can see of him. Just suppose that a general or a coach should let down his discipline and allow everyone to dress as he pleased. Suppose that he allowed his soldiers or players to shave or not, according to how they felt. If they looked like hobos, they would probably act or fight or play like hobos. The general might rule that instead of saluting their superior officers, soldiers could shout obscenities at them and call them pigs. If soldiers looked like freaks out of the circus sideshow, that is the kind of an army they would make.

This idea of excellence in appearance is also a pretty good one for every part of life. Not only should we keep our homes clean and orderly, but we should dress our minds and attitudes in righteousness. The Lord has said that cleanliness is next to godliness. The scripture says that God "cannot look upon sin with the least degree of allowance." (D&C 1:31.) The Lord has also made a commitment to harmony and unity. He said to his disciples: ". . . if ye are not one ye are not mine." (D&C 38:27.)

Every one of us should be properly groomed and our bodies should be kept clean, healthy, and well-dressed. Recently I interviewed a young man who has been a part of this modern phenomenon where some young people band together to dress in ludicrous clothing, let their hair grow, refuse to bathe, and make themselves about as personally unattractive as possible. I asked this young man if he would explain his behavior to me. He was not very coherent. I asked him if he would feel better if he took a good, hot, soapy bath, had a haircut, and did some useful work to provide for his needs and help build up his sunken chest. Perhaps he ought to go to school to beautify his thoughts and prepare himself to make some worthwhile contribution to the world.

He said that his reformation would make his friends feel uncomfortable in his presence. He said they would accuse him of desertion. I asked him what he would be deserting that would be so important to them. Then he tried to explain to me as best he could about the stand that these young people had taken for rebellion. They were committed to tear down the establishment and refuse to do what would please their parents. He said that if he got a haircut and looked respectable or went to work, it would be a visible sign that would cause his friends to reject him. I felt very sorry for this sunken-chested, low-thinking, physically lazy young man who was making a weak attempt to untwist his attitudes. It seemed to me that he must never have had a manly experience in his life, or certainly he would be well rid of those so-called friends who had helped to bring him to his unpleasant state. He seemed like a half-reformed gangster who was afraid to break with the mob.

Many young people join together for protection in their evil, immoral purposes. Then, no matter how wrong they are, they can still get some satisfaction from the praise and support that they give to each other. It is pretty difficult to help, discipline, or even make suggestions to a mob. Criminals and sinners have found that they have more power in a group than if each one were to stand on his own feet. One of the first steps to being a hippie is to put on the hippie uniform.

In the beginning of our world's history, Cain took an oath in which he agreed to serve Satan. In our day many people gang up for that same purpose. Some of these groups actually call themselves by such names as "Hell's Angels" and "Devil's Diciples." Some of these groups have initiation requirements that compel the candidate to take a human life or destroy the virtue of a woman against her will. Their outside dress usually indicates what they are on the inside.

Recently I was asked to interview a man who had made application for employment as a schoolteacher. After discussing some character questions and his academic preparation, I asked him if he would tell me the reason for his unconventional hair style. He said, "I suppose I just like hair." I said, "What are some of the other reasons?" Then he said, "Jesus had long hair, didn't he?" I said, "I suppose that he did, but if he did it was for a completely different reason. In those days everyone had long hair. They also had a different kind of dress, a different kind of footwear, and rode on the backs of mules."

The applicant said, "If I get this job, will I have to cut my hair?" I said to him, "I'm not the one who decides either of those questions, but so that you may present your own side of the case to your prospective employer, I will tell you what I am going to say in my report. Whether you cut your hair or not, I would not hire you. In my opinion, your primary problem is on the inside. The guise you are wearing on the outside is just a manifestation of what you are underneath the whiskers."

Then I tried to explain to him what seems to me to be one of the most serious problems of our world, and his group is the one that is being hurt the most. We are presently living in a world that is being torn to pieces by deadly ideological warfare. There are some people who feel that they have a kind of divine right to tear down the establishment and destroy property belonging to other people. Some think that if they don't agree with the government, it becomes their privilege to try to destroy it.

They feel that it is their privilege to fight law and order, steal food, throw rocks at the police, and call law enforcement officers obscene names. What a dreadful sin against themselves, for these young people commit themselves to rebel against their own parents while they themselves need guidance so badly. In their immaturity, they feel that they have a right to overthrow authority, rebel against education, fight against government, destroy morality, and displease God. These rebels scoff at our finest social conventions. They are often unemployed and unemployable. They have a dreadful shortage of basic ideals, character, ambition, and industry on the inside, a shortage that is vividly pictured on the outside. It is certain that everyone in each group does not do *all* of these things personally, and yet they wear the uniform and support the causes of those who do.

All of us must be judged by the company we keep. Suppose that while our nation was fighting the German madman Hitler, a soldier had appeared in the ranks wearing a Nazi uniform, waving the swastika, and shouting "Heil Hitler"; someone might have taken the occasion to believe that this man was either out of his mind or that he was trying to get himself executed. While the Communists are talking about burying us, if some American soldier should go about waving the banner of the hammer and sickle, there might be some question about his loyalty. His portestations that he didn't believe *all* that some Communists did would be completely beside the point. Likewise, if someone insisted on going into the army with a sloppy appearance, smelly clothing, and uncombed hair, he might well expect to have some problems.

What chance would any army have to protect its rights if even one soldier were allowed to scoff at military discipline? This probably applies in every other field. No one would want to be operated on by a doctor who hadn't washed his hands or taken a bath. No one would want his children to be at the mercy of a teacher who had his mind dressed in immorality, sedition, rebellion, and negative attitudes. Everyone who engages in this great enterprise of living ought to clothe himself in the uniform of humanity at its best. Certainly anyone who wears this uniform of evil should not object to being judged by that for which it stands.

Recently I visited in the home of a man who is the president of a bank. He and his wife are wonderfully intelligent people. Both have come up by hard struggle from very lowly beginnings, have gotten good educations, and have built fine characters into themselves. They are both very good church members and each carries a big load of civic responsibilities. Their children are all well-behaved except one boy, who had chosen to put on the dirty uniform of rebellion and follow this senseless course of evil. His appearance fitted him for some kind of circus sideshow. He was blackmailing his parents with threats. He would accept no discipline. If they didn't do as he said, he would run away and join a camp practicing complete immorality and degradation. He knew that his parents would submit to any of his evil demands to prevent such a thing from happening to him.

However, they could not help but feel terribly ashamed of him. Though they were having their hearts broken, they would have given everything to be able to remove this foul disease from his heart. They realized that their permissiveness is not the answer. In fact, there doesn't seem to be any answer. If he breaks his last tie with respectability, he will probably sink to the depths attained by his dope-addicted associates. But if his parents treat him kindly, he will probably leave them sooner or later anyway because of the terrible malignancy that is already forming in his soul.

By way of contrast, what a thrill to see some fine young man wearing the uniform of cleanliness, respectability, and industry. How inspiring to see someone nobly wearing the uniform of his country. Instead of bitterness, hate, and rebellion, his heart is filled with loyalty, patriotism, and devotion. We too can enlist in the service of God and put on the uniform of righteousness and acquire a love of truth, justice, and accomplishment.

INDEX

and hate, 189-90; God, 190, 193; jobs, 189-90; courage, 191; great character traits, 191; great wealth and power, 191; is great redemptive force, 253; is accumulative, 272; the earth, 275.
Lowell, James Russell, 223, 270
Loyalty, 175-76
Lucifer, see Satan
Luke, 70
Luther, Martin, 208

-M-
MacArthur, Douglas, 146
Magic, 195ff
Magic of Believing, The, 199
Malius, Joseph, 251
Man, destiny of, 92; paper, 213ff; whole, 284ff
Man, the Unknown, 114
Mandino, Og, 273
Mao Tse-tung, 213
Markham, Edwin, 108-109
Martin, Edwin Sanford, 207
Mary of Nazareth, 238
Mayflower, 181
McCartney, Clarence E., 216
McEvoy, J. P., 246
Mein Kampf, 265
"Memorial Day," 149
Memories, 58ff, 269-70
Methvin, Eugene H., 73
Midszenty Report, 73
Miles, C. Austin, 174
Milton, John, 202, 204
Mind, 244ff
Money, 268ff
Morality, 16
Moreland, John Richard, 245
Moses, 99, 156, 172, 218, 250, 291
Mother, poem about, 157; love of, 158
Mother's Day, 158-59
Mount of Olives, 253, 294
Mount Sinai, 12, 16, 20, 44, 85, 113, 149, 154, 210, 218, 221, 251
Music, power of, 72; acid-rock, 73
"My Name Is Legion," 207

-N-
Napoleon, 167, 205, 279

New morality, the term, 96
New York Times, 74
Nixon, Richard M., 220
Noah, 95, 218

-O-
Obedience, blind, 76ff
Objectives, 4ff
Odyssey, 71
Opportunities, 184ff
Othello, 47

-P-
Paper, piece of, 219ff
Paradise Lost, 204
Parents, 154ff
Pathros, 273ff
Patton, George W., 297
Paul, apostle, 2, 24, 26, 50, 70, 86, 91, 92, 93, 107, 128, 132, 136, 138, 145, 176, 203, 204, 205, 211, 218, 248, 280, 285, 287, 295
Pauley, Gay, 180
Peace, the word, 97
Pericles, 144
"Perseverance," 226-27
Personalities, plurality of, 207ff
Peter, apostle, 5, 26, 79, 99, 172
Pharisees, 290
Pilate, 126
Pilgrims, 182
Pilgrim's Progress, The, 203-204
Pitkin, Walter, 188
Pledge of allegiance, 50
Plurality, our human, 207ff
Poe, Edgar Allan, 118
Poets, 232ff
Pope, Alexander, 97
Powder Ridge Pop Festival, 74-75
Power, age of, 24ff; will, 29ff; soul, 216ff
Powers, 1ff
Practice, 17
Principle, the word, 10
Principles, 1ff, 10ff; of gospel of Jesus Christ, 16, 18
Principles of Education, 10
Principles of Successful Salesmanship, 10
Promise books, 19ff